Colonial Affairs

Colonial Affairs

*Bowles, Burroughs, and
Chester Write Tangier*

Greg A. Mullins

THE UNIVERSITY OF WISCONSIN PRESS

The University of Wisconsin Press
1930 Monroe Street
Madison, Wisconsin 53711

www.wisc.edu/wisconsinpress/

3 Henrietta Street
London WC2E 8LU, England

Printed in the United States of America

Library of Congress Cataloging-in-Publication Data
Mullins, Greg.
Colonial affairs : Bowles, Burroughs, and Chester write Tangier /
Greg Mullins.
    pp. cm.
    Includes bibliographical references aand index.
    ISBN 0-299-17960-5 (cloth : alk. paper)
    ISBN 0-299-17964-8 (pbk. : alk. paper)
    1. American literature—20th century—History and criticism. 2. Bowles,
Paul, 1910–1999—Knowledge—Tangier (Morocco) 3. Burroughs, William S.,
1914–1997—Knowledge—Tangier (Morocco) 4. Chester, Alfred, 1928–1971—
Knowledge—Tangier (Morocco) 5. Americans—Morocco—Tangier—History—
20th century. 6. Authors, American—20th century—Biography. 7. Tangier
(Morocco)—In literature. 8. Tangier(Morocco)—Biography.
I. Title.
PS159.M67 M85   2002
813'.540932642—dc21   2002004269

Publication of this book has been made possible by the generous support of the
Anonymous Fund of the University of Wisconsin–Madison

Contents

Preface

My interest in the sexual politics of colonialism first arose not in relation to North Africa but rather in relation to East Africa, where I served as a Peace Corps volunteer in the mid-1980s. Over the course of the two years I spent living in Kenya, not only did I witness the time-worn but seemingly irresistible use of sexual metaphors to describe and explain colonialism, but I also came to appreciate the extent to which metaphors of colonial conquest and domination can express sexual experience. I credit my Kenyan friends at the school where I taught with privileging one lesson about the operation of colonialism in sex: when the single, male teachers at the school would gather to exchange stories about the women they dated, someone would inevitably inquire whether a date had culminated in a successful "colonization." Deployed in this way, the trope is more indicative of some normative conceptions of domination than it is descriptive of the complex experience of either colonialism or sex. Nonetheless, the trope provides an aperture through which we can begin to see the maneuvers and negotiations that take place between players or sides in a struggle for power that overflows the boundaries that attempt to separate sexuality from politics. Indeed, this book proceeds from a vantage point that has already seen these boundaries overwhelmed, a position that allows me to take for granted the abstracted blurring of colonial and sexual domination and to turn my attention more precisely to some contests and compromises that take place upon one field of sexual politics in a particular colonial space at a particular time.

The sexual politics that concern me here are those represented in the writings of three American men who sought sex with men in the city of Tangier during the years roughly from 1945 to 1965: Paul Bowles, William Burroughs, and Alfred Chester. My reasons for locating a study of homosexuality and colonialism in Tangier will become apparent in the following chapters; less readily apparent, I presume, is the relation of this study to my own experience. In many ways, this study works out the answers to questions that in Kenya I was unable both to pose and to evade: unable to pose because I lacked the conceptual tools that queer theory and colonial theory now provide me; unable to evade because of the neocolonial position into which Peace Corps volunteers are inserted. They are questions quite similar to those that Frantz Fanon implies in *Black Skin, White Masks* without quite being able to utter. Fanon argues that the social order—and, within that order, racism—structures the psychosexual realm of identity and desire in colonial contexts and that investigating one's own subjectivity provides the starting point for an intervention into the social. As Fanon undergoes a self-analysis of his positions as a raced and gendered subject, the suppleness of his analysis, which is always in danger of rigidifying under the codes of race and gender, becomes altogether too brittle concerning matters of sexuality and sexual identity. In his curious, unconvincingly phobic remarks concerning male homosexuality, Fanon seems on the verge of putting his finger on the destabilizing potential of homosexual desire (156, 180). Following the elaboration of a colonial structure that traps its subjects within a heterosexual matrix and fixes them in terms of black versus white and male versus female, Fanon's rather offhand comments regarding homosexuality seem to gesture toward questions he is incapable of posing: what queer turn does homosexuality exact on colonial systems? Can homosexual desire in colonial relations best be understood as operating parallel to a heterosexual matrix, or is there a difference in homosexual desire that calls for a new conceptual model? Fanon writes as if homosexuality is a threat that must be contained in the process of his self-analysis, but I wonder whether that threat might not be turned against the colonial system that his analysis attempts to resist.

I should point out that when my friends in Kenya referred to colonialism as a metaphor for sexual domination, the effect was intended to be comical; nonetheless, some serious questions arise from their playful use of language. If in a heterosexual relationship between two Kenyans today a man codes himself as the colonizer and codes his partner as the colonized, how are these terms to be mapped back onto the historical colonialism experienced in Kenya? If the historical colonizers, both male and female, are positioned in a romance with the historical colonized, both male and female, their relationship can hardly be characterized as heterosexual in any normative sense. Rather, the trajectories of desire that are theoretically possible—and were, in fact, practically experienced—among the players in the historical drama of colonialism defy schematic characterization. Neither a heterosexual model in which male Europe penetrates female Africa nor a homosocial model in which European and African men are engaged in a relationship "between men" can exhaustively explain the polyvocality and the perversity of sexual desire under colonialism. That is not to say that these models are unimportant; both are useful frameworks for understanding aspects of colonial sexuality, and the dynamics of relationships "between men" (to invoke Sedgwick's work on triangulation) especially need further exploration. But the study of colonialism and sexuality calls most urgently for unraveling the knot of multiple and contradictory desires one strand at a time. This study examines one such strand: homosexual relationships between men who occupy the positions of colonizer and colonized.

Objections to this statement will immediately arise, for the subjects of this study are Americans and Moroccans, and the United States did not colonize Morocco. Moreover, the historical period of the study, from roughly 1945 to 1965, crosses over the date of Moroccan independence in 1956 and includes the aftermath of colonialism. Has postcolonial theory not already exhausted the usefulness of categorizing diverse and often contradictory experience into an ahistorical, Manichean struggle between colonizer and colonized? Yes, I would say, but also no. Yes, the time has come to think with greater accuracy about specific national, cultural, and historical encounters. Twentieth-century American neocolonialism arises from and produces a different set of relations than, say, seventeenth-century Portuguese colonialism or nineteenth-century British colonialism. Sexual tourism in Morocco arises out of a different culture and history than, for example, sexual tourism in the Philippines. The sorts of questions posed in this book are attentive to specifically American encounters. But as Fanon discovered when he traveled from Martinique to metropolitan France, there are forces at work that efface the distinctiveness of any single colonial system. In spite of the overwhelming flow of information that contradicts such a naive view of the world, even today global political and economic systems are discursively bifurcated into a "north" standing in opposition to a "south," which is impossibly but resolutely also a "west" opposed to an "east." The tool that cleaves the world in this way is race, and this tool operates by defining "whiteness" as the absence of any "color," a definition that lumps together all "colors." As Fanon points out, the metropolitan need to shore up the boundaries of "whiteness" enforces an erasure of differences within colonial settings, such as those marked by social class or by a color hierarchy. In Paris, Fanon found, his subjectivity was denied by the racism that fixed him as an object with the simple phrase, "Look, a Negro!" Moreover, this dualism in racial discourse, which is sustained in the postcolonial era, is uneasily but consistently mapped onto another dualism: colonizer versus colonized. The specificity of American postwar experience in Tangier cannot be analyzed adequately without taking into consideration how these more general discursive formations of race and colonialism shape experience.

Rather than interrogate common assumptions about racial difference and colonialism, Bowles, Burroughs, and Chester take these categories for granted; what makes their texts interesting is how each author works out his own relationship to race and colonialism. Of special interest is the negotiation that takes place as men from different sexual cultures come together in a racially and politically charged setting to seek sex and sometimes friendship with one another. North Africa provides a logical place to locate a study of representations of sexual acts and desires between men. The encounters that Bowles, Burroughs, and Chester represent in their texts form part of an extended body of literature concerned with sex between European and North African men. Bowles, Burroughs, and Chester make significant contributions to this body of literature and bring fresh perspectives and insights to the experience of sexuality under colonialism. While I am interested in the fantastic underpinnings of Western sexual experience in Morocco, I am just as interested in the economic, social, and political relations between Moroccans and foreigners that have made it possible to shift a variety of sexual fantasies into the realm of experience. The sexual culture of a certain segment of Moroccan society accommodates even while it condemns sex between European and Moroccan men, and the history of sexual tourism in Tangier places sex within a larger context of colonial relationships and financial transactions. Ultimately, I centered this study around Tangier for the same reason that sexual tourists have long been and continue to be drawn to Tangier. As a border town between North Africa and Europe, it is a site where cultures, sexualities, bodies, fantasies, and politics meet and emerge more complex for having encountered one another there.

Acknowledgments

I am grateful to many people for the advice, guidance, and support they offered as I wrote this book. Special thanks go to Henry Abelove, Donald McQuade, and Dorothy Wang, who encouraged me at crucial junctures to pursue this project and whose friendship and advice have sustained my work over the years. Fernando Arenas has seen this project develop from its infancy and he, more than any other person, encouraged me as I moved through the initial drafts. I could not have written a chapter on Alfred Chester without the help of Edward Field, who not only brought Chester's stories and essays back into print but also provided me with a copy of his edited manuscript of Chester's letters from Morocco. I remain indebted to Edward both for his generosity and for the invaluable advice he offered as I prepared this book for publication. William Cohen first introduced me to Edward Field and to the work of Alfred Chester, and I am grateful for his ongoing support. Ten years ago, Eric Peterson first suggested I read Paul and Jane Bowles. I could not have guessed at the time that his comment would lead eventually to a book on American expatriate writing!

Over the time I worked on this book, many people offered insights, questions, mentorship, and advice. The book originated as a dissertation at the University of California, Berkeley, and I am grateful for the institutional support I received as a graduate student there. Special thanks go to the members of my committee. Susan Schweik and David Halperin jointly directed the dissertation, and David Lloyd and Michael Lucey provided intellectual guidance and mentorship, as well. Other Berkeley faculty members also helped create the intellectual environment out of which this book emerged, and among them I wish especially to mention Carolyn Dinshaw and Carolyn Porter. Through courses, comments on my work in progress, and memorable conversations, this group of mentors helped me establish the theoretical foundation for my research and the contours of my major arguments.

The University of California provided financial support for travel to Columbia University's Butler Library and for two fellowships: the Dean's Dissertation Fellowship and, in conjunction with Friends of the Bancroft Library, a

Bancroft Library Fellowship. As these grants suggest, I conducted research at the Bancroft Library and at Butler Library, both of which hold rare publications and manuscript material related to Paul Bowles and William Burroughs. I am grateful to librarians at Berkeley and at Columbia for their assistance on this project. I also wish to thank Rebecca Johnson Melvin and the staff of the University of Delaware Library, Special Collections Department, who assisted my research in their Edward Field Alfred Chester Archives, Paul Bowles Papers, and Paul Bowles Collection. The collections in all three libraries helped me round out my understanding of the historical contexts in which Bowles, Burroughs, and Chester lived and wrote. Librarians at The Evergreen State College, including the interlibrary loan office, also assisted my research on innumerable occasions.

Faculty, staff, and students at The Evergreen State College provided a wonderful intellectual community during the years in which I revised my original project into a book. I wish especially to thank Julie Douglass and Kana Shephard for their administrative assistance and my faculty colleagues Nancy Allen, Caryn Cline, Virginia Darney, Ruth Hayes, Hiro Kawasaki, Lance Laird, David Marr, Alice Nelson, Brian Price, Evelia Romano, Sam Schrager, Nancy Taylor, and Tom Womeldorff. Several other people provided crucial support as I revised the manuscript and prepared it for publication. I am very grateful for the assistance offered by the editorial staff at the University of Wisconsin Press. The comments provided by the Press's anonymous readers and by Felice Picano were very insightful and guided my revisions in important ways. Illustrations were provided by Ira Cohen, the Paul Bowles Archive at the Swizz Foundation for Photography, and the University of Delaware Library, Special Collections. I'm grateful to Ira Cohen, Neil Derrick, Rebecca Johnson Melvin, Felicitas Novoselac, of Artists Rights Society/Pro Litteris, and Letizia Enderli, of the Swizz Foundation for Photography, for their help with illustrations and permissions. In addition, Ira Cohen generously shared his memories and insights about Alfred Chester, Paul Bowles, and the American expatriate community in Tangier. Special thanks to Jeffrey Chester, executor of the Alfred Chester Estate, for allowing me to quote from Alfred Chester's unpublished letters.

David Shengold, Mark Brack, Doug Kruse, Lisa Schur, Neal Charles, and Hugh Simmons offered housing and transportation during my research travels. In addition, they encouraged my work through conversation, advice, and friendship over many years. Many other friends and colleagues also shared insights, questions, and conversations that helped me refine my ideas about colonialism, sexuality, literature, and politics; additional friends and family members provided encouragement to write and revise. I wish especially to mention Allen Hibbard, Frank Ken Saragosa, Tico Arenas, Josianna Arroyo, Francisco Lopes, Jorge Silveira, Simon Stern, Rob Wesling, Ben Reiss, Ann-Marie

Weis, Sydney Levy, Maria João Pombo, Michael Boland, Roger Furrer, Lisa Skow, Jay Hotchkiss, Kim Haines, James Wilson, Loren Mullins, Iola Mullins, Susan Mullins, Doug Mullins, and Marie Mullins. Finally, Jeffrey Santa Ana made it possible for me to revise my work and produce this book. I cherish the intellectual stimulation and emotional support of our life together. Thank you, Jeff!

Colonial Affairs

1

Colonial Desire in the "Interzone" of Tangier

William Burroughs coined the term "interzone" to refer both to the manuscript that became *Naked Lunch* and to the International Zone of Tangier, where he lived while writing it. In *Colonial Affairs,* I refer to Burroughs's term in order to draw attention to the location from which William Burroughs, Paul Bowles, and Alfred Chester wrote and to the dislocations that brought them to Tangier and sustained their writing. All three authors created literary "interzones" that reflected their experience living in a city that had been detached from Morocco and was governed by a coalition of European powers until 1956. Suspended between nations, cultures, and languages, the interzone is a place of intermediacy and ambiguity, a place that remains outside standard narratives of nationhood and identity. It proved to be an expedient location for Bowles, Burroughs, and Chester to sort out the multiple crises of identity, desire, and loss that motivated their writing. I also analyze the works of Larbi Layachi, Mohammed Mrabet, and Mohamed Choukri—Moroccans who collaborated with Paul Bowles to write autobiographies, short stories, and novels. Among other topics, these Moroccan authors write about their interactions with American tourists and expatriates and about Tangier's sexual economy. I focus on their translated works, for these texts offer an excellent opportunity to explore how desire, sex, and sexuality are negotiated in Tangier precisely through translation and how these negotiations both construct and call into question narratives of national, racial, and sexual identity. By analyzing both conscious and unconscious responses to life in the "interzone," I explore the

3

impact of Tangier's colonial and transnational social structure on key literary strategies adopted and invented in postwar American literature. Moreover, I argue that
this group of texts offers readers transformative models of male subjectivity that
creatively redefine masculinity, desire, and identity.

William Burroughs had been living and writing in Tangier for more than
two years when, in October 1956, he announced in a letter to Allen Ginsberg,
"I am really writing Interzone now, not writing about it."[1] From 1923 to 1956,
a coalition of European powers governed Tangier and called the city "The International Zone of Tangier." Burroughs shortened this name to "interzone"; the
fact that he used it to refer both to the city and to the manuscript he was writing indicates how closely he associated the text with its context. At the time
Burroughs wrote this letter to Ginsberg, the "international" era was coming to
an end as independent Morocco reabsorbed Tangier into the nation. The historic political events unfolding around him, however, meant little to Burroughs—he had stopped writing about the material city of Tangier and had
begun creating an imaginary interzone through the manuscript that would
become *Naked Lunch*. In the process, Burroughs transformed his personal experience as an expatriate in Tangier into a classic work of postmodern literature.

Paul Bowles and Alfred Chester also lived in Tangier during the postwar
years, and they also "wrote interzones" that responded to the multiple pressures
and pleasures of expatriation there. Burroughs's *Naked Lunch*, Bowles's *Let It
Come Down,* and Chester's *The Foot* present three strikingly different literary
visions of the city, but all are shaped by shared expatriate experience. When
Burroughs and Bowles settled in Tangier, it was a kind of free port, with a population equally divided between Europeans and Moroccans and an economy
based on smuggling and questionable financial transactions. The European
powers had "internationalized" the city in 1923 in order to keep any one power
from establishing a military presence on the coast overlooking the Straits of
Gibraltar. This "international" status reinforced the sense that Tangier was a city
apart from the world; on the edge of a continent, overlooking two oceans, caught
between Africa and Europe, between Islam, Judaism, and Christianity, Tangier
was a place where nations, languages, and cultures could mix promiscuously.
The treaty that established the International Zone created a weak administration incapable of enforcing laws efficiently, so illegal commercial activity flour-
ished, including the buying and selling of sex and narcotics. Encounters between
people from different nations, cultures, and religions were transacted, in part,
through sexual activity and drug use, which served to break down other social
and psychic barriers. Boundaries that defined sexuality and sexual identity were
challenged, and in some contexts even the boundaries that defined self and other.

Tangier appealed to a particular type of expatriate. Previous generations of
American writers had settled in metropolitan centers of Europe, such as Paris; the
postwar writers I discuss in this book abandoned centrality. They left New York

during an era when the rest of the world looked to that city as a global hub of culture, and they preferred to live in a place so scattered in its allegiances that it looked toward no focal point—not Europe, but not exactly Morocco; not the West, but not exactly the East; a place where sex between men could take place, but not exactly a place free of sexual constraint, Tangier provided the site for a productive confusion of binary logics and preconceptions. In the free trade zone of Tangier, freedoms began to multiply. With the breakdown of national structures, kinship relations, ethical systems, and disciplinary regimes also began to decay and to reappear in new forms. Tangier was a place that was displaced in multiple ways: its geography, cultural heterogeneity, diffuse political system, and illicit economy all combined to loosen the city from its moorings but to send it in no particular direction. Bowles, Burroughs, and Chester were attracted to this loose and "free" city, and they fled the repressive atmosphere of the culture of conformity in postwar America. Because they were sexual rebels moving in decidedly bohemian literary circles, neither their lives nor their artistic visions fit into dominant narratives of postwar American culture. Marginalized at home, they created new homes for themselves on a different margin—in a city that celebrated rather than censured eccentricity. The interzones they wrote were located in Tangier, but it was dislocation that brought them to Tangier and sustained their writing.

Written so far from America, the interzone literature of these three authors remains on the margins of American literary history. While both Bowles and Burroughs continue to attract a devoted readership, neither author is usually included in university curricula that survey canonical American literature. Alfred Chester is a more obscure figure, since his psychosis and early death ended his literary career just when his talent was beginning to be recognized. It is impossible to guess what Chester might have written had he lived longer; what is clear is that, from the time he sailed for Tangier, his writing became less and less palatable to mainstream tastes. *Colonial Affairs* does not argue that any of these three authors deserves a critical reassessment that could lead to anything resembling literary canonization. On the contrary, I argue that their writing is of interest precisely because it is produced outside the United States and stubbornly remains on the margins of American literary history. Expatriate writing tends to challenge the boundaries of national literature, a tendency that is registered in criticism of such "binational" writers as Nabokov, Conrad, and Henry James. The principal texts of these authors nonetheless reside rather comfortably in various narratives of national literary history. Interzone literature, on the other hand, contests totalizing narratives of nationality and also of language, culture, identity, and sexuality. Burroughs, Chester, Bowles, and Bowles's collaborators create new narratives, and, through them, imagine alternative ways of being. In the white heat glare of colonial discourse—a discourse that attempts always to rigidify the roles of colonizer and colonized—interzone literature forges new forms of affect, desire, and deterritorialized subjectivity.

Tricking Tangier

The International Zone of Tangier was created as a compromise between the competing interests of the European powers (and, to a lesser extent, the United States), but in the postwar years it also came to perform a particular function within the global system. Guarantees of free trade, together with a weak central administration, meant that the city became a center for offshore financial transactions. Tangier served as a kind of release valve for transnational capital that needed to circumnavigate national restrictions on commercial activity and profit. It also served as a refuge for people who needed to escape limitations imposed by national authorities. All kinds of criminals washed up on Tangier's shores, including William Burroughs, who left legal complications behind when he fled the United States and Mexico. While they were never charged with criminal activity at home, in Tangier Bowles and Chester also used drugs and engaged in sexual activities that were illegal in the United States. Narcotics and prostitution were prohibited in the International Zone, but the justice system was weak and favored foreign residents. As I explain in the next section of this chapter, until 1956 a dispute between a Moroccan and an American would be decided in the United States consular court. Moroccans were understandably reluctant to file complaints.

Tangier was an especially attractive place for foreigners to live during the postwar years because of its proximity to Europe and its long history of sexual tourism and intercultural exchange. Its residents were able to experiment with and even to invent forms of promiscuity that were not available elsewhere. A thriving economy of commercial sex ensured that sexual adventure was readily available to the wealthy in Tangier and that national, cultural, and linguistic divisions were bridged through intimate physical contact. In the chapters that follow, I argue that sexual relations were not just one among many realms in which Tangier's residents encountered confusion, ambiguity, and the deterioration of bound experience. More than a metaphor for social and psychic mixing, sexual promiscuity provided the avenue through which the cultural, historical, and political indeterminacy of the International Zone was compressed into interpersonal contact. The psychological flexibility and ambiguity of interzone literature arises not only from expatriate experience in general but from sexual experience in particular. Analysis of sex and sexuality in the writings of Bowles, Burroughs, and Chester provides a lens through which it is possible to examine the interzone as both a historical product and a psychological phenomenon. Expatriate writing in Tangier articulates the desire to exceed national and other forms of identity through representations of sex, and especially through representations of marginalized forms of sex and sexuality. Furthermore, the assault on identity waged by interzone literature raises the possibility that alternative modes of existence can rescue us from the repressive norms imposed by postindustrial, heterocentric consumer society.

The various interzones inhabited by members of the expatriate literary community were established in dense and often contradictory relation to sex and sexuality, identity and desire. Interzone texts written in Tangier corroborate the abundant biographical evidence that queer sexualities strongly shaped expatriate life there.[2] Terminology concerning sex, sexuality, and sexual identity presents special problems in the lives and texts of the authors I examine. I speak at greater length about the word "queer" in chapter 3, where I consider Burroughs's use of this term. When I use the word queer, I do so with the weight of queer theory in mind, so that in my writing queer refers to forms of sexuality that refuse to be contained by norms of heterosexuality. The texts I analyze are centrally concerned with sexual desires and acts between men, and, in accordance with the definition just given, I call such desires and acts queer. But these desires and acts do not necessarily generate a sexual identity such as "gay" or "bisexual." Burroughs and Chester were quite open about their homosexuality and demonstrated a self-conscious sexual identity. Bowles, on the other hand, disliked the tendency in modern, urban societies to think about sexuality in terms of identity. He liked to surround himself with Moroccan men who similarly believed that the biological sex of one's sex partners didn't necessarily prove anything about one's identity. This attitude is also represented in the texts of Mrabet, Layachi, and Choukri.

Regardless of how Bowles, Burroughs, and Chester understood the meaning of sex and sexual identity, the fact remains that they were drawn to live in Tangier for similar reasons. On a practical level, American dollars could purchase a comfortable standard of living at a bargain price in Tangier during the 1950s and early 1960s. On a no less practical level, during this period the United States provided an inhospitable environment for men who sought sex and love with other men—whether or not they identified themselves as homosexual, and whether or not one's sexual identity was proclaimed or whispered—whereas in Tangier sex between men was not heavily policed. Tangier held another, perhaps less "practical," fascination for all three authors: in Tangier, they could pursue sexual relationships with men who were coded through regimes of colonial discourse as "racially" and "sexually" different from themselves. The culture of the Cold War consensus and of McCarthyism may be largely responsible for the exile of Bowles, Burroughs, and Chester, but the potential for "colonial" erotic exploration in Tangier contributed to their decision to seek refuge there.

Not only intellectuals and artists but also less visible gay tourists and expatriates, together with Moroccan lovers and hustlers, collectively developed a thriving sexual subculture in Tangier during the postwar years. This subculture was especially appealing because it was so complex and multiform. The multiplicity of languages, cultures, and political relations that characterized the International Zone also produced a heterogeneous sexual culture. Not only could American expatriates explore sexual pleasures prohibited at home, but also they could find themselves lost in the ambiguous dynamics of sexual expressions beyond their experience. But the indeterminacy and fluidity of interzone sexuality was counterbalanced by the rigidity of conventional colonial relations. Even an experimental sexuality that attempted to dissolve the boundary between self and other ran up against the codification of difference in terms of race, nationality, wealth, religion, and masculinity. Other sexual pursuits embraced rather than rejected the conventions of colonial desire, which were formed through stereotypes about the foreign "colonizer" and the local "colonized." The structures of colonial desire are easily replicated across time and across place because they arise not from a local articulation of sexual culture but rather from a preestablished stereotyped understanding of sex as a relation of domination and submission in which the exotic other is potently erotic. Thus, Americans accustomed to the eroticization of racial difference at home can readily transfer and even intensify that structure of desire when residing in a "colonial" space such as Tangier.

While *Colonial Affairs* is not primarily biographical, I do draw on biographical evidence to advance certain arguments about the literature of Bowles, Burroughs, and Chester. By raising the issue of colonial desire in relation to their private lives, I do not wish to suggest that Bowles or Burroughs or Chester were "sexual colonizers" or that seeking sex with men in Tangier is morally suspect. Rather, I wish to argue that, when these Americans became expatriates in Tangier, they encountered a sexual subculture in which difference was eroticized through constructions of race, nationality, wealth, religion, and masculinity. While in Tangier, Bowles, Burroughs, and Chester developed personal responses to social and sexual roles constructed in advance by colonial discourse. In the process, they wrote highly imaginative and deeply perceptive fictional representations of desire, identity, and sex in the colonial space of Tangier. References to the personal lives of the authors are of use to me insofar as biographical evidence helps illuminate the conflicts and pressures that their fiction attempts to sort out. The sexual tensions and contradictions that Bowles, Burroughs, and Chester experience and about which they write arise precisely out of the dissonance between the rigid, stereotyped roles structured by colonial discourse and the multiplicity and indeterminacy so tantalizingly promised in the interzone.

Tangier's sexual subculture developed in relation to an unusual "international" variety of colonialism, and, in order fully to understand the literary responses to sexual fantasies and practices in Tangier that Bowles, Burroughs, and Chester fashioned, we must keep in mind the historical pressures that produced the International Zone. In the next section of this chapter, I provide an overview of Tangier's political history and of American involvement in Tangier. Following this overview, I define "colonial desire" more elaborately, with reference to recent scholarship in colonial discourse studies. More specifically, I explore the theoretical problems posed by sexuality that is both colonial and queer.

International Colonialism, American Empire

Michael Rogin convincingly argues that American political culture is organized by a form of collective amnesia that sustains a general blindness about how the Republic is shaped by imperialism and how it acts like an empire. Drawing an analogy to the purloined letter of Poe's story, in "Make My Day!" Rogin explains how Americans can see the evidence of imperial practices—slavery and territorial conquest in the past, global military and economic domination today—and ignore it at the same time. One of the principal assumptions of American exceptionalism is that our national experience is shaped by domestic democratic institutions and is in this way differentiated from the experience of Britain and other monarchical and imperial societies. But in order to sustain this particular narrative of American national experience, we must selectively remember—or even forget—a significant part of our history. For example, the wars waged against Indian nations in the course of westward expansion are remembered as domestic, rather than as foreign, struggles. Other imperial adventures—such as America's participation in the international administration of Tangier—are almost entirely dismissed from the national consciousness.

Like the purloined letter in Rogin's analogy, our imperial history is obscure because it is obvious, but, because it is obvious, it can also be brought usefully into consciousness. In this section, I provide an overview of colonialism in Tangier and of American political and economic interests in Tangier. Bowles and Choukri were very conscious of this history and its legacy for contemporary Moroccan and foreign residents. While Layachi and Mrabet were not formally schooled in history, their writing suggests that they were keenly aware of the burden colonialism bestowed on their lives. Burroughs and Chester lived in Tangier as temporary residents and were far less concerned with its history than was Bowles. But whatever personal knowledge each author had of the history of Tangier, all lived there as participants in an unfolding historical drama that had begun in the fifteenth century. In order to understand the role of colonialism in their lives and their writing, we must equip ourselves with a basic understanding of that history.

The internationalization of Tangier in the twentieth century traces its roots to the very beginning of the global system as it was forged through European colonialism. In 1471, Portugal invaded Tangier and made it a garrison and trading center for its emerging empire. Portugal protected the city not only against Moroccan attempts to reclaim it but also against rival European powers that also sought preferential or exclusive trading privileges with the North

African interior. Tangier was governed by Spain under the terms that united the Iberian states under the Spanish crown from 1580 to 1640, but, when Portugal reestablished its independence, it also regained Tangier. The costs of securing the city against assaults by Moroccan armies were mounting, however, and in 1661 Portugal turned Tangier over to the English as part of the dowry of Catherine de Braganza, wife of King Charles II. The English defended the city until 1684 but, in the face of mounting military pressure, finally abandoned their strategic outpost to the sultan of Morocco, Mulay Ismail. After this defeat, the English reversed their hostility toward Morocco and forged an alliance, having concluded that Tangier would serve English interests better if it was in Moroccan hands than it would under the control of any European rival. This policy formed the basis for the eventual internationalization of Tangier; after 1684 no single European power would ever again be able to exert direct and monopolistic control over the city.

Over the course of two centuries of European occupation, Tangier came to be populated almost entirely by Europeans; after the English withdrawal it was repopulated by Moroccans, but in some ways Tanjawis (the residents of Tangier) continued to look to Europe. The economy of the city was based on international trade, after all, and the sultan transformed the city into a center for diplomacy. He preferred to keep foreign diplomats far from his centers of power in Marrakesh, Fez, and Meknes, and the foreigners preferred to live in a thriving port city near Europe, where they could facilitate the expansion of trade relationships. In the eighteenth century, these foreign diplomats began to assert more and more influence over the city and its population. To a great extent, their influence was a direct result of treaties negotiated with the Moroccan sultan that granted extraterritorial rights to foreigners and to Moroccan subjects employed by foreigners. France negotiated such a treaty in 1767, and the other European powers quickly followed suit; the Treaty of Marrakesh, signed in 1786 and ratified by the United States Congress in 1787, secured extraterritorial rights for United States citizens and their protégés (Stuart, *The International City of Tangier,* 22–23). From that time until Moroccan independence in 1956, American residents in Tangier were not subject to Moroccan laws or taxes, and disputes between Americans and Moroccans were tried in a court of the United States consulate.[3]

Granting extraterritorial rights to foreigners severely weakened the sultan's sovereignty. His authority was particularly diluted in Tangier and other ports, and in Tangier the foreign legations slowly took over key departments of city administration. Representatives of Portugal, Sweden, Great Britain, Venice, Denmark, Holland, Spain, France, and the United States formed the Sanitary Council of Tangier, which first met in 1792 in order to lobby for quarantines on ships that might carry the plague. In 1805, the sultan granted this organization the right to regulate health and sanitation, and by 1893 it was responsible for cleaning and paving the streets, improving sewage, constructing slaughterhouses, and building a water supply. Together with the international construction and administration of the Cape Spartel lighthouse, the Sanitary Council paved the way for the creation of a formal international administration for Tangier in 1923.[4]

Examples of such cooperation among the colonial powers in the late nineteenth century are rare. While the powers were engaged in fierce competition for exclusive control of territory and markets elsewhere in Africa, in Tangier they experimented with a multilateral form of imperial government. France and Spain both would have preferred to seize the strategic port at Tangier for themselves, but the objections of Great Britain made it impossible to pursue these designs. Germany and Italy also sought to expand their influence in North Africa and particularly over the Straits of Gibraltar, but, having arrived late upon the scene of colonial competition, they too satisfied themselves with an internationalized—one could say neutralized—Tangier. When, in 1904, Great Britain, France, and Spain negotiated the division of Morocco into spheres of influence, these three principal powers agreed that the north coast would remain unfortified and that Tangier would maintain an international character.[5]

After the division of Morocco into French and Spanish zones of influence, the United States began to intervene in the colonization of Morocco. The United States had maintained open-door trade agreements with the sultan of Morocco since 1786 and wanted to protect its trade against encroachments by France. While American and European business interests had benefited from the weakness of the Moroccan state (and from the open markets and extraterritorial rights this weakness allowed), by the end of the nineteenth century the sultan's sovereignty had decayed to such an extent that the United States feared that Morocco could be absorbed into the French empire. Most intercontinental African trade was already monopolized by the colonial metropoles, and the United States, under the presidency of Theodore Roosevelt, understood that American national interests in free trade were threatened. Along with Germany, which wished to protect its own interests, the United States convinced France to organize an international conference in 1906 in Algeciras, Spain, to negotiate the colonial status of Morocco. At Algeciras, a convention was signed that supported the de jure sovereignty of the sultan but the de facto authority of France and Spain over their respective zones.[6] From the point of view of the United States, the accord successfully affirmed the legality of existing treaties, so free trade and extraterritorial rights would continue. The Algeciras treaty did not prevent France from establishing a protectorate over Morocco in 1912, but it did provide the United States with a legal basis for objecting to French monopolistic practices and for insisting that open-door trade policies be maintained.

After France secured its treaty of protection in 1912, the status of Tangier remained to be determined. Negotiations to formalize the international administration of the city date from this time but were interrupted by World War I. Finally, in 1923, France, Spain, and Great Britain drafted the Statute of Tangier (revised in 1928), which established the International Zone of Tangier. The statute abolished the diplomatic corps in Tangier and all foreign extraterritorial rights, but it guaranteed the neutrality of the city and free trade privileges for all nations. A legislative assembly was established that consisted of twenty-six representatives: four French, four Spanish, three British, two Italian, one American, one Belgian, one Dutch, and one Portuguese member, plus six Muslim and three Jewish subjects of the sultan.[7] In order for the Statute of Tangier to be implemented, all interested foreign governments had to abandon the consular privileges they had accrued over the course of the nineteenth century. All nations agreed to do so except the United States, which maintained its consulate and its extraterritorial rights and never took its seat on the new legislative council. With only one vote on the council, the United States felt that it could retain more influence in Tangier by refusing to sign the statute and basing its claim to free trade on preexisting treaties. The American consul in Tangier cooperated with the new international administration, however, and recognized its authority in practice, if not in law.[8]

While a detailed historical analysis of American diplomatic and economic interests in Tangier is outside the scope of this chapter, the brief overview I have provided does suggest the main contours of those interests. The United States has pursued a remarkably consistent policy toward Morocco from the eighteenth century to the present day. While Morocco has never been a primary trading partner of the United States and while, up until World War II, the United States acceded to European dominance of North Africa, successive American governments have nonetheless diligently protected American access to Moroccan markets. Unable to control overseas markets directly through a closed imperial system of its own, the United States, and American industry, understood that its long-term prosperity depended on opening up Europe's empires to international competition.[9] Even in the late nineteenth and early twentieth centuries, when the United States experimented with developing its own formal overseas empire, President Roosevelt understood the importance of keeping Morocco's ports open to American goods and so intervened in Europe's quarrels over Morocco. Roosevelt helped bring about the Algeciras conference out of concern for trade with Morocco—but, even more important, out of concern that the principle of free trade be defended. That principle would eventually replace closed imperial systems as the basis for organizing trade between centers and peripheries of power.

This overview of Tangier's political history helps illuminate some of the tensions and contradictions that American expatriates encounter when they settle there. To return to Rogin's analogy, Tangier encapsulates the problem of the purloined letter. Through a series of international agreements and negotiations, the United States government emerged as a significant participant in the informal and formal colonization of Morocco; from 1787 to 1956, United States citizens and their protégés exercised extraterritorial rights identical to those held by Morocco's "official" colonizers. But few Americans would think that United States–Moroccan relations are marked in any way by the experience of Europe's colonial expansion. The American Republic, and the citizens who inhabit it, are thus able to criticize European colonialism while also benefiting from it. Upon the collapse of formal colonial empires in the second half of the twentieth century, the United States was able to advocate national independence for areas formally under European control, while simultaneously expanding neocolonial structures of economic dominance and dependence. American expatriates in Tangier have the option of seeing or not seeing this "purloined letter," but in either case they are affected by it—as is the literature written by the American expatriate authors who reside there.

Tangier's political history is shaped in a more specific way by the contradictions of American foreign economic policy. This policy has advocated free trade from the early nineteenth century (protection from official and unofficial piracy) through the colonial period (open access to markets France wished to control exclusively) and up to today. Ironically, from 1787 to 1956, this advocacy of free trade occurred in the context of treaties that extended American sovereignty into the political and legal system of another nation. The extraterritorial rights once enjoyed by American residents of Tangier and their Moroccan protégés do not in themselves contradict the principle of free trade (that markets should be open to all without government manipulation through quotas and tariffs), but they do indicate where power lies. Until 1956, transactions between Americans and Tanjawis—whether commercial, financial, or personal—were conducted under United States law. To the extent to which such trade was "free," its freedom was brought into being through very specific forms of political and juridical domination. When considering the lives of Americans who lived in Tangier during this period, one must wonder to what extent their "freedoms"—including the sexual freedom Burroughs and others celebrated—were secured through domination, as well. In seeking sovereignty over their own bodies and sexual desires, did American expatriates compromise the sovereignty of the Moroccans among whom they lived?

While this question arises when we consider the relation of individual Americans to the history of United States foreign policy and international colonialism in Tangier, it is too complex to be answered within the framework of political history alone. In the chapters that follow, I argue that colonial relations of power play a crucial role in both the lives and the literature of Bowles, Burroughs, and Chester but that this is not a simplistic role in which an individual American replicates the political structures of American economic domination. The operation of power in international relations and interpersonal relationships is too diffuse and too complex to be embodied in such a way. Rather, I argue that American expatriate writers inhabit the legacy of American and Moroccan political history. As residents of Tangier, they participate in the social structures of colonialism and discover that their interactions with Tanjawis are of necessity shaped by the psychology of colonialism. Far from being "free" from history, sexual relations, too, are shaped by this psychology.

Bowles, Burroughs, Chester, and other American expatriates in Tangier struggled with competing demands to identify with the colonial position they temporarily occupied and simultaneously to disidentify with that position and with the formal structures of European colonialism that were being disassembled during the 1950s and early 1960s. Bowles, Burroughs, and Chester each arrived at a different understanding about the position he could most comfortably occupy as a foreign resident in Tangier, and these differences are registered in the literature they wrote. Before turning to analysis of specific works of literature, however, I outline more specifically the theoretical issues posed by colonial psychology, particularly regarding race and sex. American expatriate literature written in Tangier is shaped in relation to transnational discursive formations of race and racism and of Orientalism. The fiction of Paul Bowles, William Burroughs, and Alfred Chester attempts to represent the complex negotiations that take place during cultural and sexual encounters that are experienced also as racial encounters. The complexity of these negotiations arises in part from the way in which American notions of race are mapped onto the colonial scene, while at the same time preconceptions about the Orient and about European colonialism help to shape American notions of racial difference.

Queering Colonial Sexuality

Scholarship on colonialism and colonial discourse has long concerned itself with the function of gender in systems of political domination, whereby the masculine "colonizer" dominates the feminized "colonized"; more recently, analysis has also turned to the role played by sexuality in imperial systems.[10] In a series of articles, Joseph Boone explored the ways that colonial, patriarchal, and heterosexual systems of domination are articulated through one another and how the homoeroticism of Orientalism challenges narratives of authority.[11] In *The Rhetoric of English India,* Sara Suleri demonstrated through a reading of E. M. Forster how the close proximity of male friendship to male love, coupled with the urgency of desire and the impossibility of its fulfillment, sustains the pervasive, hazardous, and frustrating homoeroticism of colonialism. Her argument goes a long way toward establishing the centrality of homosociality and homosexuality in colonial discourse without, however, attending closely to the ways in which that centrality is produced and attenuated. While, as Suleri argued, homoeroticism does indeed disrupt normative heterosexual narratives of empire, this work is effected from the margins of empire—and from quite specific margins at that. It is true that the "Orient" has long been construed in the "West" to be a place where sexual decadence can flourish, and, as Joseph Boone has shown, this construal has informed widespread and diverse yet homogenizing notions about sodomy and effeminacy in the East. But I argue that much is lost if we read the master text of colonial sexuality without closely examining specific margins—and experiences of marginality—in historical and cultural contexts. By specificity I mean much more than tracing the relation, regarding North Africa and the Near East, between discourses of colonialism and Orientalism. The experiences of Paul Bowles, William Burroughs, and Alfred Chester in Tangier are shaped in important ways by Orientalist notions, but each author's representations of friendship and sex describe a particular relationship to race, sex, and colonialism that is grounded in the writer's formation as an American in Tangier during the postwar years. Moreover, these writers do not readily accede to the demands of an overdetermined Orientalism. While they step into a situation that casts them as foreign and white and therefore a "colonizer," they write interzone texts that critique binary structures of dominance and that imagine new forms of subjectivity.

When Bowles, Burroughs, and Chester left the United States for Tangier, they brought with them the rather cumbersome baggage of a racial identity forged through three hundred years of American experience. The sexual fantasies and acts that all three men pursued in Morocco were shaped both by American formations of race and racism and by Tangier's insertion into a mostly undifferentiated Orientalist discourse. The function of sex and sexuality in racial and Orientalist discourse is particularly undifferentiated; Abdul JanMohammed explains that the lack of density in American discourses of "racialized sexuality" is a result of the imperative not to acknowledge the permeability of the racial border or the frequency and ease with which it is crossed. He contrasts the density of discourses that produce white bourgeois sexuality in the United States with the loud silences that surround racialized sexuality and concludes that, "Whereas bourgeois sexuality is a product of an empiricist, analytic, and proliferating discursivity, racialized sexuality is a product of stereotypic, symbolizing, condensing discursivity" ("Sexuality on/of the Racial Border," 105–6). Racialized sexuality, he continues, is managed and understood through allegorical structures, which explains why it is expressed primarily in literary forms—even when the topic of racialized sexuality is expressed in juridical or psychoanalytical discourse, that expression is processed through metaphor or analogy. It is no wonder, then, that the most interesting critical work on colonialism and sexuality has been performed in relation to literary texts.

As Boone and Suleri recognize, homosexuality tends to destabilize the allegories and analogies through which the terms of "racialized sexuality" or "colonial sexuality" are commonly understood. Within the logic of patriarchy, binary relations of power between colonizer and colonized are quite easily mapped onto gender relations of male and female. Within the logic of heterosexuality, male sexual dominance of women becomes part of this mapping. But the potential for women to desire women, for men to desire men, and for any of a number of nonnormative sexual acts to take place outside a heterosexual configuration of power confuses the logic of allegory and the clarity of metaphor. The potential for homosexuality to destabilize imperial or patriarchal relations of power, however, is not necessarily realized as an anti-imperial political position. Desire's instabilities, including the instability of homoeroticism and homosexuality, have existed within imperial relations of power for hundreds of years, so destabilizing potentials must have some role— perhaps even a supportive role—to play within colonial systems. Bowles, Burroughs, and Chester were all constrained to occupy the role of expatriate "colonial" in Tangier; each author accepted and rejected the role in his own way, forging his own relationship both to the binarisms of "colonial desire" and to the potential for desire to destabilize facile binarisms. None of these authors pursued a nationalist anti-imperialism, because they criticized nationalism as much as imperialism. Neither did they pretend there was an easy way "out" of colonial discourse and racialized sexuality in Tangier; rather, they created literary interzones that overlapped the material relations of Tangier. In this new fictive space, fantasy, affect, and desire exceed the constraints of material colonial relations.

The pressures experienced as one is thrust into the position of the "colonial" subject of desire, the response of Bowles, Burroughs, and Chester to those pressures, and the literary expressions that emerge out of those responses are the subjects of inquiry in the following chapters. Throughout the following analyses of literary forms and biographical/historical locations, attention is repeatedly drawn to the common site of these authors's expatriation. It is Tangier that brought Bowles, Burroughs, and Chester together, and it is their specific experience in postwar Tangier that shaped their literary visions. While Tangier may at first appear to be an odd place—perhaps even a queer place—for American writers to expatriate themselves, on a closer appraisal it seems a logical and perhaps even necessary destination for this group of writers. Living precariously on the margins of American society at home, Bowles, Burroughs, and Chester sought another kind of marginal space abroad, a space where they could live and write comfortably. All three men found a certain kind of freedom in Tangier—at the very least, they found the freedom to have sex with men and to experiment with drugs with little chance of official police harassment.[12] Half of Tangier's population was European before independence in 1956, and even after that time a foreign bohemian community remained, so expatriate writers could build social networks supportive of their own cultural formations while also coming into daily contact with Moroccan culture. While all three authors were fascinated in their own ways by the strong traditions of Islam and Moroccan culture in the city, Tangier was an especially attractive place for foreigners to live because of its proximity to Europe and its long history of sexual tourism and intercultural exchange. The appeal of Tangier was that it perched between cultures and nations. While the experience of Bowles, Burroughs, and Chester in Tangier was mediated by the structures of a "generic" colonial discourse, that discourse was also troubled by the very "in-betweenness" of Tangier. Not Europe, but not exactly Morocco; not the West, but not exactly the East; a place where sex between men could take place, but not exactly a place free of sexual constraint, Tangier provided the site for a productive confusion of binary logics and preconceptions. Perhaps such indeterminacies lent Tangier a special appeal for American expatriates seeking a "colonial" experience. After all, the American experience of colonialism is to stand simultaneously outside and inside its structures: to critique European imperial expansion while competing with—and eventually superseding—European influence over global markets.

Speaking from the Margins

As I have shown, the United States was a significant participant in the division of Morocco and colonial administration of Tangier, but the colonial experience of Morocco has been of little interest to the American public. France and Spain have experienced a sustained engagement with Moroccan people, history, culture, and politics, and their historical involvement in North Africa is registered in contemporary cultural and political upheavals, for example, those involving immigration to Europe. While Morocco played an important role in American postwar geostrategic military planning, it did not figure prominently in the American cultural imagination. Generally speaking, the idea of "Morocco" continues to function in the United States either as a dreamscape lifted from the *Arabian Nights* or as a backdrop for the film *Casablanca*. In the postwar years, Washington was acutely aware of Morocco's economic and political importance to United States interests, but for most Americans Morocco was then and remains today a blank space—a nation considered only marginally relevant to American culture and politics.

It is precisely this blankness that interests me, because I am curious what can and cannot be said and heard about the United States from the margins of its postwar "empire." The question is, how can we go about reading or hearing from this blankness? Certainly not by training our eyes on the centers of culture and of power, for these centers constitute themselves by making the margins obscure. One could extend the sort of history I have sketched into a meta-narrative of United States imperialism—but examining diplomatic maneuvers will not necessarily reveal the internal contradictions and complexities of colonialism in culture. I have turned to historical analysis in this introduction because it helps clarify the variety of pressures that is exerted upon individual actors in a "colonial" scene. In the subsequent chapters I examine highly subjective—even subject-forming—experience, especially in the realms of sexual fantasy, activity, and identity. By closely examining the personal experience—and the literary representations of that experience—of three Americans in Tangier, my argument works from the margin to the center. The personal and even idiosyncratic expressions of Bowles, Burroughs, and Chester cast an oblique but penetrating light on cultural formations not only in Tangier but also "back home" in the United States.

The chapters that follow are shaped by a persistent question: while interzone texts are written from margins described both at home and abroad, what relation do these margins have to each other? I address this question through historical, biographical, and textual analyses of interzone writings. I begin with a chapter on Paul Bowles, the pivotal figure in the expatriate literary community. Bowles represents expatriation as an uneasy exile from national culture and from the very possibility of social integration. In several short stories and novels, but especially in *The Spider's House*, he described the self as constituted in isolation from an object of desire that remains unapproachable. Bowles's literary treatment of expatriation critiques the nostalgic fantasy for a lost colonial era; I examine this fantasy and explore how and why it is produced in the face of colonial desire.

In a chapter on William Burroughs, I argue that Tangier is not so much the "setting" of *Naked Lunch* as it is a geopolitical corollary to the crisis of subjectivity Burroughs explores in his postmodern classic. Academic criticism of Burroughs tends to focus on the ways his experimental writing presents a critique of language and subjectivity, but such formal analyses overlook the importance of global politics and expatriation to the emergence of his critique. By paying close attention to the personal, geographical, and historical context in which Burroughs wrote, I demonstrate that his postmodern vision arises in relation to the dispersal of power in the global system and to his dislocation from the United States. I further argue that, in *The Wild Boys,* Burroughs's fantasy of a postnational future demonstrates how he translates his personal sexual identity and desire into a kind of political manifesto.

Like Bowles, Chester also explored political relations through romance, but unlike him, Chester did not come to "reasonable" terms with the demands of identity and desire in an expatriate setting. In a chapter on Chester, I trace his refusal to "reason" in *The Exquisite Corpse,* in which he turned to surrealism to invent an alternative universe, one that collapses the distance between subject and object. In *The Foot,* Chester wrote about his love for a Moroccan man and the aftermath of that relationship; he invoked the terms of fetishism in order to dispute those terms and to claim autonomy from the framework of colonial relations. Densely psychological, Chester's writing provides the most interior perspective on interzone writing.

In each chapter I trace a tense relation between two modes of experience in Tangier. Mark Twain wrote of Tangier, "We wanted something thoroughly and uncompromisingly foreign—foreign from top to bottom—foreign from centre to circumference—foreign inside and outside and all around—nothing anywhere about it to dilute its foreignness—nothing to remind us of any other people or any other land under the sun. And lo! In Tangier we have found it" (*Traveling with the Innocents Abroad,* 26). On the one hand, the impressions of Bowles, Burroughs, and Chester are all shaped by banal and undifferentiated discursive formations of Orientalism. Twain's description of Tangier efficiently illustrates this relation to the city and its inhabitants. On the other hand, Bowles, Burroughs, and Chester also relate to Tangier through a more complex mode of experience. They discover in Tangier an "interzone" of diverse, proliferating, and often contradictory desires and pressures. At the same time, processes of interaction and exchange in the multilateral interzone are also subject to the binary regime of racial and colonial discourse. I explore the tension between these two modes of experience throughout *Colonial Affairs,* but especially in the concluding chapter.

In that chapter I decenter the implicitly "national" frame of my own project by analyzing a group of translations that Paul Bowles rendered of stories told to him by Moroccan collaborators. Mohammed Mrabet and Larbi Layachi told their stories to Bowles in an unwritten variant of Maghrebi Arabic, which he translated and edited. Mohamed Choukri writes in standard Arabic but published his autobiography, *For Bread Alone,* in collaboration with Bowles. The collaborative texts produced by these men provide an excellent site to explore how identity and desire are negotiated in Tangier precisely through translation and how these negotiations both construct and call into question national narratives. These "transnational" and "translational" texts characterize the suspension and ambiguity of the interzone and at the same time provide fresh perspectives through which to analyze the phenomenon of American expatriation in Tangier. Mrabet, Layachi, and Choukri call attention to the "colonial" conditions of their literary collaboration and unsettle facile assumptions about sexuality, politics, translation, and literature.

2

Paul Bowles
Colonial Nostalgia, Colonial Desire

Over the past fifty years, Paul Bowles achieved fame as a vaguely eccentric, charming, highly original gentleman expatriate. His enduring popularity, while rooted in his stories and novels, owes a great deal to this authorial persona. Until his death in 1999, Bowles represented the alluring possibility that one could leave America, live a lifestyle out of synch with postindustrial consumer society, and substitute for it a bohemian existence dedicated to literature, ideas, and fine conversation. Moreover, Bowles represented the possibility of living this idealized lifestyle in Tangier, a "colonial" setting. Today, Tangier bears little resemblance to the place Bowles first saw in 1931.[1] A lively, sprawling, modern city, Tangier has lost much of the exotic appeal that excited European and American tourists during the colonial era. Nonetheless, Paul Bowles's authorial persona continues to be associated with the bygone era of colonial privilege enjoyed in the midst of Islamic calls to prayer, ancient whitewashed buildings, and narrow, dark, mysterious streets. Bowles's enduring popularity owes a great deal not only to his association with this idealized world but also to the loss of this world in the postcolonial era. In short, Paul Bowles is widely associated with nostalgia for colonialism.

Bowles recognized an upsurge in colonial nostalgia in the 1980s, insofar as this yearning was registered in the questions asked of him by visitors. In 1986, he complained about the numerous European television and radio interviewers who invariably asked him about life in the International Zone: "It's strange, this sudden surge of interest in day before yesterday. Nostalgia for simpler times?"[2] During the 1980s and 1990s, colonial nostalgia was readily apparent in United States culture in a number of films and books, most prominently *Out of Africa* (1985).[3] In 1991, Michelle Green published a gossipy book about the expatriate scene in Tangier that resurrected the city's reputation for giddy wealth, homosexual exuberance, and freedom from the bourgeois values of home. Green's *The Dream at the End of the World: Paul Bowles and the Literary Renegades in Tangier* helped to anchor Bowles in the popular American imagination as the gracefully aging reminder of a bygone era of decadence in colonial Tangier.

The single most forceful representation of Paul Bowles's image to American and European audiences in recent years, however, is Bernardo Bertolucci's 1990 film version of the 1949 novel *The Sheltering Sky*. This film participates in the wider cultural phenomenon of late-twentieth-century colonial nostalgia, but it also registers with precision how and why the authorial persona "Paul Bowles" appeals to a nostalgic sensibility. This persona is explicitly foregrounded by having the aging Bowles read parts of his novel as the film's narrator. In addition, Bertolucci dresses Bowles in clothes from the 1940s and has him sit quietly in the background, a "visible spectator" wistfully watching the characters he created forty years earlier come to life.[4] Bowles's protests to the contrary, Bertolucci believes that Port is Paul and Kit is Jane Bowles, and in order to emphasize this interpretation he locates the film in Morocco, with the opening and closing scenes in Tangier (the novel is set in Algeria and begins in Oran).[5] To be more precise, the film begins with a short sequence of black-and-white shots of New York in the 1940s, as if to remind us that Bowles first conceived the plot for this novel in New York at a time when he longed to return to the desert he had seen in the 1930s and also to remind us that the metaphor of desert in which novel and film turn is rooted in the spiritual and intellectual crisis of postwar Western society.[6]

The film version of *The Sheltering Sky* is multiply framed around geographical and temporal dislocations. The appearance of Paul Bowles on the screen evokes the melancholy of those dislocations and suggests that, through memory and through artistic expression, the past can be recaptured. The melancholy yearning for the past with which the film opens rejects modernity and urbanity, evoking wistful regret. As the word "yearning" suggests, this nostalgia is ultimately about desire. Colonial nostalgia is saturated with desire, which, while diffuse, contains a specifically sexual manifestation. Images or memories of colonialism that romanticize relations between colonizer and colonized are in a very real sense romances: erotic investments shape those relations, and, when desire is frustrated, it is replaced with sustained melancholia.

In this chapter, I explore in detail the erotic underpinnings of colonial nostalgia. With reference to psychoanalytic theory, I argue that such nostalgia

Paul Bowles and Mohammed Mrabet, Tangier, 1986 (Photograph by Ira Cohen)

arises from an unacknowledged loss of a disavowed desire for the colonized other. I analyze *The Spider's House* and key short stories to demonstrate that, while nostalgia pervades Bowles's work, the texts critique this way of relating to history and to politics. Paul Bowles insightfully explores the paradoxes and dilemmas of colonial desire in his fiction. This does not mean he is responsible for the romantic nostalgia other people project onto his life, but neither does it mean that Bowles finds a way to live in Tangier outside the constraints of colonial discourse. His personal relationships complexly and artfully engage the troubles of colonial desire. I offer biographical analysis when references to his personal life illuminate his fictional exploration of these issues. I conclude the chapter by examining the psychological bridge between American-style racism and colonial discourse, questioning how one can get away from "home" and why one would want to.

Love's Loss: Mourning

Renato Rosaldo defines "imperial nostalgia" as a mourning for the loss of an imagined purity in "traditional" non-Western culture.[7] Rosaldo points out that anthropology has traditionally sought its legitimation through the declared mission to preserve knowledge of non-Western cultures that are rapidly changing and, in changing, are disappearing. This humanistic understanding of anthropology makes the ethnographer out to be a sort of translator who makes "primitive" culture comprehensible to the West through language, through writing. Contemporary anthropology has had to acknowledge its own relation to colonialism, and the mission to "preserve" and "translate" knowledge is now thought of as the production of knowledge. Rosaldo reflects upon his own field work and witnesses himself as a participant in the cultural transformations occurring among the Ilongots in the Philippines. By exploring his own subjectivity as an anthropologist engaged in field work, Rosaldo calls into question the humanistic understanding of an ethnographer as a detached and neutral "translator" and contextualizes his own work as ideological production. From a contemporary perspective, we can see that the traditional desire of anthropology to "save" non-Western cultures is a desire that there be "primitive" cultures, that they be fundamentally different from Western cultures, that prior to the period of European global expansion these cultures be self-contained and static, and that these cultures be in the process of rapid decline since European contact.

While anthropologists have always tried to dissociate themselves from colonials of various stripes, and while there are important and substantive differences between the activities of anthropologists and those of missionaries, administrators, settlers, and travel writers, in their romance with "traditional" societies, anthropologists participate in the sort of nostalgia common to these "fellow travelers."[8] In mourning the loss of that which they have helped to alter, Westerners demonstrate a yearning for an authentically "traditional" non-West: that is to say, for authentic difference against which the West can come to know itself. In *Orientalism,* Edward Said traces this yearning for difference through European discourses of "The Orient," including North Africa. One trope through which the demand for "authentic" difference is clearly visible in the case of Africa as a continent is the trope of "discovery." As the European scramble for Africa heated up in the nineteenth century, accounts of European and American travel and exploration there began to proliferate. Even up to this day, one of the central tropes of travel writings on Africa is the familiar fantasy of being the first white person on the scene and hence the witness to a "virgin" land and an "untouched" culture.[9] There is a deep-seated desire in the West to believe that Africa was a "closed" continent before the Portuguese navigations "opened" it to the West. Even the earliest European travel writings demonstrate the fallacy of this notion. When the Scottish explorer Mungo Park wrote about his travels through present-day Senegal, Mali, and Niger in the eighteenth century, he repeatedly inscribed his fantasy to be the first white man on the scene. At the same time, he complained bitterly about the incessant harassment he received from Africans who knew exactly who he was: a European, a Christian, and an infidel who did not belong in Africa and whose uninvited presence there was clearly a threat.[10]

Port, the hero of *The Sheltering Sky,* is a twentieth-century Mungo Park. Like Park, Port wants to gain knowledge of Africa and is somewhat unnerved by evidence that Africans already have extensive knowledge of him. Port is, however, a product of his century, and, unlike Park's, Port's encounters with Africans are starkly devoid of sentiment.[11] Also unlike Park, Port cannot so easily evade the evidence that countless Europeans have preceded him to Africa. At best, he can only disavow this evidence; he avoids speaking to a French colonial administrator who once lived in a town he hopes to visit "for fear of losing his preconceived idea" that the town "was isolated and unfrequented" (*Sheltering Sky,* 175). Port is quite bitter in his nostalgia, for he believes that World War II has irrevocably damaged Algerian culture in the northern cities. As Kit puts it, the effect of war is that "The people of each country get more like the people of every other country. They have no character, no beauty, no ideals, no culture—nothing, nothing" (8). This is exactly the reason, insists Port, to travel deep into the Sahara, where war and modernity have not touched the "authentic," "traditional," and—in his mind—backward desert inhabitants. Even before this journey begins, we are reminded that Port's romance with premodernity is a fantasy of his own (or of his culture's) construction. When he is amazed to find a traditional Arab café in Oran, the Algerian with whom he is sharing tea corrects him: "The war was bad. A lot of people died. There was nothing to eat. That's all. How would that change the cafés?" (22).

Unlike Port, in his long years of residence in Morocco Paul Bowles became increasingly less a traveler and more like an anthropologist: very well informed about Moroccan cultures, fluent in the national languages, critical of Western cultural colonialism, and very well aware of the complexities of his own relationship to the country in which he resided. He was like an anthropologist in other ways, as well. His translations from Maghrebi Arabic, especially of those stories based on traditional folktales, are a kind of anthropological work, insofar as they attempt to preserve in writing an oral tradition that is under siege because of television and other social change. Likewise, the series of recordings he made for the Library of Congress of traditional Moroccan music attempted to preserve a "vanishing" art. Bowles's efforts to preserve Moroccan music and oral stories resemble anthropology from earlier rather than later in the twentieth century. Bowles did not adopt Rosaldo's self-reflective understanding that he was involved in the production of new forms of knowledge; on the contrary, he retained a deep interest in establishing difference between "primitive" and "modern" people. When asked why he was more interested in working with illiterate than with literate Moroccans, Bowles replied, "The literate are less interesting. They have generally absorbed French ideas from their professors."[12] In this remark we see an ideological orientation that could as well have come from Port: distaste for the cosmopolitan sharing of ideas in the modern world and preference for a "pure" traditional way of life.

If it was French ideas in particular that Bowles preferred not "contaminate" Morocco's youth, perhaps the reason was the "French" idea of existentialism that describes so well the unwelcome intellectual and spiritual crisis in which he found himself—a crisis that is rather famously the subject of his major novels. Bowles's writing is firmly grounded within modernism, and in particular two avant-garde movements within modernism: surrealism and existentialism.[13] It is in the formal experimentation and innovations of modernist art that Edward Said is able to locate the response of modernity to the pressures exerted upon Europe by imperialism. According to Said, as Europe (and, by extension, the United States) entered the twentieth century, it became increasingly clear in the colonial metropoles that the natives would never cease resisting colonialism and that the dream of absolute hegemony was illusory. "When you can no longer assume that Britannia will rule the waves forever, you have to reconceive reality as something that can be held together by you the artist, in history rather than in geography" (*Culture and Imperialism,* 189–90). Said then points to the formal innovations in high modernism as the literary response to this reconceptualization: circularity, juxtaposition of incongruities, and irony. I wish to suggest that this reconceptualization is also visible in the avant-garde movements of surrealism and existentialism, especially insofar as both movements attempt to formulate an aesthetic through refiguring and reimagining the troubled relationship between consciousness and Europe's other.

The West has long had a vested interest in conceiving of the native, colonized other as unapproachably distant from itself, and the discourse that sustained a simultaneous civilizing "mission" and economic exploitation was predicated upon this distance between "us" and "them." By the twentieth century, however, the violence of colonialism had begun to take a toll on this discourse itself, especially on the humanism of which it was a part. After all, the native was human, too, just like "us," and this point became increasingly inescapable as contact between colonizers and colonized proliferated. Said points especially to the momentous impact on Europe as more and more "natives" made it their home. For modernist literature, this means that, "Like the fascinating inverts of Proust's novel, [Leopold] Bloom testifies to a new presence within Europe, a presence rather strikingly described in terms unmistakably taken from the exotic annals of overseas discovery, conquest, vision. Only now instead of being *out there*, they are *here*, as troubling as the primitive rhythms of the *Sacre du printemps* or the African icons in Picasso's art" (*Culture and Imperialism,* 188). And, now that "they" are "here," inside "us," the unity of consciousness is put into question. Surrealism responds to this crisis by abandoning consciousness and by seeking to reconstruct transcendence through an unconscious connection between self and other, between the West and its others. Existentialism responds with a crisis of being with the other that is "resolved" through disavowal, through an attempt to banish the historicity of this crisis in a revitalized ontology of self-consciousness.

Freud offers a psychoanalytic argument about the specific mechanism whereby the West's other comes to haunt it not only from within the West but from within the psyche. He speculates that the ego is formed, in part, through the incorporation of lost love objects (he focuses particularly on parental figures), and he describes the mechanism for this incorporation as the process of mourning.[14] Judith Butler makes use of Freud's logic to demonstrate how the taboo against homosexuality helps to produce both the ego and gender. Prohibitions against cross-gender identifications and same-sex desires enforce the loss of love for one's parental figures, but "The loss of the other whom one desires and loves is overcome through a specific act of identification that seeks to harbor that other within the very structure of the self. . . . [I]n effect, the other becomes part of the ego through the permanent internalization of the other's attributes" (*Gender Trouble,* 57–58). Desire is transformed into identification, but, if desire is ambivalent in the first place, that ambivalence is sustained in identification.

In another context, Butler discusses another taboo, that against miscegenation, and explores the ways in which desires are fostered and forestalled around race because of this taboo. Through her reading of Nella Larsen's *Passing*, Butler describes how the "whiteness" of Bellew is constructed in and through his desire for Clare and his disavowal of that desire. This is an ambivalent desire insofar as Bellew on the one hand needs to possess a black woman in order to define his own whiteness, masculinity, and heterosexuality and on the other hand must avoid all contact with racial others if his "whiteness" (and that of his children) is to be "pure." This ambivalent desire is prohibited by the taboo against miscegenation, which, like the taboo against homosexuality, enforces a loss. Such a loss results in mourning, an incorporation of the lost love object, and ultimately an identification that is itself subject to prohibition and censure.[15] Butler does not dwell upon the process of mourning that Bellew must surely undergo (perhaps because he "loses" Clare only at the end of the novel). In "Passing, Queering," Butler is more concerned with the issues raised by *Passing*, that is to say, with the marking and unmarking of sexuality and race in the United States, and consequently she does not consider what it might mean for Bellew's cross-racial desire to turn into cross-racial identification. But this psychic mechanism for internalizing the other is of interest in colonial contexts, where the possibility of "going native" always lurks as a promise and a threat. The colonizer's subjectivity and social power are constituted in his difference and distance from those who are colonized and named "natives." The colonizer needs these others; as in the case of Bellew, this need is also a desire, a specifically sexual desire. But because desire can so readily be transformed into identification, colonial desire must be constantly policed lest it lead to a breakdown of the psychic and political barriers that constitute the colonizers in opposition to the colonized. Desire for the colonized other must be disavowed, but this disavowal is experienced as a loss of the love object, and from loss arise mourning and melancholia. At this point, we can see yet another face of colonial nostalgia: not only a vague desire on the part of the postcolonial world to go back in time and not only a yearning to witness or experience the "purity" of traditional non-Western cultures, but also a melancholia inspired by the unacknowledged loss of a disavowed sexual desire for the colonized other.

Love's Loss: Betrayal

In his twenties, Bowles worked primarily as a composer. He studied with Aaron Copland, and supported himself by writing theater scores. Rather suddenly, when he was living in New York in 1939, he decided to write a short story, "Tea on the Mountain," which deals with an American writer in Tangier and her erotic relationship with a Moroccan boy. Mjid, a student at Tangier's Lycée Français, invites the American on a picnic in the hopes of seducing her. She accepts the invitation, decides not to keep the appointment, then compulsively purchases the picnic meal and shows up in spite of her resolve. Mjid makes several sexual advances, and the woman does not exactly refuse him, but whatever desire exists between them is frustrated, not acted upon. The two converse, but seem unable to "connect" with each other in any significant way. The failure of sex is, most obviously, a commentary on the difficulty of communicating across cultures and of knowing or understanding one's other. As the American woman and the Moroccan boy look across the Straits of Gibraltar to the mountains of Spain, they see a geographical divide symbolic of the cultural gap between them; this gap frustrates their desire but at the same time inspires and animates their desire. Mjid wants the woman because she is "European"; when she objects that she is American, he responds, "All the better" (*Collected Stories,* 19). For her part, the woman comes to realize during the course of the day that "The idea of such a picnic had so completely coincided with some unconscious desire she had harbored for many years. To be free, out-of-doors, with some young man she did not know—*could* not know—that was probably the important part of the dream. For if she could not know him, he could not know her" (22).

I will return to the provocative question of anonymity and desire raised by "Tea on the Mountain" after first analyzing melancholia, disavowal, and colonial desire in Bowles's texts. "Colonial desire" is neither monolithic nor universal, and the same is true of the colonial nostalgia that may spring from it. While one can accurately say that the West defines itself as "the West" through a disidentification with "the non-West" (with, in this case, areas colonized by Europe), one cannot easily generalize how or when that disidentification will reverse itself into an identification, or when identity will shift registers into desire. These reversals and shifts are contingent upon historical and cultural contexts. For example, the psychological situation in a settler colony like Algeria or Kenya in the 1920s was quite different from that of the neocolonial tourist economy of Morocco in the 1960s. Whether the desire under discussion can be properly understood as homosexual, as heterosexual, or as adhering to neither of these classifications also makes a considerable difference when one analyzes its relation to identity, and whether or when desire is subject to disavowal. It seems, for example, that in Tangier's flourishing sexual marketplace disavowal is not necessary—although it is certainly possible to disavow one's desire even in the midst of acting upon it. Such a disavowal can even intensify the appeal of colonial eroticism.

The melancholia of colonial desire is complexly portrayed in Paul Bowles's favorite short story, "The Time of Friendship."[16] The story is set in the Algerian Sahara in the 1950s just as the war for independence was heating up; Fräulein Windling is a school teacher in Switzerland, but she spends her winters in a small and remote Saharan oasis. She is forced to leave suddenly one winter, never to return, when the French close the area to civilians in their war against the independence movement. The title of the story refers to her friendship with Slimane, who is fifteen years old at the time Windling is forced to leave. At the end of the story, Windling returns to the safety of Switzerland, while Slimane joins the guerrilla army. The "time" of their friendship properly speaking is the colonial era, before the war for independence gets under way: when this time is finished, both colonialism and friendship are at an end, for one depends on the other.

"The Time of Friendship" is a sad story, saturated with all three of the aspects of colonial nostalgia I have outlined. Fräulein Windling's annual journeys south into the Sahara are conceived of as journeys back in time. Like Port, she dislikes the northern port city through which she enters Algeria. The "ragged European garments of the dock workers" are a "grim" reminder that colonialism has modernized the country while impoverishing its inhabitants, and this makes the city "unhappy." She prefers the seemingly primitive, static and pure culture of the desert, for the city is a "full-blown example of the social degeneracy achieved by forced cultural hybridism" and "The change, even from the preceding year, was enormous; it made her sad" (344). Windling romanticizes the lives of the people she stays with in the Sahara, telling her Swiss pupils, for example, that the inhabitants of the desert fashion everything they need for life out of the "baked earth, woven grass, palmwood and animal skins" that are found there (337). She neglects to mention that, if this was ever true, it is certainly no longer true: the women carry drinking water in empty oil tins, slowly poisoning themselves from the refuse of industry. For Windling, neither Europe nor Africa benefits from industry; she experiences modernity as loss of humanity's connection to nature and believes that in the Sahara people still maintain this special connection: "What we have lost, they still possess" (338). This loss not only is a result of exchanging "nature" for "civilization" but also has a corporeal, even a racial, component. "She coveted the rugged health of the natives, when her own was equally strong, but because she was white and educated, she was convinced that her body was intrinsically inferior" (338).

There is another kind of loss that is central to this story: the loss of friendship between Windling and Slimane. Even before the friendship is finished, however, there is another component of their relationship that is irrecoverably "lost" because it is cut off before it can flower. The encounters between Windling and Slimane are infused with a subtle erotic charge. Allen Hibbard notes that in an early draft of this story the erotic subtext of "friendship" is much more obvious, but Bowles censored passages that would bring this desire out of the closet.[17] In the transition from rough draft to published story, Bowles enacted a kind of authorial "disavowal" of sexual desire, a disavowal that Windling also enacts within the story.

The earlier draft also explicitly draws a connection between Windling's desire for a Maghrebi boy and her identification with the desert and its inhabitants. Her first sight of the desert was a "transfiguring experience" (338), and she perpetuates this transfiguration by wearing local clothes, disguising her "white . . . intrinsically inferior" body and romantically flirting with her potential to "go native." Moreover, the early draft indicates that this dressing up is also at times a cross-dressing: "[S]he had once dressed up in men's clothing, bournous and all, and ridden horseback with a group of Moungara all the way to Sidi Moungari, where she had spent the night outside the shrine, rolled in a camel's blanket" (quoted in Hibbard, *Paul Bowles,* 56). In this behavior, Windling is like Isabel Eberhardt, who successfully masqueraded as a man and traveled in North Africa between 1899 and 1904. Unlike Windling, Eberhardt was quite honest about her sexual desires and married an Algerian man.[18] At a time and in a place where the sexual activities of most women are carefully policed and where male-male sex is quite common, disguising oneself as a man would seem to open up the possibilities for a woman to have sex with a man—or at least with boys. But Windling does not want just sex, nor does she want just any boy—she wants an "authentic" relationship based upon equal sharing, mutual understanding, and love. Her idea of romance is doubly romantic; it is based both on the possibility of merging her identity with the people of the oasis and, as we shall see, on transforming her beloved into herself.

Windling's age is never specified in the story, although she is characterized as something of a schoolmarm: a middle-aged and single woman who does not seem overtly interested in sexual liaisons. She assumes a "teacherly" attitude toward the young boys in the oasis, remaining courteous but distant from them and demanding that they show her respect. It is in making this demand that her erotic relationship with Slimane is initiated, for in order to impress her authority upon the boys she begins to stare them in the eyes, to make them the object of her gaze. She looks particularly at Slimane, and he returns her gaze—in fact, he begins to come to her hotel and stand outside her door, watching her work. She welcomes the reciprocity of his stare and eventually initiates conversation and friendship with him. The desire between them that is transacted by looking is also figured through the photographs that Windling takes of Slimane and that she asks him to take of her. The passing of the camera between them and the willingness of each to be taken as the object of the other's gaze suggests a desire for "equality" in their relationship. Like Mungo Park, who celebrates the exchange of looks that take place in his encounters with African women, Windling tries to shape a sentimental narrative of her presence in Africa, as if the politics that separate "colonizer" from "colonized" can be eliminated in the face of love or friendship.[19] For example, she has to purchase many gifts for Slimane in order for his father to allow him to spend time with her, but she convinces herself that Slimane "wanted nothing, expected nothing" except companionship (*Collected Stories,* 343). She ignores the economic basis of her relationship with Slimane and celebrates a romantic ideal of reciprocity.

Windling's desire for Slimane is figured not only through her gaze but also through epistemology: she wants to know him, and she wants him to know her. In order to attain this exchange of knowledges, she tries to teach Slimane to read but abandons this project to use him as a "guide, bearer and companion," a role that is "more suited to his nature"—or at least more suited to social expectations (342). In conversations on many long hikes in the desert, Windling talks about the "cleanliness" and "honesty" of the Swiss, but her favorite topic of conversation is religion, and she tries to present a very favorable account of Christianity. She also attempts to lecture Slimane on Islam, but he rebukes her advances on this topic, insisting that she cannot possess knowledge of sacred matters. The topic of religion becomes something of a battleground in the exchange of knowledges between them. Windling insists that Slimane must know the "truth" about Christ (that he is the Savior, not just another Muslim prophet). So she determines to celebrate Christmas one year (it turns out to be her last year) with Slimane and to make Christian rituals accessible to him by "translating" them into a Saharan context. She calls her celebration a "feast" to make it analogous to Maghrebi religious festivals, and she builds a crèche using local materials so that "it would look like a Moslem religious chromolithograph" (347). By so doing, she attempts to merge her own religious identity with her idea of the Sahara and of Slimane's life.

Windling invites Slimane to join her in the hotel dining room on Christmas Eve, after which she plans to show him the crèche and tell him the story of the nativity, with place names and details altered to make it sound like a Maghrebi legend. After she has dazzled him with the great "truth" of the nativity, she plans to dazzle him again by taking his picture at night with her newly acquired camera flash unit. Windling meticulously plans the evening in the hope that, in a moment of religious epiphany achieved through the merging of Christian tradition with local material, Slimane will understand her and she him, and that their friendship will deepen and solidify. Unfortunately for her, material reality impinges upon this fantasy. Slimane is not allowed to dine with her, because "natives" are not allowed to eat in the hotel dining room. She sneaks him in after the proprietor is asleep, and the famished Slimane is indeed dazzled by the crèche, not because of its religious truth but because it is decorated with oranges and chocolates—the food he has been hoping to find at this Christian "feast." When Windling goes to fetch her camera, Slimane helps himself, first devouring the sacred scene and then using the clay camels and wisemen to enact a pretend battle between the French army and the Algerian patriots, whom he dreams of joining. Windling is appalled at the destruction of her crèche at the hands of her "barbarian" friend but is even more appalled at the loss of her fantasy, which signals the end of their friendship:

Across the seasons of their friendship she had come to think of him as being *very nearly like herself*, even though she knew he had not been that way when she first had met him. Now she saw the dangerous vanity at the core of that fantasy: she had assumed that somehow his association with her had automatically been for his ultimate good, that inevitably he had been undergoing a *process of improvement* as a result of knowing her. In her *desire to see him change*, she had begun to forget what Slimane was *really like*. "I shall never understand him," she thought helplessly. (354, emphasis mine)

In a moment of vindictiveness, Windling takes a flash picture of Slimane before he has time to pose or even to recognize the instrument that makes it possible to take pictures at night. He is dazzled once again, this time by the new and unwelcome blinding light of the flash. But ultimately Windling does not blame Slimane for eating the crèche, for she realizes that he is hungry, that in the desert "food is not an adornment" (354). Rather, she blames the failure of her Christmas "feast" on cultural misunderstanding and on an essential difference between herself and Slimane. Later, she also blames the end of her friendship on the independence movement, which Slimane insists on joining, as if modernity and violence put a stop to her colonial romance.

What Windling does not notice is that it is the regulations of colonialism itself that have enforced a schism between her and Slimane. She does not understand that colonialism creates Slimane as a barbarian, barring him from a place at the dining table and producing the appetite that he satiates with the oranges and chocolates. Neither does she understand the more profound sense in which colonialism creates Europe's others and at the same time prohibits desire for those others. Colonial discourse produces the colonized other as essentially, fundamentally, and racially different from Europeans in order that the West can know itself in opposition to them. The gulf of difference that colonial discourse opens between colonizer and colonized demands that the West try to know and understand its others and simultaneously forecloses the possibility that such knowledge can be attained. As the long passage from the story cited earlier illustrates, this discourse also impels Westerners to "educate," "civilize," or "change" colonial subjects while at the same time making assimilation impossible (by insisting that difference is racially determined). The desire between Windling and Slimane (which is figured through the exchange of glances and knowledges) and the identification between them (which is figured through her cross-dressing and through her fantasy of similarity: "she had come to think of him as being very nearly like herself") both fall victim to these double binds of colonial discourse. Wherever disidentification may potentially shift into identification, or wherever identity may potentially shift into desire, these identifications and desires must be disavowed if the binary colonizer/colonized is to remain intact.

The friendship between Windling and Slimane seems to end together with colonialism—that is to say, with the beginning of militarized struggle against France (the story ends when Windling unwittingly helps Slimane run away from home to join the guerrillas). In a more profound sense, however, their friendship ended before it ever began: the colonial discourse that produces this friendship prohibits the exchange of knowledges of which it is supposedly constituted as a sentimental companionship between "equals." The failure of Fräulein Windling to acknowledge her desire for Slimane and to act upon it is, at its heart, the result of a culturally enforced disavowal of sexual desire for him. This original loss happens long before the story even begins and accounts for the melancholy with which the story is saturated. Desire is everywhere present in the story, but nowhere possible. Windling is nostalgic not merely for the winters she will no longer be able to pass in the Sahara but also for the boy she loves but can never have. Tellingly, the story ends with Windling hoping that Slimane will find an early death in the battle for independence. Since her romance is over, and now that she recognizes the impossibility of a sentimental friendship between colonizer and colonized, she joins Port in the twentieth century and fights sentiment with coldhearted unsentimentality. Since Slimane is lost to her, she wishes that he be conveniently, irrecoverably lost for all time.

The narrative structure of this story forecloses the possibility of the reader coming to know Slimane—of understanding, for example, what identity and desire mean to him. The story is told in the third person but close to the consciousness of Windling, and the reader is not allowed access to Slimane's consciousness. Does he think of Windling as a friend? As a potential lover? What do sentiment and affect mean to Slimane? Are reciprocity and mutual understanding important to him, or does he think of himself as a seasonal employee? Like Fräulein Windling, we will never know what goes on in Slimane's mind. In contrast, *The Spider's House*, Bowles's novel-length treatment of colonial nostalgia, does provide the reader with access to a Moroccan boy's consciousness.[20] The narrative technique of this novel—which shifts in its third person proximity from Stenham to Lee to Amar—echoes a suggestion made in the novel that there may be a crack in the façade of colonial discourse, a way not of bridging the difference between colonizer and colonized but of conceiving of this encounter in entirely different terms.

Like Fräulein Windling, John Stenham—the protagonist of *The Spider's House*—has a severe case of colonial nostalgia. Unlike Windling, he is dryly unsentimental in his nostalgia, much like Port in *The Sheltering Sky*. Stenham is an American writer and a long-term resident of Fez, where most of the novel takes place; he speaks Arabic as it is spoken there and among foreigners is considered something of an expert on the city and on Morocco generally. His love for the city, however, extends to its inhabitants only en masse—he does not have a single friend among the Fassi. The closest he comes to friendship is his relationship with a generous middle-class patriarch named Si Jaffar, whom Stenham treats as a native informant. Stenham adores Fez because it looks medieval, and he cherishes the trance dances of the Jilala and other religious sects because to him they are primitive, even barbaric. He dreads what he views as the increasing modernization and "Westernization" of Moroccans, for if Moroccans were "rational beings . . . the country would have no interest; its charm was a direct result of the people's lack of mental development" (*Spider's House*, 210). Ensconced in a comfortable hotel in the old city of Fez, Stenham desperately tries to keep his own modern, rational, and Western subjectivity detached from the Morocco he adores only insofar as it is "Oriental."

In the 1930s, Stenham had believed in social progress—he had even joined the Communist Party. When he became disillusioned with Stalinism, he turned to another totalitarian worldview: that the decadent modern West is essentially different from the pure and primitive East. The youthful confidence he had placed in depression-era communism is one response to the contradictions of imperialism. In response to the West's recognition of its colonial other, Stenham's brand of communism disavows this other and the crisis of its presence by recuperating a doctrine of human progress outside the discourse of liberal humanism. When he leaves the Party and with it his optimism for social progress, Stenham follows the heroes in Bowles's previous novels by becoming an existentialist. As we have seen, existentialism is in its own way a response to the crisis of subjectivity resulting from imperialism; ironically, in his turn toward Orientalism, Stenham finds solace for his postwar existential malaise, for his Orientalism provides the discourse of human inequality (West versus East) that he needs to legitimize his desertion of political and social action in favor of preoccupation with his own consciousness and daily existence.

Stenham is not nostalgic for colonialism in the same way that Fräulein Windling is. He does not seek a sentimental relationship with an individual Moroccan, and he certainly does not romanticize the possibility of equality in any of his relationships. Rather, he yearns for a time before colonialism and wishes to witness a medieval Fez that—he imagines—has no contact with Europe. Moreover, he does not wear Moroccan clothes or identify with the Fassi; he wants to see and know this premodern Fez and to know himself in opposition to it. The other American in the novel has a completely different understanding of colonialism and modernity. Lee is a wealthy young woman who does believe in social progress and modernity, and she apologizes for colonialism by suggesting that the average Moroccan is better off with "the hospitals and electric lights and buses the French have brought" (188). Lee sympathizes with the Istiqlal, the Independence Party waging an armed struggle against the French, because she believes the future lies with these young "Westernized" men. For Lee, the mass of Moroccans "were backward onlookers standing on the sidelines of the parade of progress; they must be exhorted to join, if necessary pulled by force into the march" (252). Her zeal is compared to that of a missionary, and her gospel is industry and progress.

Like "The Time of Friendship," *The Spider's House* takes place during the last throes of French colonialism, during the armed struggle for independence. The novel opens in Fez on the eve of the feast of *Aïd el Kebir* in 1954, one year after the deposition of Sultan Sidi Mohammed Ben Youssef by the French and his exile to Madagascar. In his role as a religious leader, the sultan traditionally presides over this feast, and his forced absence provokes mass demonstrations against the French.[21] In the days leading up to *Aïd el Kebir,* most foreigners flee the city, or at least secure themselves in the Ville Nouvelle, where the colonists reside. Stenham remains in old Fez, fervently ignoring the political changes taking place around him and immersing himself in the book he is writing about the seventeenth-century court of Sultan Moulay Ismail. He is like a lover who refuses to abandon his beloved; more accurately, he is like a fetishist who refuses to relinquish his fetish.[22] Fez is a blank screen upon which Stenham projects his desires. The city is neither an object nor a site of desire but rather the representation of a style in which Stenham seeks his pleasure: "He would have liked to prolong the status quo because the décor that went with it suited his personal taste" (286). The fetishization of Fez includes an abstract appreciation for a static culture but erases the lives and desires of the people who live in the city and produce its culture. Stenham's existentialism and his identity as a Western man are contingent upon perpetuating this very unsentimental relation to his fetish.

Lee, on the other hand, fetishizes the young men of the Istiqlal Party who are fighting for Morocco's place as a modern nation state in the world order. She is no more interested than Stenham in befriending Moroccans or making individual contact; like Stenham's, her idea of Morocco is an abstraction designed to substantiate the vision she holds of her own subjectivity. She constructs a worldview based on the idea that all of humanity is basically the same and that differences between North and South are a matter of the modern technology that the North holds and through which it holds the South in subservience. Placed together, Stenham and Lee represent a discursive shift that occurs in the movement from colonialism to neocolonialism, a shift from a West-East axis to a North-South axis, from a discourse of civilization versus barbarity to one of development versus underdevelopment.

The third principal character of the novel, and the owner of the third consciousness in proximity to which the narrative voice speaks, is Amar, a fifteen-year-old boy who is divided in his loyalties among Islam, Istiqlal, and Stenham. Amar expresses a personal worldview radically different from those held by the Americans. He comes from a religious family and is blessed with a mystical gift that allows him to see events in a divine light. When he stumbles into an

Istiqlal hiding place and befriends their leader, Moulay Ali, it is for Amar an event sent by Allah. The same is true when he meets Stenham and Lee in a café just outside the city walls. All three characters seek refuge in the café because French troops have surrounded Fez and are preparing to storm it. Stenham approaches Amar in hopes of finding out from him what is happening and whether a route of escape can be found. Lee realizes that Amar is in as much danger or more than are the two Americans and insists that Stenham help the boy. Stenham's idea of help is to give Amar money, for, within the terms of colonial discourse, "What else can you give him?" (261). Lee rejects the constraints of this discourse and offers to take Amar in a taxi to their hotel, where all three can hide from the military assault. Through this gesture, Lee rather romantically hopes to "save" Amar, but the unsentimental Stenham insists on giving Amar enough money to pay for their cafe bill and taxi, turning him into a native guide and underlining the economic nature of their relationship.

Up until the moment when Stenham and Lee meet Amar, which is to say halfway through the novel, the two Americans are engaged in a very troubled courtship. As Americans, they are thrown together in the novel as if it were logical or natural for them to fall in love, but most of their conversation consists of arguments for or against Moroccan independence and modernity. When they meet Amar, a rather bizarre triangulated desire is initiated whereby Stenham and Lee pass their attractions and repulsions to each other through Amar. He becomes the sign of their respective fetishes.

This triangulated love affair climaxes in the mountains outside Fez when the three decide to flee the city's violence and attend a religious festival at Sidi Bou Chta. As Stenham comes to know Amar as a person, he discovers a very moral and complex individual who does not conform to his preconceptions about what Moroccans, en masse, are like. In particular, he is astonished to discover that Amar is sentimental (he rescues a drowning dragonfly) and sincere (not at all hypocritical in his religious beliefs and practices). This discovery leads to a crisis and reversal in Stenham's entire worldview. After encountering Amar, Stenham can no longer think of Moroccans as "an objective force, unrelieved and monolithic . . . both less and more than human" (335), because Amar proves to him that Moroccan society produces individuals instead of masses. Stenham is suddenly able to identify with Amar as an individual: "But in that case the Moroccans were much like anyone else, and very little of value would be lost in the destruction of their present culture, because its design would be worth less than the sum of the individuals who composed it—the same as any Western country" (336). At this point Stenham resolves to leave Morocco, for he realizes that Fez (his fetish) and Amar (the sign of his fetish) are not blank screens upon which he can project his desires but are "like" him, the "same" as the West, which is to say, they are possessed of their own reality and their own subjectivity.

Lee also experiences a crisis and a reversal at the religious festival, not from coming to know Amar but from experiencing her distance from the festival participants as a Western spectator:

What she was *looking down upon* here tonight, the immense theatre full of human beings still *unformed and unconscious*, bathed in sweat, stamping and shrieking, falling into the dust and writhing and twitching and panting, all belonged unmistakably to the darkness, and therefore it had to be *wholly outside her and she outside it . . .* she was up here observing it, *actively conscious of who she was*, and very intent on remaining that person, determined to let nothing occur that might cause her, even for an instant, *to forget her identity*. (314, emphasis mine)

Her romance with modernity comes to an end; in a sense, she reverses positions with Stenham, abandoning her faith in progress and humanity in favor of an Orientalist discourse that she has previously disavowed. Now it is Lee who grounds her identity as a modern and rational being in opposition to savage humanity. The collapse of her fetish also leads to a reversal in her vision of him who signifies that fetish; now, when Lee looks at Amar, she sees "the alert and predatory sub-human, further from what she believed man should be like than the naked savage, because the savage was tractable, while this creature, wearing the armor of his own rigid barbaric culture, consciously defied progress" (345). Now fully engulfed by the terms of a discourse that divides colonizer from colonized, Lee abandons her sentiment for Amar and reorganizes the basis of her relationship with him as that of patron and client. She gives him money—all of her money—and tells him to buy a gun and join the Istiqlal. By so doing, Lee still hopes to recuperate Amar as a sign of her fetish, to corrupt his purity as a barbarian and to "pull him by force" into the march of progress.[23]

Amar takes the money but does not buy a gun. He does not seem to realize what sort of games the Americans are playing with him, or, if he does, he does not care. For Amar, Stenham is a potential friend and Lee a potential sex partner, but his desire does not flow through the circuit of the Americans's triangulation. The festival at Sidi Bou Chta is hardly momentous for Amar; the dancing is uninteresting, just "people jumping up and down like monkeys" (369). He is primarily interested in getting back to Fez and contacting his family, who are prisoners within the city walls. In hopes of getting assistance, he travels to the Istiqlal refuge. The leader there, Moulay Ali, promises to help Amar but then betrays him. The police are preparing to raid the sanctuary, and in order to create a diversion Moulay Ali asks Amar to play a song on his flute. As he plays (and as the members of the Istiqlal escape), Allah connects "his heart to other people's hearts" (393). Amar does not realize at first that he is being left to face the police alone, for he is immersed in his melancholy music; "the longing for someone who could understand him . . . came out in the fragile strings of sound" until an image of "the person for whom he played" materializes in his mind (393). This person, it turns out, is Stenham: "He had been a friend; perhaps with time they could even have understood one another's hearts" (394).

Amar recognizes that his association with Stenham may lead to sex. When he escapes with Stenham and Lee to their hotel, he wonders "if he would have to share the man's bed. It was well known that many Christians liked young Arab boys" (271). As it turns out, this is not Stenham's desire, or rather, his desire is more complicated than this. Nonetheless, within the terms of colonial discourse, the relationship between Stenham and Amar is intelligible only as a relation between patron and client, one that certainly includes financial dependency, probably includes servitude, and possibly includes sex. When Amar is discovered in the hotel by a French waiter, this is how the waiter interprets the situation, winking as he brings room service for two and announcing, "*Votre serviteur discret!*" (290). Both before and after his "discovery" of Amar's individuality, Stenham remains embedded within the terms of colonial discourse and can think of himself only as a patron and of Amar only as a client. Amar, on the other hand, is not so restricted, because he sees and lives in the world through an entirely different discourse, that of Islam. To Amar, Stenham is sent by Allah, an intervention that benefits Amar materially but that also holds out the possibility for a sincere friendship. If Amar does desire Stenham, or identify with him, it is on an entirely different set of terms from those that form Stenham. After Moulay Ali's betrayal, Amar finds Stenham, who, together with Lee, is preparing to leave for Casablanca and Europe, and Amar asks to go with him. Stenham misunderstands Amar's request because his affections are centered on Lee; he cannot conceive of an affective relationship, even a friendship, with Amar. Stenham relates to Amar in the only way he knows: he asks Amar to help with the luggage. Stenham drives Amar as far as the city's edge, then tells him that he must walk back. "Back to where?" asks Amar, for the Fez that both loved no longer exists—the French have assaulted it, and independence will transform it. Nonetheless, just as Fräulein Windling leaves Slimane, Stenham abandons Amar to the violence of the rising struggle for independence.

Bowles's early short story "Tea on the Mountain" introduces themes of colonial desire and nostalgia that develop in his fiction throughout his career. "The Time of Friendship" represents desire muted and refigured through sentiment into an idealized friendship. *The Spider's House* further explores the possibility of friendship between an older foreigner and a younger Moroccan, including the possibility that an affective bond between the two might sidestep the constraints of colonial discourse. Windling's aspiration for friendship is betrayed when Slimane does not—cannot—reciprocate. He does not betray her so much as does colonial discourse, which creates a desire that can never be fulfilled. The youthful and religious Amar disregards the structures of colonial dominance that surround him and pursues friendships with both Moulay Ali and Stenham. But whatever disregard Amar might have for colonial relations of power, his aspirations for friendship do not provide an alternative structure for interpersonal relations. Both Moulay Ali and Stenham betray him. While his spiritual life gives him an alternative worldview, and while he is fully capable of sincere and compassionate friendship, the friends Amar would make are too thoroughly constrained by relations of power for his amiability to be more than a wistful gesture.

Subject to or Subject of Desire?

Bowles acknowledged that he had always set out to deceive his readers. He compared the life of a writer to that of a spy insofar as a "spy *is* devious and, as much as is possible, anonymous. His personal convictions and emotions are automatically 'masked.'"[24] I argue that masking sentiment and maintaining anonymity are as important to Bowles's sexual life as they are to his writing. While Bowles disapproved of literary scholarship that would connect his life with his texts, his readers are often at least as fascinated by his life as by his writings. Rather than indulge the curiosity of those who would like to know the intimate details of his personal life, Bowles wrote an autobiography—*Without Stopping*—that William Burroughs thought should more aptly be called "Without Telling." Only late in life did Bowles speak on record and in detail about his sexual relations with men, including his relationship with Ahmed Yacoubi.

The secrecy with which Bowles lived his sexual life should not be equated with sexual repression. In "The Delicate Prey" (1948) and *Let It Come Down* (1952), Bowles suggests that repression is not an attractive option to pursue. This is most memorably the case in "The Delicate Prey," in which a bandit castrates, then rapes a defenseless boy. Another example comes at the climax of *Let It Come Down*, when Dyer, who two nights before has seduced Daisy in a majoun-induced stupor, is aroused once again by the same drug but, instead of seducing or raping Thami, drives a nail in his ear and through his skull. The emergence of homosexual desire at such moments and its transformation into violence points to a prior repression. Exploring this dynamic makes for gripping fiction but living a life of such repression would be understandably miserable. We would be misguided to think that Bowles's desire for secrecy indicated repression of this sort.

Rather, we can more accurately recall the remark Bowles once made that, while he never lied about his sexuality, he would consider it shameful to volunteer information about it.[25] For literary critics, fascination with Bowles's life is not an idle curiosity, because understanding elements of his lived experience can shed welcome light on his texts. Port is not Paul and Kit is not Jane, but knowledge about the dynamics of the Bowleses' marriage does open up the interpretive possibilities of *The Sheltering Sky*. Similarly, appreciation of *The Spider's House* is enhanced appreciably by the knowledge that it was inspired in part by Paul Bowles's experience in Fez and by his relationship with Ahmed Yacoubi. Stenham resembles Bowles in significant ways: both are American writers, both speak the local variant of Arabic, both are drawn to Fez because of its ancient architecture and traditional culture, both strongly dislike twentieth-century modernization, both were once members of the Communist Party, and both turned away from communism and toward an Existentialist worldview. But Stenham merely presents facets of Bowles's experience without directly representing his life. The mode is self-parody, although the humor is quite dry.

Like Stenham, Bowles met an extraordinary young man in Fez, but unlike Stenham, Bowles became the patron and lover of that young man. Bowles met Ahmed Yacoubi in 1947 and was immediately impressed with Yacoubi's talents as a story teller and an artist. They maintained a relationship over the following decade, during which time Bowles helped Yacoubi establish an international reputation for his paintings. During this time, friends of Paul Bowles understood his relationship with Yacoubi to be both sexual and deeply emotional. After the two parted company, Yacoubi insisted that it had been neither sexual nor emotional (he died in 1986 at age fifty-five).[26] Bowles remained notably reticent on the subject, at least on the record, until 1994 when an interview with Simon Bischoff appeared in which Bowles spoke explicitly about love and about Yacoubi. At one point in the interview, Bowles concedes that "friendship" might be the word that describes their relationship. "Who knows where friendship begins . . . or ends," says Bowles. "I mean, he was friendly. I would say we were friends, yes, naturally. But I never expected him to care one way or the other, he didn't" ("How Could I Send a Picture into the Desert?" 227). Bowles's relationship with Yacoubi had faded by the time he wrote "The Time of Friendship" in 1962. While it would be grossly inaccurate to presume that Bowles directly identified with his character Fräulein Windling, the notion expressed earlier that a friend may or may not "care one way or the other" does evoke the dynamic between Windling and Slimane. At issue in that story and in Bowles's life is the extent to which one's desires and relationships are shaped by sentiment.

Later in the same interview Bowles proposes the word "obsession" to explain at least some of his feelings about Yacoubi. The word he struggles with and ultimately rejects is "love." "If you're in love with someone—I mean, you tell him you are, show him. That's what . . . I mean, it's that way in books and plays. But it's not that way in my life, certainly! . . . I don't think I was ever in love with anybody, to tell the truth" (231). Even though Bowles refers to "books and plays" to define love, his own fiction could hardly be characterized as sentimental or romantic literature. On the contrary, his major novels and short stories repeatedly explore the failure, inconvenience, or irrelevance of sentiment. The rejection of sentiment within the framework of colonial desire is especially interesting in Paul Bowles's life, since this antisentimentality is also the subject of his fiction.

Bowles tells Bischoff that *The Spider's House* was written with Ahmed Yacoubi in mind. "It wasn't about him as a subject," Bowles clarifies, but it was "inspired by him, suggested by him" (226). One can presume that the inspiration arose in part from the sixteen-year-old Yacoubi, whom Bowles had met in Fez in 1947. But *The Spider's House* also bears traces of Bowles's relationship with the adult Yacoubi. Bowles began writing this novel in 1954 (the same year in which its action occurs), while living with Yacoubi. The previous year, they had traveled together to New York, where Bowles helped place Yacoubi in contact with gallery owners and leading artists, writers, and other members of New York's intellectual social life. For a season, Yacoubi created a minor sensation, both with his art and with his exotic attire. Wearing traditional Moroccan clothing to openings and parties, he deliberately played upon cultural stereotypes to promote himself and his paintings as exotic expressions from the mysterious Orient.

An episode from this New York adventure survives in Hans Richter's surrealist film *8X8*, in which Bowles and Yacoubi appear as actors.[27] The segment in which they appear was filmed at the Connecticut estate of Libby Holman, a close friend of Jane Bowles. The action occurs in three places: a swimming pool emptied of water and filled with pieces of furniture (including a piano), a forest through which runs a river, and a final scene along a curving driveway. Sound is at least as important as image in the segment. It opens with the ring of a telephone, which awakens Paul Bowles from sleep and continues to interrupt and irritate throughout the swimming pool scene. Upon awakening, Bowles begins to compose a piece of music, but, when he attempts to play his composition on the piano, the irritating buzz of the telephone competes with a flute for his attention. Suddenly, Yacoubi appears playing that flute, and Bowles's face lights up as, with Yacoubi dancing enchantingly around him, he incorporates the flute tune into his piano composition. Yacoubi is dressed in an "Oriental" outfit that seems drawn from the pages of the *Thousand and One Nights*.

The imagery in the scene is rather heavy-handed (the traditional Oriental other as muse to the Western artist, whose work is undermined by the dissonance of modernity). But Bowles and Yacoubi must have been aware that they were not merely acting out stereotypes about art, inspiration, enchantment, and the Orient in order to provide a surrealist film with rich symbolic material. They were also portraying elements of the lives they lived together. After all, Bowles did draw on folk traditions in several of his compositions and stories, and Yacoubi purposefully embodied Oriental difference in order to reach

American audiences. Moreover, the musical enchantment of the scene suggests sexual intrigue and seduction.

The eroticism of exotic difference becomes even more apparent when Yacoubi suddenly strips, revealing a classically muscled body clothed only in swimming trunks. He seizes a suitcase Bowles had previously packed, climbs out of the pool, and disappears into the woods. Bowles tries to follow but is at first restrained by the incessant ring of the telephone. Only after cutting the phone cord can he follow Yacoubi. Bowles spends the rest of the scene seeking Yacoubi and calling repeatedly, "Ahmed! Ahmed!" in mournful tones. Yacoubi teases his pursuer with flute tunes that fade as he evades Bowles, and he eventually emerges in a western-style business suit. At the end of the segment, having achieved success, he is driven down the winding road in a Jaguar. Bowles, meanwhile, has been literally trapped by the forest: vines have encircled and immobilized him.

The second half of the Bowles/Yacoubi segment of *8X8* also offers crude symbolism (Yacoubi as Pan, nature as the realm of lust, desire as the "primitive" urge that entraps and defeats one's "civilized" capacities) and also parodies the personal lives of Bowles and Yacoubi. The concluding scenes evoke not only Yacoubi's successful manipulation of New York intellectuals to promote his art but also the growing personal distance between Yacoubi and Bowles during the spring of 1953. Yacoubi made use of his time in New York to establish independent relationships and contacts that would one day free him from Bowles's patronage; this freedom was expressed in sexual terms when Yacoubi involved himself in an affair with Libby Holman, prompting Bowles to return to Tangier alone.

The action and symbols of the film refer so obviously to their personal lives that we must wonder why the usually reticent Bowles would agree to make a spectacle of his relationship with Yacoubi. No doubt Bowles acted in the film in part because it does cogently represent modernist assumptions about art, civilization, desire, nature, the Orient, and so forth in surrealist terms that need not necessarily be read as biographical. But his participation in such heavy-handed symbolism and farcical action also suggests a sense of humor about the conditions of his relationship with Yacoubi. While both men inhabit the structures of colonial desire, it is Yacoubi who manipulates those structures to his advantage. Rather than objecting to the stereotypes that exoticize his sexuality, Yacoubi deploys them to enchant Bowles; through his patron he achieves material success in the West. Meanwhile, the patron is entrapped by desire, and specifically by the structures of desire enforced by the West's Orientalist discourse. He cannot resist his desire, but neither can he satisfy it. Bowles's mournful calls for Ahmed in the forest suggest not only that he is lost in desire but that his love object has always been and will always be lost to him. But unrequited love in this scene is neither sentimental nor romantic. The emo-

tional dryness of *8X8* could not be further removed from the nostalgic opening of Bertolucci's *The Sheltering Sky*. The erotic relation represented in
Richter's film is not at all nostalgic, for it is not an unacknowledged loss of a
disavowed desire. On the contrary, colonial desire and unrequited love are
entirely conscious; they are cleverly manipulated by Yacoubi and willingly
mocked by Bowles in this self-parody.

Ultimately, the kind of colonial desire represented in *8X8* is less subtle and
interesting than that represented in Bowles's fiction. The fiction explores more
tortured psychological relationships, including repression in "The Delicate
Prey" and *Let It Come Down* and disavowal and nostalgia in "The Time of
Friendship" and *The Spider's House*. The value of comparing these works to
Bowles's life lies in achieving a better understanding of Bowles's characteristic evacuation of sentiment. In "The Time of Friendship," Windling learns to
reject affect at the end of the narrative when she can no longer sustain her nostalgic relation to Slimane and colonialism. Stenham takes up where Windling
left off, as it were. When the novel opens, he has already reached an understanding of his relation to the inhabitants of a colonial space that admits no
possibility of sentiment. Stenham's crisis is the inverse of Windling's: at the
end of the novel he encounters genuine sentiment in Amar, and this challenge
to his worldview leads him to end his nostalgic "romance" with Morocco. Stenham does not open himself up to affect at this point in the novel—neither his
rude treatment of Amar nor his combative and parched relationship with Lee
offers any hope along these lines. For Stenham as for Bowles, removing one's
self from sentiment is a way of coping with and accommodating the psychological constraints of colonial relations.

Amar, on the other hand, is able to maintain a capacity for sentimentality,
and he offers a perspective on colonial relations that is wholly disinterested in
nostalgia. Of the three main characters in *The Spider's House*, Amar seems to
have the clearest vision of affective and erotic relations, at least in part because
he understands the contours of colonial discourse without feeling bound to follow them. He understands that an erotic relationship with either Lee or Stenham is possible, but he is interested neither in pursuing sex nor in running away
from it. Amar has no need to disavow desire for men or for women, and so he
need not mourn the loss of such desire. In this sense he resembles Ahmed
Yacoubi in *8X8*, who similarly understands the structures of colonial desire
but who manipulates them rather than being overwhelmed by them.

Bowles's relationship with Yacoubi was the most extended he had with a
Moroccan man and is consequently the most documented, but on a few occasions Bowles wrote or spoke about other sexual experiences. He characterized
these as being devoid of sentimental attachment, suggesting that pursing sex
without emotional intimacy provided him with an effective way to live in a
colonial space without suffering from the paradoxes of colonial desire. As we

will see, William Burroughs and Alfred Chester write insightfully about anonymous sex in their fiction, and anonymity plays a central role in the way they fashion expatriate lives. Burroughs and Chester explore the potential for sex in the interzone to transform sexuality, desire, and subjectivity. Bowles is less a visionary and more of a critic in this regard; his fiction critiques the norms of colonial nostalgia, while in his personal life he finds ways to live comfortably in Tangier, both during the colonial era and after independence.

Bowles accepts the role he is expected to play as a wealthy foreign patron of his Moroccan sex partners. As he tells Bischoff, "All relationships I ever had, from the beginning, had to do with paying" ("How Could I Send a Picture into the Desert?" 227). Within the sexual economy of Tangier, Bowles purchases not only sex but also anonymity. In a letter written in 1983, in response to a question about his sex life, Bowles responds, "I think what people really want to know is: With whom have you been to bed? To answer that, it would be necessary to have known their names."[28] Anonymous sex with racially and culturally other men provides Bowles with pleasure unencumbered with intimacy or emotional attachments. Bowles explains the function of anonymous sex in his early story "Tea on the Mountain," when the protagonist of that story dreams of being "free, out-of-doors, with some young man she did not know—*could* not know. . . . For if she could not know him, he could not know her" (*Collected Stories,* 22). She would pursue reciprocity of pleasure but not reciprocity of knowledge, because knowledge could disturb both the eroticism of the encounter and the fulfillment of her desire to be "free." Colonial desire arises through eroticization of difference (especially of difference conceived in terms of race and culture and power), and if that difference is compromised through recognition of sameness, the erotic relation will crumble. Moreover, the protagonist of "Tea on the Mountain" pursues anonymous embraces because they leave her "free" to act as a subject of colonial desire. Ironically, she can act upon this "freedom" only by operating within the terms of self and other produced by colonial discourse— that is, by remaining subject to colonial desire.

In "Pages from Cold Point" (1947), Bowles writes about anonymity, knowledge, sentiment, and male homosexual desire in a colonial context. This story takes place in an Anglophone West Indian island apparently under colonial rule. It concerns a white American man who has inherited a large amount of money from his deceased wife and has expatriated himself to the island along with Racky, his sixteen-year-old son. The father fancies himself a hedonist and seems to be gay but is apparently not interested in pursuing sex with men on the island. Racky, on the other hand, seduces boys and men from the surrounding area with a skill that belies his youthful innocence. After the police complain to the father about the son's behavior, he decides to send Racky to boarding school in the United States. Before preparations can be made, however, Racky seduces and then blackmails his father. At the story's end, the father gives Racky most of the inheritance money and takes him to Cuba, where he is last seen in the company of a handsome man. The hedonist is outwitted by his son, who knows how to expertly manipulate power for sex and sex for power.

In 1947, Bowles sailed for North Africa, where he intended to write *The Sheltering Sky*. Before leaving New York, Bowles already had devised its title and plot, but during the voyage he refrained from starting the novel in order to write "Pages from Cold Point." In a sense, this story serves as a counterpoint to *The Sheltering Sky*. The plenitude of Racky's sexual adventures contrasts sharply with the sexual desert of Port's and Kit's relationship. In the original version of the story, Racky is called Rocky, and the solidity of this "rock" stands in opposition to the emptiness of the novel's "sky" (see Hibbard, *Paul Bowles,* 33). The empty sky protects us from the emptiness beyond it, and throughout the novel it reminds us of lack, of unfulfilled and unacknowledged desire, of nostalgic yearning for what is lost. Rocky/Racky, on the other hand, suggests the possibility of avowed desire, of completion and satisfaction. This satisfaction takes place, of course, within the constraints of colonial discourse, and that is not a problem for Racky. He has a precise understanding of how to manipulate age and youth, pale skin and dark skin, wealth and want in the pursuit of his desires. "Pages from Cold Point" is a wickedly amusing story, devoid of the existential anguish and confused colonial nostalgia of *The Sheltering Sky*. It does not suggest that there is a way to excuse oneself from desire or from colonial discourse; on the contrary, it suggests that pleasure is readily available within the structures of colonial desire.

The Way Home

At age twenty-three, Bowles returned to the United States after an extensive journey through Algeria and Tunisia. The following year, he left again for further travels to Spain, Morocco, and Central America. While in the United States, in 1933, he compared the experience of living at home to that of living abroad. Regarding sex, to Aaron Copland he complained, "Where in this country can I have thirty-five or forty different people a week, and never risk seeing them again? Yet, in Algeria, it actually was the mean rate." It was not the unavailability of sex in the United States that bothered the youthful Bowles so much as the lack of anonymity, and sex expressed just one dimension of his difficult relationship to his own culture. "I hate America because I feel attached to it," he continues, and later, "here I look at the landscape, and it looks back at me." Bowles experienced his connection to America as intimate in a horrifying way. At home he was scrutinized, the object rather than the subject of knowledge. The pressures that constituted him as an American immobilized and haunted him, so that even when he was abroad he woke up sweating at night, having "dreamed of being in America, which reminded me somehow that I had escaped from prison and the guards were on my tail."[29]

As he aged, Bowles expressed his relationship to the United States in gentler terms. Nonetheless, even toward the end of his career, he continued to write about travel and expatriation and to write about them as extremely difficult, even painful, psychological dramas. In the novella "Too Far from Home," published as the title story of his *Selected Writings* (1993), Bowles returns to desire, nostalgia, sentimentality, and anonymity to explore the psychology of an American seeking refuge from home in North Africa. The bridge between North Africa and America in this story is the bridge between colonial desire and American formations of racialized sexuality. In this story, he diagnoses once again the problem of racialized sexuality for a traveler who is tormented by the paradoxes of colonial desire and who, unlike Bowles, must return home because of them.

In many ways, this novella revisits the concerns that run throughout Bowles's major works of fiction: the experience of "exotic" travel, an existential and epistemological anxiety that flirts with insanity, the disavowal of desire, and nostalgia in and for a colonial space. In these ways, the white American protagonist, Anita, bears some resemblance to her predecessors: the unnamed woman in "Tea on the Mountain," Kit in *The Sheltering Sky*, and Fräulein Windling in "The Time of Friendship." In "Too Far from Home," Anita travels to the Niger River valley, where she is forced to confront her sexual desires, to question her identity, and to sort out her attitudes toward African Americans and Africans. Anita comes to the desert because it is less expensive than a sanitarium: she wants to recover from her recent divorce and "the rest of the trouble," whatever that might be (*Too Far from Home*, 299).

She could more usefully have seen a therapist, for Anita brings with her a great deal of fear and guilt, especially regarding sex and race, and she projects her interior turmoil onto the people and the land she encounters. At first, it seems "quite natural" that her Malian servants are black, because in the United States she always has had black servants whom she thinks of "as shadows of people, not really at home in a country of whites." As time passes, Anita is shocked to realize that, in Mali "the blacks were the real people and that she was the shadow" (298). The reconceptualization of herself as a racial minority, which erodes but does not topple her sense of racial superiority, is a fundamental challenge to Anita's subjectivity. This challenge does not resolve her interior turmoil but rather heightens the pressure on the guilt and fear she experiences as a white American woman.

There is a sexual dimension to Anita's crisis of being, and her sexual desires are shaped by her formation within an American discourse of racism. Anita has a troubled relationship with Sekou, who is introduced to her as "a kind of chief" but whom Anita thinks of as "a kind of servant" (296, 305). She takes an immediate dislike to this reserved and gentle man and soon begins to accuse him of watching her sleep at night; her sexual desire for Sekou is carried over into the context of American racism, so that her desire is experienced as guilt and transmuted into fear, specifically the fear of rape. Anita remains unconscious of the extent to which sexualized racial violence, deeply rooted in American society, structures her desires and her guilt. Rather than confront this legacy, she perpetuates further sexualized violence against two American college students.

She first encounters these two "nearly naked youths"—from Yale, no less—when they speed into town, causing an accident that wounds Sekou's leg. Anita is extraordinarily angry about the incident, and she screams at the boys, whom she calls monsters, "You've gone too far from home, my friends, and you're going to have trouble. . . . And I hope I'll have a chance to see it" (307). Indeed, Anita does see the trouble. She experiences a sense of "elation" when, walking in the desert a few days later, she sees in a hidden declivity "a senseless sculpture in vermilion enamel and chromium . . . the cycle had skidded, hurling the suntanned torsos against the rocks" (311). Repulsed yet fascinated by her desire for Sekou, attracted to and angry with the boys, she avenges the first accident by not helping at the scene of the second. A few days later, Anita learns that the boys have been discovered; both died of exposure after several days of suffering.

Soon after, Anita prepares to leave Mali, but before she leaves she wishes to clear her mind of the "doubts and fears" that trouble her, and so she resolves to speak with Sekou. Sekou becomes the therapist in her desert sanitarium. He tells Anita that she is wrong to be angry with the students—that anger is useful to no one and that she should forgive their carelessness. He explains that one night he dreamt that he asked her to forgive them, but in the dream Anita refused. Anita does, belatedly and tearfully, forgive the monsters whom she now calls boys; she is grateful to Sekou but at the same time is disturbed that his "intense desire had, through his dream, put him in contact with the dark side of her mind" (326). She is disturbed because Sekou supposedly knows nothing about her, yet mysteriously is able to know the innermost emotions and the deepest motivations that remain obscure even to herself. However, Anita's conscious mind is able to reassert control, and, by recuperating a sense of anonymity, she rebuilds her sense of subjectivity. The story concludes with Anita "reviewing" the "painful story" of her behavior with the college boys and with Sekou: "Sekou knew much of it, but she knew it all, and she promised herself that never would anyone else hear of it" (327).

At the beginning of the story, Anita thinks of Africans as basically the same as African Americans, which is to say she thinks of them as servants or as "shadows," but, after her conversation with Sekou, she thinks of Africans as "real people," and of Sekou as a better person than herself. Both the fear and loathing she experiences at the beginning and the admiration and idolization she feels at the end are based in desire—a desire for Sekou as a black man, a desire that she never acknowledges or acts upon. She does, however, become somewhat sentimental about this desire. Anita's conversation with Sekou takes place just as she is preparing to leave for the United States, and, after she parts company with him, she is melancholy. What she had once experienced as fear she now experiences as loss. This moment of leave-taking inspires in Anita a newfound nostalgia for the desert she so recently detested: "She had begun to care for the flat sand-colored town, knowing that she would never see another place quite like it. Nor, it occurred to her, would she ever find another person with the same uncomplicated purity of Sekou" (326). Unlike Fräulein Windling, for whom the time of friendship is finished when she leaves Algeria, Anita discovers her sentimental attachment only at the moment of departure, a discovery that promises a sustained nostalgia for Mali and Sekou—or, rather, for her memories of what Mali and Sekou represent for her.

"Too Far from Home" is a beautifully crafted story and is classic Bowles: the major preoccupations that pass through all his major fiction are brought together once again. The journey into the desert is a journey to work out one's inner chaos on foreign topography and in the face of colonialism's others. The crises of being and of knowledge produced in the postwar, postcolonial, and postindustrial West are experienced as physical and psychic dislocations, threatening insanity. Sanity is recuperated within the constraints of colonial discourse, which shapes desire and the obligation to disavow desire for racialized/colonized others. Here, as elsewhere in Bowles's work, displaced desire emerges as violence, and unfulfilled desire is registered as nostalgia. What does it mean to go *too* far from home, and who in this story goes too far? Certainly the Yale students, who die from a combination of their own inflated sense of entitlement and self-confidence and a compatriot's cruel vengeance. Anita goes too far with her revenge, and probably not far enough with her therapy, but she does not go so far from home that she cannot return, that she cannot be reabsorbed into the troubles from which she would escape. As for Paul Bowles—he found equilibrium in his expatriate life, and stability in his fictional rememberings of that life. For Bowles, expatriation and anonymity were balms applied to his troubled relationship with America and to the sexual agitation that he named without naming: Paul Bowles could not get far enough from home.

3

The Sexual Re-Orientations of William S. Burroughs

Forty years after he made his literary debut, William Burroughs's cameo appearance in the film *Drugstore Cowboy* underscores the extent to which his image as this century's consummate literary junky perpetuates his fame and his popularity. Burroughs's status as an icon of underground drug culture continues to influence literary criticism, as well: whether censorious or celebratory, critics consistently read Burroughs as a social outlaw, a radical provocateur, or a hallucinogen-inspired visionary. The fact that Burroughs's name, image, and texts continue to be associated with narcotic use comes as no surprise; after all, he began a long career of fictionalized self-representation with the novel *Junky*, and his first successful novel, *Naked Lunch*, was inspired in part by opiate use and withdrawal nightmares. But as I demonstrate in this chapter, it is more accurate to describe Burroughs as a literary ex-junky, because his writing matured during and after withdrawal, and he denounced addiction of all kinds. Moreover, when Burroughs ceased to organize his identity, experience, and literary vision around addictive opiates, he replaced them with sex—and specifically with homosexual sex—a shift that is registered by the title and subject matter of his second novel, *Queer*.

Given this exchange of drugs for sex, why is it that the iconic figuration of Burroughs continues to be that of the exemplary literary junky, and not the exemplary literary queer? Granted, the novel *Queer* remained unpublished until 1985, but even *Junky* suggests that, as Burroughs moved away from addiction, he moved toward homosexual desire, and in *Naked Lunch* and later novels Burroughs's sexual fantasies assume an increasingly prominent and central textual function, decisively modifying the hallucinogenic imagery of earlier texts. Another seemingly unrelated question might help shed light on this puzzle: why is Burroughs rarely discussed as an expatriate author? In spite of the fact that approximately half of Burroughs's prodigious corpus was written overseas and that travel of various sorts is a recurrent theme in his work, even the best criticism of Burroughs ignores the geographical locations and geopolitical implications of his writing. Furthermore, no critical attention has been paid to the fact that travel is frequently accompanied in Burroughs's work by sexual adventures involving young male partners of various "third world" origins.

Whether one wishes to celebrate Burroughs's texts as countercultural triumphs or dismiss them as frivolous Beat ravings, it is relatively easy to deal with Burroughs by focusing on the personal and literary uses he makes of narcotics. Much more difficult, but also much more rewarding, is a serious examination of sexuality and politics in his work. The field of literary criticism has shifted sufficiently in recent years to make such an examination possible, but even the first wave of queer theory has avoided discussing Burroughs's sexual politics, in spite of the fact that he is one of the most prominent middle-century, self-identified queer public figures. Critics have hesitated to explore sexuality and politics in Burroughs because his texts so persistently and complexly evade ideological classification—except when they express appallingly simplistic and simply appalling political positions. The best known of such positions concerns the absence of women in Burroughs's utopian visions, which he explained in the 1970s by claiming that women are evil. Burroughs later tempered his view of women, but readers who wish to interrogate the politics of his writing still encounter blunt racism and derogatory representations of women and effeminate men in the midst of his sometimes radical and sometimes reactionary political opinions.[1] Burroughs is easier to handle as an exemplary junky, it would seem, than as an exemplary queer. In this chapter, I neither congratulate nor chide Burroughs for his opinions, because neither apology nor reproach helps explain his intricate and often contradictory political ideas. My aim is to think of Burroughs as exemplary of nothing other than himself—and to analyze the formation of that "self" as it is represented in volumes of his writing about sexuality and subjectivity in "colonial" contexts.

Burroughs's political expressions are complexly formed in response to the confluence of factors that also shape his writing: his drug use, his sexual experiences and fantasies, his interior conflicts, and his travels in Latin America and in North Africa. In order to analyze this convergence of personal, cultural, and historical pressures, in this chapter I read Burroughs's letters against his fiction, make reference to his life experiences, and locate his writing in historical and cultural context. The most insightful criticism of Burroughs's work has, in the past, ignored his biography. Ironically, much of his fame as a writer is based on widespread knowledge about his life, especially regarding his drug addiction and the death by gunshot of his wife, Joan, in a drunken William Tell routine. His biographers have rendered complex portraits of Burroughs's life that nonetheless supply little critical leverage for understanding his enduring appeal and critical significance.[2] Critics who base their arguments on his biography usually do so in a hostile maneuver to discredit Burroughs on moral, rather than literary, aesthetic, or political, grounds.[3] By contrast, most of the critics who describe Burroughs as an important and insightful contemporary writer ignore his place in history, and the biographical journeys that his texts write and rewrite, focusing instead on the artifice of his fiction.[4] The exception in this group is Jamie Russell, who insightfully analyzes queer sexuality in both Burroughs's life and texts. I argue in this chapter that Burroughs's writing practices, and the political ends to which those practices are directed, emerged under the pressure of very specific personal experiences, especially as Burroughs traveled and lived in "colonial" spaces. These experiences include the painful process of coming to terms both with his sexual desire for men and his internalized fear of effeminacy, the frustration of pursuing unrequited love, and the struggle to define his own relationship to the international politics attendant upon the ascendancy of postwar American hegemony over former European colonies like Morocco.

For the first half of his writing career, William Burroughs lived as an expatriate, first in Latin America, then in North Africa, and finally in Europe. Throughout his travels, Burroughs sought freedom from the limits that constricted his queer sexual identity, desires, and acts, but his understanding of what sorts of limits restrain freedom, and what might constitute "freedom" in sexual and other arenas, changed over the course of the years. As he traveled and wrote his way through the three principal locations of his expatriation, Burroughs gradually discovered his distinctive literary voice, and he made an explosive entrance into American literary history as an early and important postmodern novelist. This chapter examines the impact of Burroughs's "queer expatriation" on his writing and especially analyzes *Naked Lunch* as a signal text of American literary postmodernism, asking what it means for American culture that this text should be produced by a queer American junky, going through withdrawal, in Tangier in the late 1950s. To answer this question, I locate the author in relation to those categories—"queer," "American," "(ex)-junky"—that are used to define him and that he uses to define himself. I also examine Burroughs's personal history and his relationship to the political and cultural history of the period. As much as his flight south to Mexico and east to Tangier was a flight away from the discourses that regulate identity and experience, in exile Burroughs discovered that he could not escape so easily and that his attempt would have to be pursued not through travel or sex or drugs, but through remembering his experiences—and his fantasies—and writing about them.

William Burroughs, Amsterdam, 1979 (Photograph by Ira Cohen)

Good Trips, Bad Trips, and the Final Fix

Burroughs's writing career began in flight and recorded that flight. He attempted to evade legal authority and American society in general, but it is also clear that, during the years of rewriting that journey in his early books, Burroughs sought an escape from himself. His first book, *Junky* (1953), was written in Mexico City and dryly narrated the principal events of his experiences with drugs (especially opiates) that helped propel him into exile there.[5] The prose is direct and unadorned, the narration linear and rendered in the first person. The author of *Junky* was originally given as William Lee in order to protect Burroughs's family from notoriety, and the narrator in the book carries this name.[6] Aside from the distance between author and narrator afforded by this pseudonym, the narration is Burroughs's most conventionally autobiographical, which is to say his least "inventive," book. Burroughs employed a straightforward narrative style in an effort to represent accurately both his experiences as a junky and his state of mind in the late 1940s and early 1950s. *Junky* describes the development of a habit that leads the narrator to engage in petty theft and pushing to support his habit, and the development of a reputation with the New York City police that impels Lee to skip town. While the narrative does not advocate the use of heroin (the horrors of addiction and withdrawal are rendered with disconcerting precision), neither does it vilify or demonize Lee. In fact, in a way Lee is something of a model patriarchal subject. Far from twisting in the winds of mid-century angst, Lee possesses a stable and self-sufficient identity and consciousness. Drug use centers Lee and organizes a universe to revolve around him—or, more precisely, around his need for the next fix. As Burroughs indicated twenty-five years later, "'Lee' comes across as integrated and self-contained" precisely because he is addicted; "Lee on junk is covered, protected and also severely limited" (introduction to *Queer,* xii). The same substance that makes it possible for Lee to experience a sense of centeredness, security, and independence from other people exacts the price of chemical dependency: if the junk is withdrawn, his sense of security will collapse.

Lee's prejunk history is not recorded in *Junky*, so we see not where he came from but only where he is: fixed in a static cycle of need and relief, frozen in a cycle of consumption that repeats itself monotonously until his supply runs out. Junk has taken Lee on an interior journey, deep into himself. He has traveled to a place of security, but a security purchased at the cost of near-complete alienation from other people. Lee does not need other people; he needs only junk. His alienation includes a reduced need for sex, because "Junk short-circuits sex" (*Junky,* 24). He can connect only with a "connection": "When you are on the junk, the pusher is like the loved one to the lover" (139). Lee is obsessed with the pusher because the pusher can provide the substance that replaces and makes insignificant sexual desire and sexual relations, the material that in fact makes all social relations seem unnecessary. This is not to say that Lee uses junk specifically to avoid social contact. Lee, narrating Burroughs's experience, makes it clear that this explanation of obsession and need is not a psychoanalytic explanation of motivation; the need for a fix is a physical need so powerful that it displaces his psychological relationship with the world.

But while psychological motivations and needs may be displaced, junk cannot obliterate them altogether; neither does the use of opiates ever completely "free" Lee from society. Rather, junk reorganizes and simplifies his psychological needs and social relations around satisfaction and denial, around replenishment and frustration. The world is divided into two groups of people: those who help secure a constant supply (Lupita the pusher, fellow addicts like Bill Gains and Old Ike) and those who stand in the way of the next fix (policemen, incorruptible doctors, moralistic pharmacists). In Lee's world, all that is "real" is his need for junk; what we would commonly understand as "experience" in the "real" world is hallucination for Lee. This inversion is quite literal and prefigures the collapse of the real and the imagined in *Naked Lunch* and later works: among many other instances, Lee tells the story of how he threatened to shoot a policeman in a seedy Mexico City bar. Lee is in a hysterical rage, although he cannot remember why, or even what he had been talking about that incited such belligerence. When he comes to his "senses" in the "real" world, he stops fighting: "The scene was unreal and flat and pointless, as though I had forced my way into someone else's dream" (130–31). Before reaching this point, Lee is acting in his own "dream" world, preparing to kill "the recurrent cop of my dreams—an irritating, nondescript, darkish man who would rush in when I was about to take a shot or go to bed with a boy" (130). Junk organizes Lee's life in a parallel universe wherein the next fix is always his most important priority. Lee would kill the dream image of authority and denial; he very nearly kills a real policeman who momentarily occupies the same time and space as his dream cop.

That this dream cop is recurrently construed to stand in the way of both taking a shot and going to bed with a boy indicates that in Lee's mind the sanction of authority establishes a linkage, and possibly an equivalence, between these two actions. Moreover, in this dream those actions (hypodermic injection and sexual penetration) stand metonymically for two related desires: the desire for drugs and for sex. While junk short-circuits Lee's sexual desire, that desire is not extinguished but is rather restructured by drug use. When he is "fixed," Lee does not seek sex at all, but, to the extent that he does look for sex with boys while using opiates, he seeks encounters that involve a minimal amount of emotional investment or intimate exchange. Junk provides Lee with a self-image and sense of psychic integration, while casual pickups in the Chimu Bar provide him with sexual pleasure. Sexual experience is transformed, however, when Lee goes through periods of withdrawal, a theme that figures prominently in *Queer* but is already sketched out in *Junky*. Withdrawal brings junk-sickness, one of the side effects of which is spontaneous orgasm, "an extremely unpleasant experience . . . putting the teeth on edge" (*Queer,* xiii). Lee's loss of control over his sexual activity is echoed by the loss of control over his emotions; he becomes "uncontrollably sociable," forcing "intimate confidences on perfect strangers" and making "the crudest sexual propositions to people who had given no hint of reciprocity" (*Junky,* 127–28). Junk-sickness also brings a heavy sense of nostalgia, which for Lee means especially nostalgia for childhood: "train whistles, piano music down a city street, burning leaves" (126). Nostalgia for a lost childhood became a principal concern in Burroughs's later fiction. Lee is no longer self-contained in this condition. He needs contact with other people: social contact in general, sexual and emotional contact more specifically. Withdrawal sends Lee on a journey outside himself, a journey through memory into his past life and through people into present time.

Throughout *Junky*, Lee's drug trips are figured as both interior journeys and external movements. Junk organizes Lee's actions around his drug habit; the pursuit of that habit entails evading legal authority, so physical escape is sometimes necessary if his drug use is to continue. He leaves New York to avoid arrest for pushing and flees New Orleans for Mexico rather than stand trial on a charge of possession. Junk responds to state and federal law with its own Law, which is to remain free of arrest and forced withdrawal at all costs. Lee could have traveled west rather than south, but Mexico exerts a quiet, irresistible appeal for him: the descent from "anglo" America to Latin America is for Lee also a movement "east" and into the Orient. On the one hand, the conflation of "South" and "East" seems a quirky repetition of Columbus's mistake, a misperception that indigenous Americans are "Oriental." On the other hand, for historical reasons, Lee associates opium and the drugs derived from it with China, and Mexico appeals to him as a source of those drugs. Very early in *Junky,* there is evidence that, for Lee, Mexico and China coalesce in some kind of dimly imagined hypothetical Orient. When he lives in New York, Lee stops by the apartment of a fellow thief and user; he describes the place as "a chop suey joint"—on the ceiling a colored wheel is painted with "the nightmarish vulgarity of Aztec mosaics" and on the wall there is a "Chinese character in red lacquer" (12–13). In the remainder of the novel—and, in fact, throughout *Queer, The Yage Letters*, and *Naked Lunch*—Burroughs/Lee never questions the linkage of symbols in his friend's modern opium den.[7] In fact, once Lee arrives in Mexico, his conception of the Orient becomes only more encompassing. As soon as he arrives in town, he seeks a "connection" at a café that looks promising because it is "unmistakably Near Eastern," and, he says, you can always find a connection to junk through a "type person" who is from "the Near East, probably Egypt" (111–12).

While one appeal of this Orient that Burroughs seeks in Mexico is the availability of junk, it attracts him for other reasons, as well. During this period of
his life, Burroughs was seeking a physical utopia, a place where he could live
and act as he wanted with interference from neither official state authority nor
unofficial moral authority. In fact, he wanted to live in a place where he was
outside society altogether, a place where he was out of place and where consequently he would be free. Sir Thomas More devised the word "utopia" from
Greek roots to suggest that it is in fact "not" a "place," but in the early 1950s
Burroughs wrote as if he could find a real, earthly utopia. The Orient, as Burroughs constructed it, is a utopia in which he could be "free," and the journey
to Mexico qualified as a "good trip" insofar as it allowed him to step outside
social restrictions. Writing to Allen Ginsberg in 1950, Burroughs enthusiastically described Mexico as "basically an oriental culture (80% Indian) where
everyone has mastered the art of minding his own business. . . . Boys and young
men walk down the street arm in arm and no one pays them any mind. . . . It
simply would not occur to a Mexican to expect criticism from a stranger, nor
would it occur to anyone to criticize the behavior of others."[8] Later that year,
Burroughs revised his initial enthusiasm after a neighbor reported his drinking and drug use to the police, but for Burroughs this turn of events simply
showed that Mexico was sometimes too bourgeois and not "Oriental" enough.
The fantasy that he could discover a society in which individuals were "free"
from social, legal, and moral norms is indicative of the state of mind of a naïve
tourist rather than a thoughtfully observant resident. Eventually, he left for Peru
in search of a "more Indian" and hence "more Oriental" utopia, but during his
first year in Mexico City he was content because "here no limits are imposed
on experience."[9] No limits were imposed on sexual experience, in his dubious
view, because the unpoliced promenading of boys and young men was the supposed sign of unrestricted sexual activity. A more accurate observation was that
no effective limits were imposed on drug experience because, even when the
police were called, a bribe could once again set one free.

But sexual and drug experiences were only part of the entire life experience
Burroughs looked for in an unbounded utopian Orient. Sex and drugs were,
in fact, meant to be vehicles on a larger trip, the means through which Burroughs could transcend both identity and desire, both bounded consciousness
and all variety of dependence. He wrote *Junky* as an exposé of the failure of
junk to help him achieve this goal; *Queer* makes a similar point regarding the
failure of sex. *Junky* concludes with Lee's resolve to leave junk behind because
it has only replaced one form of control and dependence with another. He wants
"the uncut kick that opens out instead of narrowing down like junk" (152),
and he resolves to seek this kick through a drug he has heard of called yage—
a drug used by Amazonian Indians, reportedly to promote telepathic communication. Junk enforced isolation from other people, but Lee hopes that yage

can help him connect with others, possibly bringing sexual experience and drug experience together in a harmony of plenitude. As *Queer* makes clear, the search for "telepathic contact" through yage is also a search for emotional intimacy and affection, for "contact on the nonverbal level of intuition and feeling" (*Junky*, 152). Burroughs ended his first book on this optimistic note: "Yage may be the final fix" (152).

Queer, the sequel to *Junky*, relates the principal events of Burroughs's unsuccessful search for the "final fix" in Ecuador in 1951.[10] As the title of *Queer* indicates, Burroughs's second quasi-autobiographical book makes the matter of his sexual identity a central concern. Over the course of this narrative, Burroughs, once again named Lee, gradually withdraws from his dependence on opiates while pursuing a relationship with an attractive young self-identified heterosexual American named Eugene Allerton (a character based on a man named Adelbert Lewis Marker). Lee becomes infatuated with Allerton in Mexico City and persuades Allerton to accompany him on the journey to Ecuador, all expenses paid in return for sex twice a week. It is in every respect a bad trip, in which Lee manages only to replace junk with Allerton, one form of addiction substituting for another. As the two book titles suggest, *Junky* and *Queer* were written as a pair, the first book on junk, the second one off it; as Lee's dependence on junk fades, his sexual and emotional needs increase.[11] Together, these two books record a shift from an identity organized around junk to one organized around sex.

Significantly, the narrative techniques and styles that Burroughs employs underline this shift. *Queer* is told in the third person, even though it still unfolds as though organized by Lee's consciousness (the narrative voice never speaks outside Lee's experience). While the narrative voice in *Junky* is tightly framed, direct, and self-assured, that of *Queer* is tentative and fragmented, prone to digressions and flights of fantasy. This style reflects Burroughs's state of mind as he withdrew from junk in 1951, and the third-person narration allowed Burroughs a distance from Lee that seemed necessary in order for him to commit to paper his emotional and sexual insecurities at that time. As Burroughs said, "While it was I who wrote *Junky*, I feel that I was being written in *Queer*" (*Queer*, xiv). The question is, being written by whom? Burroughs suggested that, during this period of his life, he was possessed by something he calls the Ugly Spirit and that his "concept of possession is closer to the medieval model than to modern psychological explanations, with their dogmatic insistence that such manifestations must come from within and never, never, never from without" (xix).[12] But the narrative of *Queer* invites easy, even transparent, psychoanalytic readings in ways that *Junky* resolutely refuses: the tightness of the narration in the first novel produces Lee as a hermetic shell; the diffuse narration of the second novel breaks Lee wide open, his insecurities exposed, his behavior nearly hysterical. In fact, it is the nearness of Lee's behavior to that of a hysterical drag queen that indicates that the roots of his crisis lie not only in withdrawal from addiction but also in facing his sexual identities and desires: for Lee this means coming to terms with "feminine" and "masculine" aspects of himself, with his desire for men (especially young men, and especially young "Oriental" men), and in general with his construction as a gendered and sexed subject. One rather easy (and accurate) psychoanalytic reading of *Queer* is that Lee is suffering from an extreme case of internalized homophobia arising from a horror of femininity, that he has terribly low self-esteem, and that his dysfunctional behavior is only making his situation more dramatically tragic. But *Queer* also yields a more complicated reading that is not simplistically psychoanalytic—in the sense of dogmatically insisting on the separation between internal need and external "possession."

At the opening of the twenty-first century, the word "queer" has a different meaning than it had in the 1950s. Recent queer activism and queer theory have altered not only the meaning of the word but also the way that it goes about meaning. Today, "queer" is still used as a derogatory epithet that lumps together a variety of sexual minorities under one sign of abnormality and approbation; however, the word is also employed by self-identified queers in new ways and with new meanings. Through the efforts of self-identified queer radicals, the word has been appropriated and revalued to signify the positive value of standing outside middle-class norms, especially but not exclusively in regard to sexual activity and identity. As such, various groups of self-identified queers have sought in their use of the word a basis for revitalized coalition politics and/or a basis for extrainstitutional and subversive, rather than reformist, politics. Many theorists of queer politics agree with Judith Butler that the usefulness of the word lies precisely in the fact that it decenters the "necessary error" of identity and identity politics and that the word will remain useful only so long as it is "never fully owned" by anyone, so long as it is "redeployed, twisted, queered from a prior usage and in the direction of urgent and expanding political purposes" (*Bodies that Matter,* 228).

In naming his second book *Queer* and in referring to his own sexual identity with that word, William Burroughs was not using the term in the way that contemporary queer activists and theorists use it. Burroughs did develop a critique of identity categories and their social construction, but in 1951 his critique was still nascent and not fully articulated. His understanding of identity emerged during this period through his experiences with drugs and with sex, and his writing was just beginning to work through the question of what sexual identity meant for him. Burroughs accepted his sexual desires as they came to him, and he accepted desire as the basis of an identity. In 1951, when Allen Ginsberg wrote to Burroughs concerning his own self-doubt as to whether he should "get over being queer," Burroughs replied, "I am not going anywhere from where I am, couldn't go anywhere and don't want to. . . . I am acquainted with the drawbacks of being queer. Better acquainted than you. . . . [T]he point is not how dissatisfied you are with being queer. The point is do you get everything you want in the way of sex from a woman?"[13] Burroughs used the word "queer" as it was commonly used among gay men in the United States in the 1930s and 1940s. As George Chauncey explains in his study of New York gay life during this period, "queer" could refer to all men who sexually desire other men, but it could also refer more specifically to masculine-identified men who enjoy having sex with other masculine-identified men. Used this way, the word "queer" distinguishes masculine-identified gay men from effeminate gay men ("faggots" or "fairies"). Both groups typically share as an object of desire a "normal" or "straight" man who, in his ideal manifestation, is "trade": a heterosexual man who has sex with a queer or a fairy, sometimes for money. Chauncey explains that in making their self-definitions, queers distanced themselves from fairies:

[M]any queers were repelled by the style of the fairy and his loss of manly status, and almost all were careful to distinguish themselves from such men. They might use *queer* to refer to any man who was not "normal," but they usually applied terms such as *fairy, faggot,* and *queen* only to those men who dressed or behaved in what they considered to be a flamboyantly effeminate manner. (*Gay New York,* 16)

When Lee first appears in a queer bar, in New Orleans, he makes his own relation to this schema clear. "A room full of fags gives me the horrors," he says, and, when he sees an attractive young boy, he makes sure the boy doesn't "come on faggish" before proceeding to proposition him (*Junky,* 72). The same dynamic is repeated in the Chimu, his queer bar of choice in Mexico City, which is populated with "depraved" and "repulsive" Mexican fags but where Lee meets the boy of his dreams, Angelo, who is trade: "He was not queer, and I gave him money" (114).[14]

Reading *Junky* and *Queer* today, we see that fear of effeminacy is readily apparent in Burroughs's deployment of the words "fag" and "queer." But it is also important to keep in mind that, at the time these two novels were written, mainstream psychiatry strongly endorsed the notion that homosexuality was a psychological disease. For Burroughs, psychiatry represented one line of attack by an enemy that wished to condemn and control the sexual desires he experienced as constitutive of his very selfhood. His strategy in fighting this enemy was to attack those medical and ethical discourses that construed his desires to be deviant. Burroughs's letters from the 1950s show that he refused to accept the notion that he had an internal "problem" regarding sexual desire and insisted instead that any problem there might be existed outside himself. Burroughs developed this idea of externality in part through his "medieval" notion of possession.[15] But his insistence that "problems" with sexual desire come from outside the self also had a less mystical and more sociological explanation. As he wrote to Allen Ginsberg, "The problems and difficulties you complain of in queer relationships are social rather than inherent—resulting from the social environment . . . of middle class U.S.A."[16] This statement, written in 1951, represents an early attempt on Burroughs's part to articulate the demands that social conditioning place on queer men and queer relationships. While this analysis does not engage the more complex question of how his own fear and hatred of femininity in men and women supported the "social environment" he condemned, nor how that conditioning helped produce the sexual desires he felt to be deeply rooted in his very being, his fiction and letters from the 1950s do begin to explore some of these larger issues. Specifically, he explored such issues by writing about gender identity, sexual desire, and sexual acts.

The voice of Lee in *Junky* expresses no doubt about the reality and authenticity of his masculinity, in comparison to the femininity of fags who "jerk around like puppets on invisible strings, galvanized into hideous activity that is the negation of everything living" (72). But in his letters, Burroughs indicated, at times, that he did not take his own "masculine" gender identity so seriously. When Ginsberg, acting as Burroughs's agent, asked what biographical information the publisher Carl Solomon should include in the first edition of *Junky*, Burroughs replied, "tell Solomon I don't mind being called queer. T. E. Lawrence and all manner of right Joes (boy can I turn a phrase) was queer. But I'll see him castrated before I'll be called a Fag. That's just what I been trying to put down uh I mean *over*, is the distinction between us strong, manly, noble types and the leaping, jumping, window dressing cocksucker." In pointing out that the distinction between queers and fags is to some extent a matter of deception ("trying to put down"), Burroughs recognized how "masculinity" is enacted as a rhetorical strategy. While it is true that Burroughs wanted to be called a queer and not a fag, he satirized the very distinction he insisted upon. Here, the derision of "fags" is ironic, and Burroughs went so far as to take on a campy, feminine voice. The letter continues, "Furthechrissakes a girl's gotta draw the line somewheres or publishers will swarm all over her sticking their nasty old biographical prefaces up her ass."[17] It is uncharacteristic—even rare—for Burroughs to refer to himself as a "girl," but this example of queeny camp shows his willingness to call rigid gender categories into question.

Burroughs also began to explore the part played by gender, sexual, and racial identities in the construction of sexual desire. The "queer" structure of sexual desire (a masculine-identified man who enjoys sex with other masculine-identified men) is in this limited sense built upon a logic of like attracting like. But Burroughs described a desire that is highly differentiated within this structure according to age, "sexuality," and "race." His sexual object of choice was youthful (age 18–25), "straight," and "Oriental."[18] A "straight" sexual identity was confirmed by sleeping with men for money and with women for fun; both of Burroughs's long-term boyfriends during the 1950s (Angelo in Mexico City, Kiki in Tangier) fell into this category. Both boys also fell into Burroughs's somewhat idiosyncratic notion of "Oriental": "Angelo's face was Oriental, Japanese-looking, except for his copper skin" (*Junky,* 114), and in Tangier, "Kiki looks like a South American Indian."[19] Burroughs compared the boys in 1954: "Both had very straight black hair, an Oriental look, and lean, slight bodies. . . . Lee met the same people wherever he went" (*Interzone,* 38). This seems to be true not only for Mexico and Morocco but also for Peru, from where he wrote, "The best people in S.A. are the Indians. Certainly the best-looking people. My boy is at least 70% Indian."[20] Not only did Burroughs find "Oriental" features in attractive boys with Spanish and Indian ancestry—even the Anglo-American Marker/Allerton fell into this category: his face is "delicate and exotic and Oriental" (*Queer,* 16). During the years of his expatriation in Latin America and North Africa, Burroughs rendered the concept of sexual Orientation quite literally: it is as if all objects of his sexual desire had some connection to the "eastern" utopian space Burroughs sought, a space that overflowed with masculine, boyish young men, while effeminate men were nowhere in sight. None of the objects of desire described in his letters and fiction from the early 1950s came from Asia, so that Burroughs's use of the word Orient called attention to the symbolic function of this category in the construction of his sexual desires. But during this period, Burroughs was interested first and foremost in accepting his desires as they came to him; his writing was not so much a critique of how those desires came to be constructed as it was an attempt to make them recognizable by representing them. The fact that Carl Solomon declined for legal reasons to publish *Queer* is just one indication of how controversial such representations were in the early 1950s, and in this light Burroughs's self-revelations concerning the roles of age, "sexuality," and "race" in the construction of his desires broke important ground in the history of queer self-representation.

Unlike *Queer*, the other early "autobiographical" books, *Junky* and *The Yage Letters,* were published soon after they were written; the otherwise startlingly frank self-revelations of all three books are notably silent, however, when it comes to representations of sexual acts. Besides the mention of a few tender caresses, Burroughs had little to say about what exactly happened between the sheets as he sought a utopian space in Latin America and North Africa. Since he wrote in such interesting ways about desire, the lack of information about sexual acts in his early writings was especially noteworthy; it seems that the unrepresentability of sexual acts was itself one point of these texts. But Burroughs did suggest through the realm of fantasy some outlines of what might take place during those unrepresentable acts. In *Queer*, Lee travels to Guayaquil,

Ecuador, in his search for yage and, through it, an experience of plenitude beyond limits. Of course, he also looks for sex, in the pursuit of which he walks through the city preoccupied with the question, "What happens when there is no limit?" (95). He encounters a group of "six or seven boys, aged twelve to fourteen" who watch him in an "overtly sexual" and yet "mocking" way. Lee returns their gazes with "limitless desire" and, as he looks on, he feels himself merging with the body of one of the boys, then merging with the boy's consciousness. He feels the stone floor as he and the other boys take off their clothes and begin to have sex with each other; he feels "the orgasm blackout in the hot sun" and afterward the warmth of a young head as it lies on his stomach. He then feels the desire of the boy *for a woman*. "'I'm not queer,' he thought. 'I'm disembodied'" (96–97). While, even in this fantasy, the precise acts that precipitate orgasm go undescribed, the entire process is directed toward leaving both body and identity behind through sexual activity that turns Lee into the very object he desires, an object that as a subject desires women. By being disembodied, Lee ceases to be homosexual, to be situated in his particular sexual/gender identity. Passing beyond "limits" means, for Lee, both pursuing his desires for "Oriental" boys and escaping the structures of those very desires. This escape never quite happens. Lee tells Allerton that the boys have a "maleness" that he wants; ironically, in his sexual fantasy this "real uncut boy stuff" begins in a group sex scene but ends with desire for a woman, as if to underscore the fact that "maleness" is bounded even in the fantastic state beyond limits, because it depends upon some notion of the feminine in order to be understood as masculine (98–99).

In his letters, as well as in his fiction, Burroughs wrote about the meaning of sex acts indirectly, through fantasies about those acts. Many letters have been destroyed, some on purpose, but at least those that remain have little to say directly about sex acts. It is possible, however, to read at least one account of Burroughs having sex—not with boys in Latin America or Tangier, but with a more accessible witness: Allen Ginsberg. For his biography of Burroughs, Ted Morgan interviewed both men about the sexual relationship they had in New York in 1953. He rendered this account:

What Burroughs wanted was to take the passive role. Allen was surprised to see that he could have an orgasm that way. There was nothing reciprocal in it. Having it done to him was enough. . . . He seemed to melt completely, to take on a different identity. . . . His distinction and reticence gave way to a mushily romantic, vulnerably whimpering female persona, as if he was able to contain within himself the personalities of both sexes. To Burroughs, it was another instance of being possessed by beings over which he had no control. (*Literary Outlaw,* 230)

While it would be a mistake to generalize Morgan's account into a framework for analyzing all of Burroughs's sexual experiences, the value of repeating this story lies in the way that it confirms the element of transformation—even meta-morphosis—so strongly evident in Burroughs's written sexual fantasies. Morgan's description is so vividly at variance with the hard-boiled masculine image of Inspector Lee that Burroughs cultivated over the years that the transformation seems as likely—or as unlikely—as Lee's merging into the consciousness of an Ecuadorian boy. The idea of Burroughs "melting" into a woman in bed suggests that his tough image should be taken with a grain of salt and his many misogynistic statements read in the light of a phobic reaction.

While representations of sex acts are absent from Burroughs's first three books, one sex act is repeatedly—almost obsessively—represented in *Naked Lunch* and later books. The various hanging scenes in *Naked Lunch* and the cut-up trilogy that follows all figure strangulation as the coming together of sex and death, of orgasm and metamorphosis. In his film version of *Naked Lunch,* David Cronenberg accurately translated this major interest of the novel into the scene in which a monster kills Kiki by sexually penetrating him while simultaneously tearing him apart with claws. But by filming this scene in the language of horror movies instead of using the conventions of pornography that Burroughs employed in the original text, Cronenberg lost the sense of obsessive sexual fantasy that Burroughs had achieved. The hanging scenes, like many scenes in the novel *Naked Lunch*, are scripted like films, with directions like "on screen" or "fadeout." At the end of the hanging/sex scene in "A.J.'s Annual Party," we are reminded that we have been watching porn, not "real" sex-as-death: "Mary, Johnny and Mark take a bow with the ropes around their necks. They are not as young as they appear in the Blue Movies" (*Naked Lunch,* 103). As Burroughs's hanging scenes accumulate in book after book through the 1960s, the increasingly banal repetitions further underline the obsessive quality of this particular sexual fantasy. Hanging makes its first appearance in *Junky*, when Lee compares the spontaneous orgasm of junk sickness to "the orgasm of a hanged man when the neck snaps" (94). Burroughs's various subsequent hanging fantasies all connect the involuntary orgasm that is supposed to accompany strangulation with the death of the will—in fact, with the death of autonomous male subjectivity in the throes of pleasure. Burroughs repeatedly focused on snapping necks at the moment of ejaculation, a displacement from the locus of bodily pleasure to which Cronenberg rightly drew attention as Kiki is killed *a tergo*: the anus. As Leo Bersani has argued, this is precisely the locus of sexual pleasure wherein male subjectivity undergoes disintegration and transformation. In *The Soft Machine,* Burroughs imagined death/orgasm from hanging as a route of penetration into the body and consciousness of another, and it is one means through which the narrator becomes part of an ancient "Mayan" civilization. While Bersani explored the rectum as a site of "masculine" disintegration in the face of "feminine" pleasure, and while Morgan's description of sex between Ginsberg and

Burroughs seems to be a classic instance of this phenomenon, in his fiction Burroughs disallowed the terms of such psychoanalytic analyses. Instead, he explored the potential of anal penetrative sex (figured as hanging) to actually transfer one's ego to another body, to transcend consciousness through a corporeal merging, and to transform an identity based on race as well as on sexuality and gender.

That the exploration of such transformation through the mechanism of sexual strangulation occurs in the science fiction novels that follow Burroughs's more "autobiographical" books suggests that a degree of wishful thinking is at work. *Junky* describes the failure of opiates to effect transcendence; *Queer* describes the parallel failure of sex, at least the sort of sex Lee has with Allerton. Lee has a deep emotional need for a reciprocal "telepathic" relationship with Allerton, but reciprocity is ruled out by Allerton's unwillingness to experience the relationship as anything other than the exchange of sex for money— he is trade, after all. Moreover, Lee's sexual Orientation consistently directs his erotic interests toward objects who are distanced from him through fantastic constructions of "boyhood," the "Orient," and "heterosexuality," making "contact on the nonverbal level of intuition and feeling" unlikely if not impossible. While Lee hopes to find in and through sex that mechanism that will liberate his "inner" self and make it possible to transcend all kinds of limitations, including moral restrictions and the boundedness of identity itself, erotic desire and sexual acts are themselves bounded by social structures. Lee engages in a misguided effort to escape the constructedness of identity, including sexual identity, in his search for a utopian "Oriental" space and for transformative sex in that space.

As his multiple reworkings of the hanging fantasy indicate, Burroughs did not give up this effort easily. The 1951 journey to Ecuador ended disastrously: Lee does not find yage, he is not able to connect with any of the Ecuadorian boys he desires, and Allerton remains cold and indifferent. But in 1953 Burroughs set out once again in search of yage: having experienced the failure of opiates and sex to resolve his need for transformation, he wanted to find yage as another possible source of the "final fix." On this trip, Burroughs traveled alone to Panama, Colombia, Ecuador, and Peru and he found that, in fact, yage (also known as *bannisteria caapi* and *ayahuasca*) is readily available in towns in the upper Amazon region. This journey provided the basis for Burroughs's third book, *The Yage Letters*, in which he collected and edited letters sent to Allen Ginsberg, along with Ginsberg's letters to Burroughs about his own yage experiences in 1960.

Just as *Queer* marks the beginning of the end of Burroughs's addiction to opiates, *The Yage Letters* marks the beginning of the end of his search for a literal, terrestrial utopia. As Burroughs experimented with yage first in Colombia and later in Peru, his hallucinations finally allowed him entry into the space beyond limits that he had been seeking since leaving New York seven years earlier. These hallucinations continued to exercise his fantasies of psychic and corporeal transformation:

Yage is space time travel. The room seems to shake and vibrate with motion. The blood and substance of many races, Negro, Polynesian, Mountain Mongol, Desert Nomad, Polygot [sic] Near East, Indian—new races as yet unconceived and unborn, combinations not yet realized passes [sic] through your body. Migrations, incredible journeys through deserts and jungles and mountains . . . across the Pacific in an outrigger canoe to Easter Island. The Composite City where all human potentials are spread out in a vast silent market. (*The Yage Letters*, 44)

Burroughs's journey south from the United States into the "East" culminated in this vision of a new kind of travel—"space time travel"—which became the hallmark of *Naked Lunch* and his subsequent cut-up novels. This new kind of travel occurred as "races" passed through the self, rather than as the body passed through space; as Burroughs's list of "races" indicates, the emphasis was on "exotic," "ancient," and "primitive" experience that Burroughs could not possibly have in real time—that, in fact, he could barely imagine. The success and failure of imagination is precisely the point of Burroughs's "space time travel." In *Junky*, opiates close Lee off and shut him down; in *Queer*, sex leaves him lonely and depressed; but in *Yage*, Burroughs was reborn as the future author of "all human potentials." His yage vision of the Composite City served as Burroughs's blueprint for the limitless city of the interzone before he ever set foot in Tangier.

Yage also holds another meaning for Burroughs—a meaning that went unpublished in *The Yage Letters* but that was made public in his more recent collected letters. In a letter to Ginsberg written two days before the one cited earlier, Burroughs described the sexual and corporeal dimensions of his yage hallucinations. "The substance of body seems to change," wrote Burroughs; in one vision "I turned right into a nigger." He elaborated:

The room took on the aspect of a near Eastern whore house with blue walls and red tasselled lamps. I feel myself change into a Negress complete with all the female facilities. Convulsions of lust accompanied by physical impotence. Now I am a Negro fucking a Negress. My legs take on a well rounded Polynesian substance. Everything stirs with a peculiar furtive writhing life like a Van Gogh painting. Complete bisexuality is attained. You are man or woman alternately or at will. . . . The only contact you want is sexual contact. I never experienced such sex kicks. [21]

The offensiveness of this passage is reason enough not to have published it with the other *Yage Letters* material; yet, in spite of its recourse to negative stereotypes about African American sexuality—stereotypes Burroughs presumably repeated both to parody them and to record his hallucination—this passage vividly connects the racial and sexual elements of the transformation

Burroughs sought to effect. Furthermore, in the same letter he explained a great deal about why he was so interested in transformation in the first place: "[Yage] is the drug [that] really does what the others are supposed to do. This is the most complete negation possible of respectability. Imagine a small town bank president turning into a Negress and rushing to Nigger town in a frenzy to solicit sex from some Buck Nigra. He would never recover that preposterous condition known as self respect."[22] Burroughs's sexual fantasies about race point to a need for abjection in a way reminiscent of Genet. Both Burroughs's life and his writing celebrate depravity in an attempt to displace middle-class morality; abjection of self would form a route of escape from boring and oppressive pieties. Seen in this light, Burroughs's self-identification as queer does indeed resonate with the way that word has been deployed recently by contemporary queers: by assuming a label of opprobrium, one rejects the center and champions the marginal. But the transformation Burroughs sought to effect through yage, the "negation of respectability" that is also "complete bisexuality," is very much the vision of a queer (in the older sense) white American male drug-consuming literary expatriate who grew up on the fringes of the southern United States in the twentieth century, and it is very much structured by those parameters.

The impulse behind Burroughs's search for a kind of inverse apotheosis was basically romantic, because it was based on a notion of the self as some kind of coherent, self-sufficient essence that can be set free from moral and political regulation. What Burroughs learned on his long journey from New York to Lima is that the oppressions experienced by the self cannot be overthrown simply by stepping outside one's society because the self carries with it and perpetuates those social forms and conditions that have helped form it. A vision of sexual liberation played out through stereotypes about African American sexuality is a powerful sign of this lesson. Burroughs left the United States in search of a utopian space, in the hope that, through sex with "Oriental" boys and through the consumption of "Oriental" drugs, he would be liberated from all forms of repression and control. For some months, Burroughs believed he had found this utopia in Mexico City; by the time he arrived in Lima in 1953 his optimism had been tempered. Not that he disliked Lima: in fact, he called it "the promised land for boys" and enthusiastically wrote to Ginsberg, "I have not seen any queer bars (hope I don't see any), but in the bars around the Mercado Mayorista—Main Market—any boy is wise and available to the Yankee dollar."[23] The absence of queer bars, and of the fairies who frequent them, was a predictable element of Burroughs's concept of a sexual utopia. He reveled in the idea that the Peruvian boys he flirted with and had sex with are "non-queer": "If they do go to bed with another male, and they all will for money, they seem to enjoy it. Homosexuality is simply a human *potential*."[24] What was added to his description of sex in Lima that figured less prominently in his early descriptions of sex in Mexico City is the emphasis on the *Yankee* dollar, and consequently on his position not only as a purchaser of sex but as a North American purchaser of sex from poor or working-class Latin American boys.

Burroughs's escape south into the "East" was initially an attempt to secure "independence" by placing himself in a foreign culture where he could command authority by virtue of his ignorance. Especially in his Amazonian expeditions, Burroughs parodically staged himself in the role of the European explorer/scientist, a kind of modern von Humboldt, wearing a pith helmet and collecting samples for laboratory analysis. His position as a gringo explorer of the Amazon and of seedy bars in Latin American cities would ideally place him outside North American social structures and mores, opening him up to new forms of knowledge and experience. But Burroughs discovered both in the search for yage and in the search for sex that his identity as a North American put limits on his experience and on his consciousness. When he arrived in the Putumayo region of Colombia, a region of dense forests and little economic development, he found that the Texas Oil Company had preceded him and that everyone believed he worked for this company. While this mistaken perception aided Burroughs's search for yage, it also positioned him as a representative of "colonial" U.S. interests in Colombia. Burroughs could not have cared less what Colombians thought about him, but he did begin to realize the extent to which his experience was bounded by his position as an American. In the town of Puerto Asis, he was approached by an attractive young boy who, it turned out, was a hustler specializing in North American clients. Burroughs's desires and his identity were read quite efficiently by this hustler, as well as by the Peruvian boys who were "wise to the Yankee dollar." Like the content of Burroughs's yage visions, being rolled by a hustler in the Amazon was a lesson not in new but rather in "old" knowledge and experience as a queer North American man in search of "Oriental" trade. Burroughs repeated his sexual fantasies and experiences again and again.

It turns out that yage is not the "final fix" but rather one fix among many that Burroughs sought as methods of transformation and liberation. Under its influence in Lima, Burroughs saw a vision of a utopian "Composite City," but the fantastic quality of this vision served to underscore the fact that such a place does not exist in present space and time. After the dream image faded, Burroughs was back where he started: with the same sexuality, the same gender, the same racial and national identities. In attempting to escape from middle-class, middle-American, middle-century moral values, Burroughs was attempting to escape from the very structures that had formed his identity, his desires, and his way of being in the world. It was only after seeking and failing to find a terrestrial utopia of plenitude beyond limits that Burroughs understood that social conditions and conditioning cannot be overcome by physical relocation, drug consumption, or sexual activity. This emerging realization, forged through five years of expatriation in Latin America, was the beginning of the new Burroughsian vision that is now called postmodern, the vision that he would make famous in *Naked Lunch*.

Burroughs's Interzone

Burroughs did not immediately stop consuming opiates and other drugs when he relocated from Mexico to Morocco, but his relationship to drugs did begin to change after 1954, along with his experience and understanding of sex, writing, and expatriation. In Latin America Burroughs attempted to use drugs and sex as tools that would enable him to achieve liberation from a variety of external pressures that shaped his interior being—moral conventions, the culture of conformity, and social conditioning in general. His experience in Latin America, including the failure of yage to effect a "final fix," led him to question more closely the relationship between interior being and external constraints. In Morocco Burroughs came to reject opiate use because of the loss of self-control he experienced through addiction. Indeed, he formulated a theory that any form of external control is an addiction that must be overthrown if the self is to achieve liberation. But deployment of the metaphor of addiction in this way did not immediately clarify for Burroughs the perplexing question of what the "self" actually is. In fact, this metaphor threw into greater disarray his understanding of how queer identity relates to sexual liberation, because both homosexual desire and internalized homophobia can be thought of as "addictions," and perhaps even as two antagonistic aspects of a single addiction. In Tangier Burroughs attempted to sort through a number of questions concerning subjectivity, especially regarding external control of interior life and the relation of sexual desire to personal identity. He explored these questions by having sex and writing about sex within the web of colonial relations that prevailed in Tangier in the 1950s. More specifically, he engaged in both a search for freedom from society through anonymous sexual activity and a search for connection with American friends and soul-mates through writing. In the process of writing and having sex, Burroughs came to realize that external controls were exercised over him through language itself, and he began to invent ways to fight that control through writing.

Tangier was not the promised land Burroughs had once optimistically sought in Latin America, but it was the inspiration for the "composite city" he invented in *Naked Lunch*. As Burroughs accumulated the pages of manuscript that became *Naked Lunch*, roughly between 1954 and 1958, he called his work in progress "Interzone" and referred to it as my "Tanger [*sic*] novel."[25] Burroughs's concept of the "interzone" was based on his vision of Tangier: tellingly, Burroughs dropped "nation" out of the "international zone" of

Tangier. Burroughs disliked nationalism and called for an end to the family unit upon which nations are based (*The Job*, 50–51, 98–102). By eliminating the crucial category of "nation" from his "interzone," Burroughs deflected attention from the colonial politics that sustained Tangier's special status and toward Tangier's in-betweenness as such: located at the crossroads of Africa, Europe, and the Middle East, situated between the Mediterranean Sea and the Atlantic Ocean, the meeting place of West and East, North and South, Tangier was a new Babel where dozens of languages and cultures and three major religions mixed promiscuously.

The promiscuous mixing occasioned by sexual tourism became, for Burroughs, a metaphor for understanding Tangier as a space where national, religious, and cultural interests could be blurred and where unrestrained and proliferating desire could supplant bounded identities and ideologies. Burroughs's notion of in-betweenness in the interzone engaged many of the major crises of late twentieth-century culture in general—the indeterminacy of philosophical thought due to loss of faith in any of a number of totalizing ideologies, the insufficiency of tradition to sustain culture in an age of global communication and marketing, the inadequacy of words like communism, capitalism, colonialism, and nationalism to describe accurately contemporary political systems and relations—all of these issues are represented in *Naked Lunch* through multiple and proliferating suspensions, irresolutions, and disintegrations. Above all, however, the interzone represented for Burroughs that place of in-betweenness he wanted to inhabit—the place he had sought in Latin America but had found only momentarily in his yage hallucinations. In 1955, he wrote to Kerouac and Ginsberg, "Tanger [*sic*] is the prognostic pulse of the world, like a dream extending from past into the future, a frontier between dream and reality—the 'reality' of both called into question."[26] For Burroughs, this was literally a dream come true; he was finally able to escape "reality," not by traveling to a utopian place but by residing within a frontier.

For Burroughs, to live as an expatriate in this in-between space was to exist outside social boundaries. As when he first arrived in Mexico City in 1949, in Tangier Burroughs looked for freedom through anonymity. The problem with the United States, Burroughs complained to Ginsberg, was the "continual annoyances from presumptuous cops. . . . One of my reasons for preferring to live outside the U.S. is so I won't be wasting time reacting against cops and the interfering society they represent. . . . Living here [in Tangier] you feel no weight of disapproving 'others,' no 'they,' no *Society*, consequently no resentment."[27] The dream of living outside society, of inhabiting a subjectivity independent of all others, of possessing radical autonomy and self-determination merged into reality for Burroughs insofar as he remained uninvolved in and ignorant of the society of the city in which he lived. Of course, Burroughs did involve himself in the economic lives of Tanjawis—he had to purchase shelter, food, drugs, and sex—but, even in these interactions, Burroughs attempted to remain apart from society. During his early years in Tangier, before he overcame his addiction to narcotics, drugs helped him remain outside social life. Indeed, he came to be known among Tangier's street boys as "El hombre invisible," in part because he looked so spectral when addicted but also in part because he seemed so obscure on city streets, his existence so tangential to social life. Aside from making the minimal purchases necessary for survival, Burroughs used anonymous sex as his preferred form of social interaction. In Tangier Burroughs could have sex with hustlers who were, for him, "blank" people. After one month in Tangier, he wrote to Ginsberg, "It's like I been to bed with 3 Arabs since arrival, but I wonder if it isn't the same character in different clothes. . . . I *really* don't know for sure. Next time I'll notch one of his ears."[28] This is not a complaint but rather a joke with a serious point—the pleasure of anonymity was precisely what Burroughs sought and found in Tangier, and this pleasure was heightened by remaining ignorant of and detached from the social and cultural lives of his sex partners.

Burroughs lived in Tangier long enough to develop a comfortable position as an outsider; ironically, it was as an outsider that he felt he belonged in the interzone. In 1956, during the wave of nationalism that accompanied independence, Burroughs told Ginsberg, "So long as I go with Spanish boys, it is like having a girl in the U.S. I mean you feel yourself at one with the society. No one disapproves or says anything. Whereas to walk around town with an Arab boy would be unthinkable at this point. . . . You dig no one cares what the unbelievers do among themselves."[29] Later in the 1950s, Paul and Jane Bowles, along with many other expatriates, fled to Europe when the Moroccan government began to prosecute and persecute foreign and native residents who were involved in homosexual relationships with each other.[30] Burroughs noted with irony that he could feel "at one" with Tangier society precisely insofar as he was disregarded by mainstream moral concerns. Another irony arose from the fact that, while Burroughs categorized his boyfriend Kiki, and perhaps other Spanish boys, with Arabs in his erotic organization of the "third world," Tanjawis lumped Spaniards and Americans together in the category of unbelievers or "Westerners." Burroughs sought sexual freedom in the late 1940s by leaving the "West," but he experienced this freedom in Tangier in the late 1950s to the extent that he had sex only with fellow "Westerners" as defined by the Moroccans among whom he lived. Burroughs attained the license to pursue his sexual desires by remaining suspended between domestic and foreign moral structures—another aspect of the in-betweenness that he sought in his own private interzone.

While this interzone represented in many respects a dream come true for Burroughs, life on the "outside" of society could not fulfill all of his needs. While he was perfectly happy to be "free" of disapproving others, Burroughs also yearned for the type of intimacy and connection he found in a handful of close friendships. During his initial years in Tangier, Burroughs was very lonely because his close friends all lived in the United States, and it was only through reading and writing letters that he was able to maintain his intellectual and emotional connections with them. Moreover, to write at all, whether fiction or nonfiction, Burroughs needed to have an audience, and, for most of the late 1950s, Allen Ginsberg was Burroughs's long-distance audience. Many of the ideas for *Naked Lunch* were worked out in his letters to Ginsberg, and many long passages were sent to Ginsberg for editing. In part, this method of composition merely continued Burroughs's working habits from his years of expatriation in Latin America, when Ginsberg acted as Burroughs's agent and to a lesser extent his editor; Burroughs sent Ginsberg drafts of *Junky* and *Queer*, and Ginsberg provided encouragement and editorial assistance. The composition and editing of *The Yage Letters* brought this method of collaboration to the surface of the text. But there is an important distinction to be drawn between Burroughs's earlier writing and *Naked Lunch*: in the early 1950s, Burroughs was infatuated with Lewis Marker—he dedicated *Junky* to Marker and wrote *Queer* for and about him.[31] Ginsberg was already the audience for *Yage*, but the letters were still written from one friend to another. But when Burroughs returned to New York from Peru, he fell in love with Ginsberg, and they had a brief sexual affair. While the sex did not last beyond a few months in 1953, Burroughs's emotional connection to Ginsberg and his need for intimacy did continue after he left New York for Tangier.

Much of *Naked Lunch* was written for Ginsberg in the same way that *Queer* was written for Marker; Burroughs experienced writing as a way to connect with the object of his desires. In 1954, Burroughs briefly returned to the United States in hopes of reuniting with Ginsberg in San Francisco, but a harsh rejection letter stopped Burroughs in New York and sent him back into exile. From Tangier he wrote to Ginsberg, in 1955, "I need you so much your absence causes me, at times, acute pain. I don't mean sexually. I mean in connection with my writing." During this period Burroughs had a steady boyfriend, Kiki, to address his sexual needs, but he maintained a strong emotional connection with Ginsberg. Later in the same letter, he told Ginsberg that his interzone novel would gather "all the material I have written so far on Tanger [*sic*] that is scattered through a hundred letters to you."[32] While the material in those letters imagines an interzone in which his status as an outsider bolsters Burroughs's sense of freedom, through the writing of those letters he sought an "inside" connection with Ginsberg, as if the friendship provided an emotional integration to counterbalance the severe isolation of "independent" expatriate life in Tangier.

After Burroughs received Ginsberg's rejection letter, he had a complex and painful dream, which he recorded in a letter of his own. Suffering from rejection—

and under the influence of "a small shot"—Burroughs found that his personal anxieties and political strategies began to coalesce, indicating the direction that Burroughs's thought, writing, and politics would take in *Naked Lunch*. As Burroughs related the dream to Ginsberg, it was set in North Africa. In the dream, Burroughs shares a house with a "fatuous fairy." This effeminate and campy man "pounces on every word with obscene *double entendre*," which disgusts Burroughs and makes him feel "like some loathsome insect was clinging to my body." Walking with this man he encounters two lesbians "who say 'Hello Boys,' recognizing Fairy-Lesbian status," a greeting from which Burroughs turns "in retching disgust."[33] This opening sequence rehearses a theme that is already familiar from his early novels: Burroughs's internalized homophobia is externalized as fear and loathing of women and of effeminate men. What is especially striking about this dream, however, is the emphasis placed on recognition. Not only is Burroughs disgusted by his own effeminacy and by the role of effeminacy in his sexual desires, but he is appalled to be identified as a "fairy." The fact that he is so easily recognized suggests to Burroughs that he has control over neither his desires nor his identity and that they are interconnected.

His fear of control is represented in the central image of the dream: a "Holy Man" who lives in a "Tower-like structure" controls the population of the area by broadcasting some kind of high-frequency radio waves. Burroughs wants to kill this Holy Man, but a friend appears in the dream to dissuade him, to convince him that even his assassination plot is already known and controlled by the Holy Man. Later in the letter, Burroughs identified this friend as Ginsberg. While Burroughs clearly resented having been rejected and therefore associated Ginsberg with his enemy the Holy Man, the friend of the dream also tries to help Burroughs by explaining something that Burroughs knows but does not want to admit: his identity is known, his subjectivity is controlled, and his potential courses of action are already constrained before he makes conscious decisions. This dream dramatizes the lesson that Burroughs had begun to learn during his search for yage and that he mastered in *Naked Lunch*: the self is written by external pressures, and narrative self-representation cannot transcend those pressures. Furthermore, once Burroughs began to understand the trauma of his life in terms of this pervasive text of control, he came to realize that the terms of inside and outside upon which he had based his flight from the United States and from "the disapproving others" of "Society" disabled rather than enabled his search for freedom. The penetrating vibrations through which the Holy Man exercises his power illustrate the fact that physical escape is impossible because there is no inside out of which one can step. Living as an "outsider" expatriate in Tangier did not, in the final analysis, provide Burroughs with the kind of independence he desired; neither did his "inside" emotional connection with Ginsberg.

As he concluded his letter, Burroughs told Ginsberg, "Will attempt to enlarge on this dream. May provide frame-work for novel."[34] Key images of the dream did indeed find their way into *Naked Lunch*, but even more significant is the fact that Burroughs uncovered an important lesson about subjectivity and discourse through fantasy and related that lesson in a letter. Writing his dreams and fantasies later became Burroughs's principal method of literary production and political action. In Tangier, in the late 1950s, the most immediate significance of this dream was the fact that it foregrounded "control" as Burroughs's primary concern. Neither in Latin America nor in Morocco was Burroughs able to step completely outside social organization, politics, ideology, or identity. He responded by developing a theory that explained why he was so restricted or controlled even in flight. Burroughs argued that human subjects are controlled not merely through social convention, the pressures of conformity, or institutionalized morality, but also through discourse—or, as he put it, through word and image.

This theory developed over the entire course of Burroughs's expatriate writing career. Its roots are visible as early as *Junky*; in that novel Burroughs objects to psychoanalysis and especially to the notion that his own social and sexual problems might stem from an interior conflict. Rather, he believes, any frustrations, inhibitions, and self-doubts are imposed by external sources of control through processes of social conditioning. As he experienced the horrors of opiate readdiction and withdrawal throughout the 1940s and 1950s, Burroughs began to describe external control not as conditioning but rather as addiction. He drew a parallel between the lack of self-control in a junky and that in the average person, who is subject to the "algebra of need" that enforces "image addiction" and "morality addiction."[35] By 1959, when Burroughs was putting the finishing touches on *Naked Lunch*, a new concept of control appeared—the virus—the invisible agent that invades and corrupts from within. Burroughs described addiction as a "junk virus."[36] But his notion of control through viruses developed to maturity only in the course of writing his cut-up trilogy *The Soft Machine*, *The Ticket That Exploded*, and *Nova Express*. By the end of the 1960s, it had become a full-fledged theory: human subjects are controlled through language, which Burroughs called the Word, and "the Word is literally a virus" (*The Adding Machine*, 47).

Burroughs's exploration of this theory through his writing is thoroughly discussed in Robin Lydenberg's *Word Cultures*, which focuses on *Naked Lunch* and the cut-up trilogy that follows. *The Soft Machine*, *The Ticket That Exploded*, and *Nova Express* rework material from Burroughs's Tangier "word hoard" that was not included in *Naked Lunch*, as well as adding material written in the early 1960s during his expatriation in Europe. The cut-up method of composition focuses on the materiality of language by literally cutting up pages of Burroughs's own writing and splicing them together at random, often incorporating cut-up material from other authors, as well.[37] Lydenberg reads Burroughs through and against Derrida, Barthes, Kristeva, and other theorists in order to argue that Burroughs's principal contribution to contemporary thought lies in his theory that human subjects are controlled—bodies themselves are controlled—by the virus of language. She reads his experimental, antinarrative cut-up texts as attempts to write himself out of the control of language and demonstrates that "the ideas we now recognize as characteristic of post-structuralism and deconstruction were being developed independently by Burroughs almost thirty years ago" (*Word Cultures,* xi). Burroughs drew attention to the way "reality" is produced in and through narratives, and he attempted to refashion "reality" by writing *Naked Lunch*, *The Soft Machine*, *The Ticket That Exploded*, and *Nova Express* as antinarratives that frustrate the exercise of power through language.

Lydenberg's argument is convincing—indeed, it is a ground-breaking critical treatment of these four novels—but she leaves unexplored the context out of which Burroughs's ideas and literary experiments arise. Certainly, his ideas about language were influenced by Count Alfred Korzybski (a mid-century linguist), but, for the most part, Burroughs's theoretical understanding and practical use of language arose from his life context: from his travels, his loves, his desires, his drug use—all of which were processed through writing and rewriting.

More specifically, the basic unit of Burroughs's characteristic literary voice, the "routine," was developed during his years of expatriation as he pursued impossible relationships, especially with Lewis Marker and with Allen Ginsberg. In the guise of Lee, Burroughs parodically described himself as someone who desperately wanted to love but could not and so pursued lovers "who could not reciprocate, so that he was able . . . to shift the burden of not loving, of being unable to love, onto the partner." The result of this dynamic is that "the loved one was always and forever an Outsider, a Bystander, an Audience" (*Interzone,* 64). This was precisely the audience Burroughs needed in order to write; or rather, the writing of routines is the mechanism through which Burroughs attempted to make erotic and emotional contact. To the extent that Burroughs's mature writing began with his early routines, his literary production was grounded in a sexual enterprise. *Queer* dramatizes how Burroughs went about pursuing the impossible object of his desire through writing. In order to impress Allerton, Lee entertains him with little stories: bits of gossip or humorous sketches that begin to take on lives of their own, to grow into hilarious and grotesque satiric "routines." For example, Lee "comes out" to Allerton by spinning a tale about how, when he first recognized his sexual desires, he was saved from self-hate and a self-destructive fear of effeminacy by Bobo, a wise old queen who taught him "to conquer prejudice and ignorance and hate with knowledge and sincerity and love." The mild self-parody turns outrageous as he describes how Bobo came to a "sticky end" when, riding in a car, "his falling piles blew out of the car and wrapped around the rear wheel" (40). Burroughs told another story of coming into his sexuality in a letter to Ginsberg that is included in *The Yage Letters*: he carried on an idyllic, pastoral adolescent romance with a boy named Billy Bradshinkel until Billy announced that they must stop having sex and could not see each other any longer. "Mother brought me a bowl of milk toast on a tray but I couldn't eat any and cried all night," he wrote, shortly followed by, "And I got a silo full of queer corn where that come from" (6).

Burroughs's early routines satirized and parodied, a function complementary to their intended purpose, which was to impress an audience without making the author vulnerable to rejection.[38] Directed at objects of unrequited love, these "coming out" routines both exposed and obscured Burroughs's innermost self, declaring and mocking his identity and his desire. Their humor relied upon positing an initial sincerity that was then savagely satirized, so that the emotional core of the autobiographical subject of the routine was evacuated. Sincerity was incompatible with the routine form and became a target of Burroughs's routines. For example, the negotiations that take place in the routine known as "Corn Hole Gus's Used Slave Lot" exemplify the way routines reduce an issue as weighty and profound as human slavery to a trivial joke about the empty formalism of barter and exchange, and celebrate the insincerity of social interaction (*Queer,* 67–70). The idiom adopted in many of Burroughs's routines is of a folksy, gossipy, rural white male inhabitant of the American South or Midwest—a self-parody of his own background—and he mocked the ingenuousness of this voice by making it speak increasingly bizarre, outrageous, and even obscene tales. Over the years the routines became more and more grotesque, pushed beyond the limits not only of good taste but of coherence, until they spun out of control. As they did so, the routines began to question the centrality and stability of any narrative voice. In *Naked Lunch,* Lee is no longer the sole author of routines that now take on a life of their own; in the "Benway" section, for example, while Lee begins to tell the story of how he engages the services of Dr. Benway for Islam Inc., the story veers off into Benway's own narration, then into a routine on lymphogranuloma, and it ends with a fantasy that originated in an unspecified consciousness, a fantasy of rock and roll adolescent guerrillas attacking the Louvre.

In Tangier, routines became increasingly central to Burroughs's literary production. Whenever he was withdrawing from or free of addiction, Burroughs spun off routine after routine, which appeared in the text of his letters to Ginsberg or were appended to them as discrete units. Eventually, these routines became the basic narrative units of *Naked Lunch* and provided multiple entrances into the antinarrative chaos of the whole. Making their first appearance in letters were routines concerning Andrew Keif (Paul Bowles) and KY jelly made from whale dreck, the man with a talking asshole, the detectives who come to arrest Lee (Hauser and O'Brien), A. J. hog calling in a five-star restaurant, an American diplomat in the interzone, Eisenhower as a sex junky, lymphogranuloma, and a routine on all the major religions called "The Prophet's Hour."[39] Many other routines survive only in *Naked Lunch*, as the letters in which they first appeared have been lost. Nonetheless, it is possible to trace the emotional and erotic needs that inspire these fragments of narrative in the novel.

Burroughs compared love to addiction. In the early months of his expatriation in Tangier, when Ginsberg was traveling and unable to correspond with him, Burroughs wrote to Kerouac that he was still "hooked" on Ginsberg: "The withdrawal symptoms are worse than the Marker habit."[40] Writing routines to Ginsberg was his equivalent of an apomorphine treatment for heroin withdrawal. Routines themselves became "like habit," a substitute for love, but Burroughs required a "receiver" for his routine; otherwise, "routine turns back on me like homeless curse and tears me apart, grows more and more insane (literal growth like cancer)."[41] When Burroughs mentioned literal growth, he meant it; even though most of his critics read his routines as metaphors, Burroughs consistently insisted that his writing be understood to speak literally. As Lydenberg points out, Burroughs's experimental texts undermine their own symbolic and allegorical potential in an attempt to understand the word as an object, as a literal virus that must be eliminated in order to "kick the habits of Western discourse" (*Word Cultures,* 17). Burroughs developed his ideas about "literalism" when reflecting on the form of the routine, which he declared "is not *completely symbolic*, that is, it is subject to shlup over into 'real' action at any time."[42] "Shlupping" is a concept developed in a *Naked Lunch* routine about Bradley the narcotics agent, who consumes the objects of his desire by turning into a blob of jelly and ingesting them. The idea that two lovers could merge into one being also occurs in relation to Marker (*Queer,* 100) and Ginsberg (Morgan, *Literary Outlaw,* 230–31) and suggests not only the consumptive dimension of desire but also a dream that desire itself could be fully satisfied through the fusing of subject and object. This dream is extended in the Burroughsian concept that the "real" and the "symbolic" are not two separate, interconnected realms but are rather two dimensions in space and time between which one can travel; writing is the ticket for such a trip. When Burroughs said that routines "are uncontrollable, unpredictable, charged with potential danger" for the author as well as the audience, he meant that symbolic language can shlup into reality, changing the world in unforeseeable ways (*Interzone,* 127).

Shlupping, both in love and in writing, is a precarious merging of subject and object, of the real and the symbolic. Shlupping is perhaps the best word to describe what happens in *Naked Lunch*'s interzone, as narrative voices merge into characters who sometimes become the author, as aspirations

combine with nostalgias and dreams with memories, as the novel's proliferating voices speak simultaneously from Morocco, America, and Scandinavia,
and as life and death, self and other collapse in multiple orgasms. The hallucination that Burroughs edited out of *The Yage Letters*, that experience of
being transformed into a "Negress," appears in *Naked Lunch* (109) and
underscores the racial and sexual side of shlupping in the interzone. In Burroughs's words, *Naked Lunch* is a "queer Inferno," a labyrinth of inversion
and perversion, built upon "a vast Turkish Bath under the whole CITY."[43]
He used another sexual metaphor to explain *Naked Lunch* in his "Atrophied
Preface," when he clarified his notion of the Word: it "is divided into units
which be all in one piece and should be so taken, but the pieces can be had
in any order being tied up back and forth, in and out fore and aft like an
innaresting [*sic*] sex arrangement" (*Naked Lunch*, 229).

Burroughs's assertion that the Word can be rearranged—and that the extent
of those rearrangements is limited only by the bounds of one's sexual fantasies—
is a declaration that language does not have total control over human subjects.
Shlupping is Burroughs's method for fighting the control of language, for
breaking down those narratives that produce reality, and, rather than merely
replacing them with other narratives, creating an interzone between the real and
the symbolic. *Naked Lunch* exposes the fictitiousness of all narratives, especially of those narratives that constitute what is thought of as reality. The novel
overflows with stories, but each story is a "cover story," a deception designed
to throw the agents of control off the track—and the deceptions work especially
well since there is nothing solid beneath the cover. Burroughs insisted on the
literalness of his writing because the surface of the cover story, the telling of
Naked Lunch, is all that exists. The stories of Lee, Benway, A. J., Hassan, and
the other characters of the novel overlap and merge; "Sooner or later," Burroughs
wrote in the "Atrophied Preface," all these characters will simultaneously "say
the same thing in the same words" and at that moment will "be the same person" (*Naked Lunch*, 222–23). They will cohere precisely in the dimensionless-
ness of pure utterance, just as the routines that make up the novel shlup their
way into intelligible nonsense.

Shlupping is the basis of what has come to be known as Burroughs's postmodern writing practice. Those critics who point to formal aspects of his
writing to define it as postmodern are most interested in various forms of mixing and merging—collage, collaboration, the combination of high and low culture.[44] Other critics, including Robin Lydenberg, Michael Bliss, and Timothy
Murphy, analyze Burroughs's experimental writing techniques as a way of sit-
uating his texts within poststructuralist and postmodern theorizations of language and subjectivity. Lydenberg focuses on the shlupping or collapsing of
binary logic in Burroughs and demonstrates how binaries such as
subject/object, mind/body, figurative/literal, real/ideal are deconstructed in

Naked Lunch and the cut-up trilogy. Bliss argues that the "orchestrated chaos" of shlupping in *Naked Lunch* allows Burroughs to absent the author from the text; by so doing, Burroughs pointed toward the way in which authorial "silence" can free the writing subject from addiction to the conventional referential word. Murphy analyzes Burroughs's critique of capital, subjectivity, and language by way of articulating an alternative to the confining dialectic of modernism and postmodernism. Ihab Hassan, Michael Leddy, Brian McHale, Charles Russell, and Frederick Dolan also refer to Burroughs as a significant theorist and practitioner of postmodern writing and point especially to *Naked Lunch* as a defining text of postmodern literature.

But the tendency of criticism to focus on formalistic concerns in Burroughs's texts and to define the importance of his work in terms of experimental writing per se has deflected attention from very important connections between his subject matter and the forms he invented to express his literary vision. Ironically, one of the most perceptive critical articles to discuss the subject matter of *Naked Lunch* comes from a hostile quarter. In his 1965 essay "The New Mutants," one of the first articles to conceptualize postmodernism as a literary and cultural phenomenon, Leslie Fiedler argued that "mutant" youth (beatniks and hipsters) were the heralds of a new "post-Modern" age, and that William Burroughs was their "chief prophet." Fiedler was frightened by what he perceived as a break with modernism and with the rejection not only of Judaism and Christianity but also of rationalism and humanism and the principal ideological systems of the modern age: capitalism, socialism, and communism. The new mutants, he argued, abandoned Western values of work and reason and "whiteness." Echoing the racial vocabulary of Norman Mailer's 1957 essay "The White Negro" in a censorious rather than celebratory mode, Fielder decried the abandonment of middle-class privilege by white youths who attempted "to become Negro, even as they attempt to become poor or pre-rational" ("The New Mutants," 515). Burroughs also employed the metaphor of racial transformation as degradation and abjection, especially in his yage dream of becoming a "Negress," but what Fielder condemned as "mutation" Burroughs celebrated as "shlupping." More troublesome to Fiedler than "racial" mutation, however, was sexual and gender mutation, and he was alarmed that beatnik men attempted "to assimilate into themselves . . . that sum total of rejected psychic elements which the middle-class heirs of the Renaissance have identified with 'woman'" (516). *Naked Lunch*, he said, is a "nightmare anticipation . . . of post-Humanist sexuality" because homosexuality in the novel calls into question—or "queers," as we say today—the boundaries supposedly separating male from female (517). As much as Fiedler's essay calls for the reinscription of such boundaries, he wrote as if the battle were already lost: "Even heterosexual writers . . . have perforce permitted homosexuals to speak for them (Burroughs and Genet and Baldwin and Ginsberg and Albee and a score of others), even to invent the forms in which the future will have to speak" (521).

Thirty years later, Fiedler's alarmism seems quaint, but his analysis seems prophetic. Without attending to the formal techniques of *Naked Lunch*, Fielder effectively described the novel's central critique of modernity and located sexuality as the privileged sphere within which Burroughs developed a theory and practice of "shlupping" or postmodern writing. But Fiedler imprecisely identified homosexuality as the source of Burroughs's "post-male," "post-humanist," and "post-heroic" literary vision (517); he inaccurately presumed that homosexuality itself is the cause of gender and sexual "confusion," rather than examining how Burroughs worked through identity, desire, unrequited love, and homophobia to develop his critique of language and subjectivity. Homosexual desire did not "confuse" Burroughs; in fact, Burroughs made use of his desires to locate himself and—especially in the novels that follow *Naked Lunch*—to orient his writing. The personal crisis that did "confuse" Burroughs arose as he traveled through Latin America and North Africa in search of his "true" self. Gradually, he came to realize that the truth of the self is produced by "word" and "image"—by what today we call discourse. *Naked Lunch* expresses his reconciliation with this insight. The novel recasts the struggle for transcendence as a struggle to rewrite what has already been written. It celebrates the mutability of identity as a solution rather than criticizing it as a problem.

Naked Lunch acknowledges that the struggle against exterior control is a struggle against discourse and that it cannot be waged merely through the process of writing one's own story, of substituting one narrative for another. In *Junky* and *Queer,* Burroughs attempted to do just this, to subvert middle-class morality and normativity by identifying himself under the signs first of drug use and then of homosexual desire. In *Naked Lunch,* Burroughs demonstrated that such static identifications are part of the problem, rather than part of the solution. As long as thought is processed through binary relations, and as long as one's identity is defined in relation to some other, language exercises what he called a "word lock" on human subjects. With the creation of his interzone, Burroughs broke off his search for an impossible transcendence through a final fix and turned instead to the creation of a space of in-betweenness, suspension, and unresolvability that was meant to free him from the Word. This fundamental shift in his understanding of the purpose of writing occurred in Tangier in the midst of composing *Naked Lunch*; as Burroughs told Ginsberg in 1956, "I am really writing Interzone now, not writing about it."[45]

The Wild Boys Take Over

Throughout his journeys in Latin America, Burroughs sought to inhabit a utopia in which his true self could finally emerge free of social constraints. He repeatedly described this utopia in Orientalist terms and considered the most appealing aspects of his Latin American experience to be signs that he was arriving in the Orient. His first letters from Tangier point toward more similarities than differences in his sexual and drug experiences in Latin America and North Africa, perhaps because of the fact that in Tangier Burroughs was finally "really" in the Orient—at last his search for "Oriental" boys and "Oriental" drugs was mapped onto a geographical "East." After Burroughs had spent some time in Tangier, however, the Orient becomes a less and less frequent concern in his writing. As he wrote *Naked Lunch*, Burroughs came to accept the idea that the sort of paradise he sought is not available in a mysterious, eastern city but rather has to be dreamed—or written—into existence. Moreover, Burroughs came to see Orientalism as a hoax and distraction; as he wrote to Ginsberg from Tangier, "don't ever fall for this inscrutable oriental shit like Bowles puts down."[46] Burroughs continued to desire boys like Angelo and Kiki, but his "racial" descriptions of them faded away, and he gradually began to categorize them under the politicized but deracinated sign of the "third world." This alteration in vocabulary marks a reorientation in Burroughs's writing about sex, sexuality, and politics and coincides with his realization that there is no "true" self to be liberated and no "eastern" utopia in which that liberation can take place.

Burroughs's sexual fantasies about deracinated "third world" boys became, especially in the novels that followed *Naked Lunch*, the pivot around which his writing and his politics turned. Burroughs explored the relationships among political action, sexual fantasy, and writing as early as 1954 when, in the letter cited earlier, he responded to Ginsberg's rejection of his desires by narrating a nightmare. In that dream, which takes place in North Africa, Burroughs plots to assassinate the "Holy Man" who represents the forces of control. Burroughs does not act alone but rather joins a conspiracy; to be more precise, he offers to sell his services as an assassin to the opponents of the Holy Man, who happen to be two Arabs. "One is a vigorous man in his forties, the other a Boy," Burroughs wrote: "I am immediately attracted to the boy." The impulse to join an effective insurgency movement was developed more fully in his cut-up trilogy (especially regarding the Nova conspiracy) and in *The Wild Boys* (1969). In this early dream, we are able to witness the sexual desire that underwrites the impulse. Burroughs approaches the desirable Arab boy and, as if he were a hustler, "We haggle about price, but both know money is not the point."[47] The point is to have sex and to battle against the forces of control—at the same time. In *The Wild Boys* and in *Port of Saints* (1973, revised 1980), Burroughs took his point one step further: writing itself, and especially writing his sexual fantasies, became the means by which he struggled against control.

While Burroughs lived in Morocco in the years immediately preceding and following independence and national integration, and while one might think that his own struggle against "control" would have caused him to ally himself with the Moroccan struggle against colonialism, Burroughs remained hostile to Moroccan nationalism. Witnessing the Moroccan struggle for independence fueled Burroughs's imagination, but his interest lay in a postnational world where boys from all over the world would converge for their mutual sexual pleasure. The sexual Orientation of Burroughs's early expatriate years came to an end as he ceased to seek a terrestrial Oriental paradise; it was replaced by a less racially coded desire for boys, although the objects of his desire still had vaguely "third world" origins. In *Port of Saints,* Burroughs stressed that wild boys come from all races and nations, although in doing so he singled out a significant few: "Negroes, Chinese, Mexicans, Arabs, Danes, Swedes, Americans, English. That is, they are evidently derived from racial and national stock corresponding to Negroes, Mexicans, Danes, Americans et cetera" (71). As much as the wild boys were "a new breed," Burroughs still felt compelled to define them in relation to their racial and national origins, for these affiliations and markers were part of what made the boys exciting to him. Tellingly, those races and nations Burroughs mentions correspond in nearly every case to boys he has had sex with and places he has traveled to; in his postnational fantasy, "third world" objects of desire figure prominently.

The political struggles in which Burroughs's writing was invested were neither national nor anticolonial nor ideological but rather extremely personal. The personal nature and formation of his politics should come as no surprise, since they were based on his sexual desires. For Burroughs, the personal equaled the political and vice versa, which explains why it is so difficult to characterize his politics along traditional ideological lines. Most favorable criticism of his writing points to his postmodern experimentation as a sign of radical politics, and to his politics as an articulate struggle against control. But it is a struggle that accommodates itself to certain limits. Burroughs did offer an insightful critique of power and discourse, but in the course of struggling against what he calls control he accepted rather than critiqued his desires and accepted the neocolonial political relationships through which those desires became acts. His attempt to create an interzone through writing was inspired by his experiences on the "outside" of society—that is to say, by his expatriation and especially his anonymous sexual encounters in Latin America and North Africa. Burroughs's life in Tangier and the writing that emerged from that life were supported by colonial relations of power, and Burroughs was remarkably content with his relationship to the structures of American postwar neocolonialism in Morocco.

Contentment did not come easily to Burroughs; as I have suggested, the anguish he experienced in relation to sexual desire can be traced through expressions of internalized homophobia and unrequited love in both his letters and fiction. At times he experienced desire as addiction, as loss of personal control. Through the course of the years of his queer expatriation, however, Burroughs did eventually make peace with his desires. In a 1973 interview, he described sexual desire as a personalized film "usually laid down in early childhood on a reception screen" to which a person is compulsively drawn, so that his or her sexual acts are only performed as repetitions of a prescripted sequence. The film of desire is "quite literally wired to the sex centers of the brain" (*Gay Sunshine Interviews,* 16–17). Burroughs speculated that the film could be short-circuited or reedited; but he saw no point in doing so since most people are satisfied with their personal desire films. Burroughs, in any case, was satisfied with his, and, because his politics were so highly integrated into his sexual experiences and desires, this satisfaction included accepting his position as a participant in neo-colonial political structures.

Burroughs proceeded in the interview to explain that his literary creations were projections of his own personal film. It was eros that made Burroughs's writing lively and exciting—or, as he put it, "any writer who has not mastur-bated with his own characters will not be able to make them live on paper" (17). And, I would add, much less will he be able to make them take over the world. Burroughs's political vision was his sexual vision. His battle against control was first and foremost a battle against his own repression or "early con-ditioning" (18), and the youthful "third world" warriors who fight that battle in his novels are the objects of his fervent desire. The fact that his novels rep-resent his personal desire film through writing explains why Burroughs con-strued women to be political enemies rather than allies and why he homogenized the political and economic life of diverse countries, lumping them together under the sign of the third world. Latin America and North Africa blurred into each other in his fiction, and in *The Wild Boys* one social group—street boys—comes to stand in for all the people of nations as distinct as Mex-ico and Morocco.

Written during the European phase of his expatriation, *The Wild Boys* and *Port of Saints* nonetheless continue to focus on a number of motifs drawn from Burroughs's experience in Latin America and North Africa. These two novels mark what is frequently called Burroughs's return to narrative, because, in con-trast to the cut-up trilogy, they tell their stories in a relatively accessible and linear fashion. Aspects of the cut-up technique remain, particularly insofar as repetition and juxtaposition of narrative units provide structure for both nov-els, but the pursuit of randomness has been abandoned in favor of clarity. The two novels share one principal story: a worldwide guerrilla movement of ado-lescent wild boys has seized anarchic "control" of large areas of Latin Amer-ica, North Africa, and Asia, and, joined by renegade youths from the United States and Europe, they are threatening to take over the world. The wild boys exhibit all the charms that attracted Burroughs to street boys in Tangier and Mexico City: they are young, masculine, rough, uneducated, and emotionally distant from their many sexual partners, with whom they perform intercourse at every opportunity. In contrast to his presentation in his work from the 1950s, in these novels Burroughs was far from reticent about representing sexual acts, and *Port of Saints* in particular consists largely of erotic scenes among the wild boys that focus on penetrative acts.

Like *Naked Lunch*, both *The Wild Boys* and *Port of Saints* attempt to destabilize the Word using formal techniques like fragmentation and disruption. In addition, the novels explore through their subject matter a global struggle against discursive power. *Port of Saints* foregrounds the instability of identity in its opening pages, which introduce fragments of the subplots that run through the novel. There is the American consul, who, in his frozen bureaucracy, can not even begin to unravel the mystery surrounding the identity of a long-dead American who is confused with his living brother. In addition, there is the story of Audrey, from St. Louis—the character who replaces Lee as Burroughs's alter ego—whose Mexican double grows up on the streets of Mexico City and who, not unlike Burroughs's own son, is the child of a junky father and an alcoholic mother. The characters in *Port of Saints*, like those in *The Wild Boys*, travel through space and time as actors in dramas that have no beginnings, no endings, and no fixed roles; their stories are told through congruences and incongruences of repetition, remembering, and reimagining. These two novels do mark Burroughs's return to traditional narrative forms, but they continue to question the Word. The wild boys in both novels use a language over which they exert control, "A common language based on variable transliteration of a simplified hieroglyphic script" that is incapable of assuming control over human subjects (*The Wild Boys,* 514). The wild boys are radically independent—free not only from discursive control but also from social and political structures such as family, church, and state. The demise of heterosexual institutions comes about after the wild boys develop cloning technologies that allow them to reproduce without women. But as much as identity, language, and heterosexual society are attacked and destabilized in these novels, homosexual desire among the wild boys is never questioned; rather, it is the one stable and constant factor that unifies them in their political revolution against the "North" that is also the "West."

Whereas, in *Naked Lunch,* sexual desire leads Burroughs to a theory and practice of literary "shlupping," in *The Wild Boys* and *Port of Saints* sexual fantasy provides the coordinates that organize both writing and politics. The sexual fantasies that recur throughout Burroughs's work became more explicit through the 1960s and came to assume a structural function in his texts. The handful of erotic scenes that are inexhaustibly repeated in *Naked Lunch*, the cut-up trilogy, *The Wild Boys* and *Port of Saints*—orgasm by hanging, adolescent seduction in automobiles and during long country walks, sci-fi sex with lizard boys and vegetable life forms, boys masturbating in outhouses, various initiations of younger boys by older boys, adolescent group scenes, and so on—link all six novels in a string of fantastic climaxes. That these scenes are indelibly marked as Burroughs's own fantasies indicates the extent to which even the antinarrative "chaotic" cut-up novels are organized around one authorial consciousness. *The Wild Boys* foregrounds the part played by this consciousness through the device of the "Penny Arcade Peep Show." The wild boys recruit Audrey by bringing him to an all-male homosexual carnival of delights outside St. Louis. Five of the eighteen sections of the novel are written as "Peep Shows" that Audrey witnesses, and the experience of sitting in a booth and watching pornography becomes a metaphor for both the reader's and the author's relationship to the novel as a whole. Audrey, standing in for Burroughs, represents the authorial organizing consciousness that filters through images, memories, and fantasies in order to write down and communicate self, desire, and meaning; Audrey also stands in the position of the reader, who filters through these images in order to make sense of them.

The chaos even of *Naked Lunch* and of the cut-up novels, but especially of *The Wild Boys* and *Port of Saints*, is ordered around the coordinates of Burroughs's desire. As much as critics like Lydenberg and Bliss admire the way that Burroughs managed to "silence" himself as the author of his experimental writings, his consciousness is still present as the organizing principle behind the sexual fantasies in the cut-up novels. *The Wild Boys* and *Port of Saints* recognize the necessity of this central consciousness and reconcile themselves to the convention of having an author who spins out narratives. In fact, these two novels foreground the importance of sexual desire in motivating and organizing narratives that project and broadcast the author's personal erotic film script. In a sense, Burroughs's entire writing career was an attempt to claim and proclaim his desires. Throughout his writings, he focused on the emptiness that follows satisfaction, on the constant renewal of desire, on its urgency and insufficiency, on the impermanent death of orgasm, and on desire's volatile and transient attachment to objects. In *Naked Lunch,* the shlupping of sexual desire leads to a critique of subjectivity and to Burroughs's distinctive experimental writing practices. In *The Wild Boys* and *Port of Saints,* Burroughs accepted his desire rather than agonizing over it and utilized his sexual fantasies to coordinate his writing and his politics. In these later novels, Burroughs continued to write against the Word, but he did so by elaborating fantasies about homosexual "third world" boys engaged in a global insurrection.

The interzone of *Naked Lunch* as well as the all-queer utopia of *The Wild Boys* can be described as postmodern spaces. Indeed, the surface geography of Burroughs's texts, his critique of the power of discourse, and his exploration of the instability of identity resonate with the work of many theorists of postmodernity. However, the cultural and philosophical analyses worked out in Burroughs's texts arise from his life experience as his erotic film is screened in Latin America and Morocco. Burroughs wrote his own private interzone so as to verbalize his fantasies and to create a world that conformed to his desires.

Naked Lunch begins this enterprise, which is continued in *The Wild Boys* and *Port of Saints*. In the latter novel, guerrilla cadets are given assignments by Old Sarge, who tells Audrey, "You're the writer. Well, write a wild boy takeover" (*Port of Saints,* 22). This is the assignment Burroughs gave himself, beginning with his own takeover by the wild boys. He attempted to imagine and to write himself into a queer postnational utopia, and did so by rewriting his memories. He renamed himself Audrey and traveled back in time to his adolescent years in St. Louis, where the wild boys recruit him into their anarchic revolution. This route of escape—channeled through memory and youth—underscores the fact that the adult Burroughs had no place in the world he imagined, the world of perpetually aroused queer boys stripped down to jock straps and rocketing through the desert on roller skates with weapons drawn. The author's position as an outsider was foregrounded in his fantasies, and the distance from his objects of desire was registered by age, nationality, and race. Burroughs's interzone was a specifically sexual construction that was built upon desire and that maintained suspension, irresolution, and impermanence through desire. His sexual fantasies were rooted in and perpetuated his status as an outsider, and his radical politics were directed at securing the freedom to maintain his personal film script. Both his erotic practice and his politics depended upon sustaining his distance from and ignorance of his "third world" sex partners. It was this insistent position on the outside that most clearly distinguished his experience in Tangier—and the impact of that experience on his writing—from that of Paul Bowles and Alfred Chester.

4

Alfred Chester's Multiple Exiles

Who thought Morocco up? What congregation of ecstatic angels or giggling devils sang it into being? It's better to be an old queen in Morocco than the king of New York, of all America, Europe, Mexico—provided, of course, that you're free.

—Alfred Chester, *The Foot*

In 1964, after roughly eight months of expatriation in Tangier, Alfred Chester wrote to his friend Norman Glass, "I realized last night, how curious that Bowles, Burroughs and I should be in the same city. One the past, the other the present, and the third, me, the future."[1] Chester obliquely elaborated upon the terms of this imagined chronology by declaring that "dark black death" is "a fake" and that "I am really the prophet of joy." His letter dismissed the negativity of Bowles's and Burroughs's literary visions as fraudulent, in contradistinction to his own more ecstatic expressions. The terms of fakery and reality weighed heavily on Chester's conception of writing and of self—matters to which we return later—but, while Chester suggested that artifice measures the inadequacies of his literary predecessors, his observation also comments on a range of social, psychological, and philosophical formations and allegiances that can be thought to divide Bowles, Burroughs, and Chester into "generations," or at least into representatives of those formations and allegiances. Chester's imagined distance from Bowles and Burroughs, which serves to position him as both heir and prophet, can be vividly delineated with reference to the sexual subtexts and contexts of the three authors' encounters with Morocco. If Bowles represents an old-fashioned way of being homosexual (don't ask, don't tell) and Burroughs represents a radical way of being queer (declaring and celebrating marginalization, persecution, abjection), Chester represents the hope that exuberant campiness will set us free. Similarly, if we take

Bowles to represent a "colonial" style of "insider" expatriation and Burroughs to represent a "touristic" style of "outsider" expatriation, we can see how Chester resists such dichotomous terms of cultural experience and exchange and how he strives for a new, third way of arranging his encounters with Morocco.

Among the questions that arise if we are to take seriously Chester's claim to be the future of American literature, or more frighteningly, if we understand his claim to encompass our future more generally, is whether this future is recognizable, attainable, or even desirable. Chester, after all, died of a drug overdose following a prolonged slide into insanity—and it is precisely his psychosis that shaped and informed his "prophetic" writings. Chester lived in Morocco from 1963 to 1965, and, while early signs of mental illness appear in letters and fiction written prior to this expatriation, it was in Morocco that Chester experienced his first two major psychotic breakdowns. In 1966 he returned to New York, but the homecoming did not alleviate his illness. He spent several unhappy months in Morocco in 1967 and 1968 before he was deported because of his increasingly erratic behavior. While Chester made some attempts to seek professional psychiatric help during this period, he remained unimpressed by the doctors in New York, who diagnosed paranoia, and those in London, who diagnosed schizophrenia; he turned instead to alcohol and barbiturates to silence the voices in his head and to flee from the little green men who, he believed, pursued him. After being banished from Morocco, Chester repeatedly attempted to return there, and, after several years of a peripatetic existence, he finally settled in Israel, which represented for him—in an ironic fashion—both a return to his Jewish heritage and a return to certain aspects of Arab culture that had captivated him in Morocco. The relief provided by alcohol and tranquilizers exacted its final toll in 1971; in his last essay, "Letter from a Wandering Jew," Chester contemplates his own death, but it is difficult to say to what extent his fatal overdose was intentional.

While Chester's life and death can be either appreciated or dismissed as a cautionary tale, the story told in his fiction is much greater than a parable of limits and the cost of passing beyond them. Several of his short stories, his novel *The Exquisite Corpse*, and his final novel fragment, *The Foot,* document Chester's decline in mental health but also speak critically and intelligently about issues of central importance to postwar American culture: the fracturing of subjectivity in the contemporary era, the violence enforced through the categorization of identity along lines of gender, sexuality, race, and religion, and the instability of sexual desire constituted within the terms of the same regime that polices that desire. Chester's life and writing were very much products of his times and reflect both the various locations of his expatriation and the social turbulence experienced in the postwar years as the United States adjusted to its new position in the global system. While in most respects Chester had nothing to do with his Beat contemporaries, he did share with them a critique of the value of postwar bourgeois prosperity and, having cut ties with the middle class, a sense of floating adrift. He wrote his first novel, *Jamie Is My Heart's Desire*, and some of his best short stories in Paris, where he lived during the 1950s. *Jamie Is My Heart's Desire* is set in New York, and, while the prose of this novel is carefully wrought, passages that attempt to formulate a version of American existentialism sound hollow, as if neither the author nor his characters really believe in an existential philosophy—or, for that matter, in any single theory. It is as if in writing this novel Chester wanted to assume the mask of a Sartre—as the letter to Glass cited earlier indicates, Chester wanted to lead his generation like such a figure—but that mask does not quite fit. In a similar appropriation of masks, the stories dating from Chester's Paris years take on startlingly distinct perspectives, moods, and points of view. Chester wrote his stories using several different voices during this period, all the time hoping to find *his* voice, the "real" voice that would make his writing distinctive, original, and, to use his own word, prophetic.

Chester experienced the search for his own voice as a creative and intellectual crisis until the watershed years of his expatriation in Morocco. In Tangier, at work on *The Exquisite Corpse*, Chester discovered that he had no single voice and that writing, as well as living, requires one to assume different masks at different times. Whereas, early in 1963, Chester savaged Rechy for lacking a unified voice in *City of Night*, his essay on Norman Mailer, heroism, and American culture, written later that year, celebrates heterogeneous, provisional, and shifting perspectives.[2] *The Exquisite Corpse* extends this celebration through the elaboration of a surreal world in which characters split and merge, in which names and roles and histories change without explanation or fanfare, and in which masks and costumes define rather than disguise the personality upon which they hang. Chester arrived at this vision of multivocality and superficiality through the frequently painful and difficult experience of his search for a literary voice and a social identity. In particular, the campiness of his gay sensibility informed Chester's understanding of subjectivity as a function of surfaces, roles, and masks. In addition, the tensions of being queer, Jewish, American, and bald—baldness is not an insignificant issue for Chester—also enriched and complicated his understanding of camp, of identity, and of being itself. As he wrote to Edward Field from Tangier, "The truth is you cannot be other than the creature of the situation."[3] This is a truth Chester arrived at after living in Morocco, which was a strikingly foreign place for him—a place where he was alienated from many of the connections and patterns of his previous life in Europe and America. In Morocco Chester asked himself who he was and discovered that it is hard to know oneself except in relation to the situation in which that question arises.

Alfred Chester and Edward Field, Arcila, Morocco, 1963 (From the Edward Field Alfred Chester Archives, Special Collections, University of Delaware Library. Photograph by Neil Derrick.)

Morocco did not produce Chester's identity crisis by itself; rather, the social and psychological dynamics of his encounters there—including sexual experience and drug experience—exaggerated and clarified preexisting conflicts. The anxiety provoked by experiencing identity as contingent and mutable had troubled Chester in Paris and New York as well. In fact, this anxiety both inspired him to write and kept him from writing a novel called *I, Etc.*, in which Chester attempted to express his still incoherent ideas about situational identity and split subjectivity. The story "Behold Goliath," written in Paris, provides some idea of what that novel would have looked like had Chester been able to complete it. Like *The Exquisite Corpse*, "Behold Goliath" is told in short fragments that add up to something quite insane, or at least surreal; but the story is pensive, rather than funny or outrageous or horrifying. Goliath cannot discern who he is or what is real in his world, and the story leaves one disconcerted by the impossibility of resolving these questions. *The Exquisite Corpse*, by contrast, celebrates the impossibility of resolution and treats contingency and performativity as solutions, rather than as problems.

What happened to Chester between his frustrated attempts to write *I, Etc.* and his success with *The Exquisite Corpse*? In his own words, from 1963, "I am slightly changed—Morocco, kif, Dris."[4] The writing changed and in fact became possible because of alterations in Chester's self (or at least in his conception of self) enabled by his expatriate experience. Three elements of that experience made particularly forceful impressions on him: its location in Morocco, the smoking of a Moroccan form of cannabis, and Chester's love affair with a Moroccan man named Dris. Location, drug use, and sexual experience were linked under the sign of Morocco, and, to an extent, this sign enforced an equivalence among the three elements of Chester's experience. But Chester struggled against the logic of this equivalence, which was the Orientalist logic behind Paul Bowles's literary vision. Chester entered Morocco not only through Bowles's friendship but also through his understanding of the Orient as a realm of magic, mystery, and racial difference. In the first month after his arrival, however, Chester determined that Bowles was "an old fashioned colonial type" and began to distance himself from Bowles's friendship, lifestyle, and worldview.[5] As much as he was repelled by colonial mentalities, however, Chester struggled with the fact that his love for Morocco—and especially for Dris—was constituted within racial, Orientalist terms. Displeased with the present in which he found himself, Chester imagined a future in which the law of "colonial desire" was overturned; beginning in *The Exquisite Corpse* but especially in *The Foot,* Chester attempted to write a new kind of subjectivity, one in which identity and desire become disconnected from the field of social relations. He imagined a new way of being—of being queer, of being an expatriate—by troping upon the conventions of surrealism and of fetishism.

In Praise of Fetishism

Alfred Chester lived roughly half his life outside the United States, mainly in France, Morocco, Greece, and Israel. Two periods of exile had a particularly definitive impact on his life and writing: the years spent in Morocco from 1963 through 1965, when Chester sought refuge from the New York literary scene and from the United States in general, and the years after 1966, when Chester lived in exile from his refuge, seeking to return to Morocco and recapture the happiness he had found there. This second period coincided with other forms and experiences of exile: Chester cut himself off not only from professional society but from friends, family, and, as much as possible, all human contact. In New York and in Paris, he closed himself up in his apartment, stuffed his ears with wax, and ventured out only at night. In Israel, he pared his social circle down to one friend, and even this much contact with humanity seemed excessive to him.[6] After 1966, Chester lived in exile not only from Morocco but from social relations and, indeed, from sanity. All of these forms of exile entailed a staggering amount of loss—loss of love, of companionship, of happiness, of self—and in his writing from the period Chester attempted to come to terms with these losses.

To be more precise, we can trace Chester's concern with loss only in the writing that *survives* from this period, because much of what Chester wrote after 1966 was lost or destroyed. The most important text from these years of madness and exile is *The Foot*, a fragment of a book-length project that was edited for publication in the *New American Review* in 1970.[7] Posing as journal entries dated from January 31 to February 28 (the year, we presume, is 1966, since the text was composed in that year), *The Foot* weaves together strands from several stories based on Chester's memories and fantasies of Morocco. The stories never get off the ground, as if plot, direction, and conclusion are beside the point. For example, Chester tells of the encounter of Mary Monday (Susan Sontag) with her double, which could be traumatic but is oddly devoid of feeling or drama. Another story describes his own encounter with a Moroccan beggar whom Chester believed to be his good friend Edward Field. A third story describes the death and funeral of his lover's father, an event that did take place when Chester lived in Morocco, although *The Foot* claims that the death was faked and suggests a sinister conspiracy. The line dividing memory from imagination in these stories and in the running commentary on sex, love, sanity, and Morocco in which they are embedded is unclear; what is clear is that, as inconclusive narrative fragments, they are subordinate to the larger project of *The Foot*, which is to represent and reprocess the experience of Chester's years in Morocco. *The Foot* is a plaintive elegy mourning the loss of what Chester held most dear in his life: Morocco and Dris. That the lost objects of his desire should be organized under the sign of a foot—Dris's foot, to be more precise—tells us a great deal about the process of mourning mobilized through this piece of writing, for Chester's fascination with Dris's foot is informed by the conventions of foot fetishism introduced into the popular imagination by Sigmund Freud forty years earlier.

As we have already seen in chapter 2, an object of desire constituted within the classic framework of colonial discourse is a necessarily alien and alienated object. Key short stories by Paul Bowles suggest that this necessary alienation leads inexorably to loss; characters in those stories engage the consequences of this loss through a process of mourning. Bowles's texts echo the Freudian theory that the mourning process is completed through the mechanism of incorporation, whereby the lost object of desire is incorporated into the ego of the mourner—who is then able to return to the social order. Within the colonial social order, this return is accompanied by a sustained nostalgia. While Bowles pragmatically accepted the regime that regulated relations between colonial subjects of desire and colonized objects of desire, and while his texts follow the sequence Freud described of enforced loss, mourning, incorporation, and return to sociality, Chester attempted an alternative course through a different writing practice. Chester objected to the regime of colonial discourse that structured his relationship with Dris, and he attempted to create a new

Alfred Chester and Dris, Tangier, 1965 (From the Edward Field Alfred Chester Archives, Special Collections, University of Delaware Library.)

order, a new logic of desire, and a new definition of self.[8] Like Bowles, Chester experienced a sharp and consistent alienation from the object of his desires, enforced by that gulf which splits "West" from "East"; rather than reconcile himself to this alienation, however, Chester manipulated it so as to be able to refashion the ensuing loss to his own ends. Chester's letters refer to frequent fights with Dris over seemingly trivial matters, followed by emotional reconciliations, but these events are hardly remarked upon in *The Foot*. As Chester writes in that account, "we were happy . . . why bother remembering the mosquitoes, the bloody quarrels, the torments?" (*Head of a Sad Angel,* 250). Even more striking, the final, stormy break between Chester and Dris takes place off stage, as it were: the event itself remains unrepresented in his writing.[9] While *The Foot* memorializes Chester's love for Dris, to have represented the forces, events, or issues that lead to the end of their relationship would have been inconsistent with the needs of that memorialization. Unlike Bowles's *The Spider's House* or "The Time of Friendship," which make use of memory to seek reconciliation with loss, *The Foot* makes use of memory to reshape loss, to bend it to another purpose.

Chester attempted to restructure reality through the force of his own desires. While this attempt was no doubt enacted within the sphere of his lived life and is indissociable from the decline in his mental health, my interest here is not to psychoanalyze Chester as a person but rather to interpret this restructuring as a cultural phenomenon worked out in his literary production. To reorder reality through writing, Chester turned to the conventions of surrealism, especially in *The Exquisite Corpse*—a novel to which we will return. Surrealism continues to occupy a key position in *The Foot*, but in this later work Chester also played extensively upon popular conceptions of foot fetishism. In fact, it is the mobilization of foot fetishism that enabled Chester to shape the logic of loss and mourning toward his own ends.

Fetishism in *The Foot* is imagined through a series of linkages that assign an overdetermined meaning to one particular physical object: Dris's foot. Dris is called Larbi in *The Foot*, not so much in order to disguise his identity as to rename him as a generic species: as Chester explains, Larbi means "the Arab" (*Head of a Sad Angel,* 248). To begin with, then, Dris stands in for "the Arab" in general, and "the Arab" is marked as Chester's object of desire through Dris's foot. The central episode remembered in *The Foot* occurs one night when Chester kisses Larbi's foot in the *medina* of Elkbir (the fictional name of the town, Arcila, where he lived with Dris). "That was the beginning of our—dare I call it this? dare you call it anything else!—our love affair" (262). More precisely, Chester specifies, the kiss marks the end of their first breakup (the breakup itself, of course, goes unremembered) and the beginning of a reborn love. Chester recalls feeling "so hungry for love—inexhaustible. . . . And a ham. And quite literary perhaps. But also a man in love" (263). And so he falls to his knees and kisses Larbi's foot. The joy of that moment is, he tells us, "unending"; he then pauses in his rhapsody in order to clarify that, "When I speak of Larbi, I am also speaking of Morocco. And when I speak of Morocco I am also speaking of Larbi. They are one and the same. As when Anthony says to Cleopatra, 'I am dying, Egypt, dying'" (263). Chester adds that his desire does not end at Morocco's borders: "I want to run my fingers through the hair of Morocco. Or of all Africa" (252).

The sign of the foot—Dris's foot—organizes Chester's text, and, within that text, organizes an increasingly long string of linkages: Dris—Arab—Morocco—Africa. This list expresses a certain logic of desire ordered along lines of "race" and exoticism, the specific object of desire standing in for a complex construct of Otherness. The missing link that explains why a foot should come to rule over this logic is provided by Freud in his essay on fetishism. According to Freud, "the fetish is a substitute for the penis" and not for any "chance penis" but "for the woman's (the mother's) penis that the little boy once believed in and—for reasons familiar to us—does not want to give up" ("Fetishism," 152–53). Freud placed the phenomenon of fetishism at the service of his familiar theory of castration anxiety; he conjectured that, when a little boy sees that his mother (or any woman) lacks a penis, he is terrified by the possibility that his own organ might be taken away. At the traumatic sight of a missing penis, the future fetishist turns his attention to an object, such as a piece of underwear or a shoe, or to a body part, such as a foot, and invests that object with the significance of a phallus. For a foot fetishist, any foot can henceforth stand in for the missing penis, and, in this way, "the fetish is precisely designed to preserve it [the missing penis] from extinction" ("Fetishism," 152). Chester did in fact have a troubled relationship with his mother, but *The Foot* is interested in neither her penis nor his castration anxiety; nor is Chester satisfied to turn his attention to just any foot—it is Dris's foot that interests him. Chester's text does not fit neatly into Freud's universalizing castration theory but rather makes use of the association, popularized since Freud, between feet and penises. In addition, what makes Freud's essay especially relevant to *The Foot* is the notion that fetishism provides a mechanism for controlling the effects of a terrifying loss. Chester turns to Dris's foot after such a loss—after a fight and a breakup—and he worships that foot, genuflecting before it and offering it a kiss, because that object will henceforth represent for him permanent and indestructible love—"endless" joy, to use his own words; preservation from "extinction," to use Freud's.

William Pietz notes that the various discourses of fetishism (in Marxism, psychoanalysis, and modernism) share certain themes, among which are the themes of "irreducible materiality" and of "singularity and repetition." A fetish is not like an idol, which bears an "iconic resemblance to some immaterial model or entity" ("The Problem of the Fetish," 7). Rather, the fetish is organized by a need to locate meaning in the object itself, in the object's materiality. For Chester, the foot did not express meaning as a metaphor for Dris; meaning lay in the physical existence of the foot—a material existence that shored up the boundaries of "reality." Moreover, as a fetish object, the foot brought together a variety of heterogeneous elements—a person (Dris), a bodily organ (Dris's cock), a place (Morocco), a period of time, a set of sexual desires, a discourse of Orientalism—and collected them in one single object. These and other elements were, in Pietz's words, "fixed (or fixated) by the fetish, whose power is precisely the power to repeat its originating act of forging an identity of articulated relations between certain otherwise heterogeneous things" (7–8). After Chester bends to kiss his beloved's foot—and whether or not this event "literally" took place—the foot organizes Chester's relationship with Dris, with Morocco, and with colonialism. The advantage of placing one's relationship under the power of a fetish lies in the inexhaustible capacity of the fetish to repeat the moment of its inception and thus to sustain a set of fixed relations. In this way a sense of permanence can be achieved, and a new reality—a specially tailored reality—can be brought into existence. Following the terrifying loss of his breakup with Dris, permanence and a new reality were precisely what Chester sought.

The Foot remembers neither the initial breakup (which ended when Chester kissed Dris's foot), nor the series of fights and separations Chester discussed in his letters, nor the final breakup (which more or less coincided with Chester's departure from Morocco). All of these "forgotten" episodes repeat the same intolerable traumatic event. What is important for this text to remember or to imagine is a new reality in which the loss of love is banished, and it is the fetish that allows this new reality to come into being. By fashioning Dris's foot into a fetish, Chester is able to preserve in a material object the complex set of relations that constitute his desire for Dris—and his own identity, forged in relation to that desire. The fetish is repeatedly produced as the antidote to the "forgotten" but all too real fact that Dris and Morocco have been lost. The capacity of the fetish perpetually to reconstitute its meaning in and through its materiality forestalls the process of mourning that Chester would otherwise be expected to undergo upon losing Dris and Morocco. While Bowles's texts explore the process of mourning in which the lost object of desire is incorporated into the ego of the grieving person and thus becomes a new part of that person's identity, *The Foot* refuses to allow the process of incorporation to proceed. Dris and Morocco may be gone, but the foot remains and is preserved from extinction. Since its meaning resides in its materiality, the foot is extremely resistant to transmutation and incorporation, and the fetish object sustains the relationships that led to its inception, potentially forever. As Chester tells his readers, "I want to burn that moment [of the kiss] into your mind, as it is seared in mine. I want each of you to have had that splendid moment, the unending joy of having kissed Larbi's foot at four in the morning in the *medina* of Elkbir" (*Head of a Sad Angel,* 263).

The loss of Chester's beloved could not be forestalled, but the process of mourning and incorporation could be stopped or at least frustrated. But with the object of desire gone and prevented from reappearing inside the subject of desire's ego, the subject was left both empty-handed and hollow. While Chester's strategic fetishism had the advantage of displacing loss in one form, it provoked loss in another form. The foot, it turns out, was an insufficient substitute for Dris and for Morocco insofar as it did not allow Chester to complete a process of mourning that would return him to an integrated identity capable of functioning in a social order. *The Foot* is too busy elegizing Dris and Morocco to turn its attention to the cost of sustaining elegy as a mode of human and psychological relations; however, the costs exacted on Chester's identity are registered by his increasing paranoia and schizophrenia. Specifically, the challenge posed to identity and desire when the normal grieving processes of mourning are forestalled is suggested in a letter Chester wrote to Edward Field, in January 1964. Chester wrote, "Listen, I have fallen in love with Dris. (Except when I hate him.)" This declaration of love is not new—his letters are filled with similar announcements—but it is spoken as if it were

new: not " I am in love (and have been for the last six months)" but "I have
fallen in love (for the first time)." The reason for insisting on the immediacy
and originality of falling in love is suggested by the parenthetical remark that
follows, for Chester frequently fell out of love, and, try as he might to bracket
his "hate" and to banish memories of it, it is these bracketed episodes that
enforced his need perpetually to reinvent and return to love. Chester continued, "Yesterday at this time I was ready to pick up and leave. Then I kissed
his foot. . . . I did that once before on the street in Arcila at three in the
morning." Like the first kiss, this kiss marked the end of separation and loss
and reconstituted a complex set of social and psychological relations. Chester
calls it a "love miracle" because something magical happened at the moment
of the kiss: "I was suddenly *inside* Dris. *In him.* . . . I could hardly believe it.
Bang. Suddenly I was Dris at the market. And I knew exactly who he was and
exactly who I was to him."[10] While Chester avoided processing loss through
mourning and incorporation, this letter demonstrates that he nonetheless sought
some kind of merging, an alternative way of negotiating identity and desire
through contact between the subject and object of desire. Rather than incor-
porate the lost object, however, Chester ventured out of himself and entered
Dris, not to "lose" himself in Dris but in order to know "exactly who" Dris is
and, through that knowledge, to define his own identity in relation to Dris.

While the reality Chester fashioned through kisses and through writing was
novel, it was also unstable and liable to collapse as other realities pushed in
upon it. It is not surprising, then, that the question of what is and is not real
lay at the center of Chester's reflections on his growing madness. The problem of "reality" did not begin in Morocco, however; Chester's obsession with
fakery and reality dates from his childhood, when he contracted a disease that
caused complete and permanent hair loss.[11] Traumatized by baldness from an
early age, Chester at first hid his head under a series of caps, which served
very well as long as he attended only a Yeshiva. When he began to attend public high school, however, he began to hide his head under a wig. In *The Foot*,
he wrote that the first time he put on the wig was "like having an ax driven
straight down the middle of my body. . . . Whack! Hacked in two with one
blow like a dry little tree" (*Head of a Sad Angel,* 293). From that moment,
Chester wrote, he began to live different realities in different circumstances.
Only his immediate family could see him bald, or with wig and hat: the rest
of the world was divided into those who could see him with the hat and those
who could see him with the wig. He describes the "terror of encountering one
side in the camp of the other. . . . The terror felt when a man leaps at you from
some midnight hedge with a knife in his hand" (294). Although he tried hard
to wear the right head piece for the right crowd, Chester inevitably met "hat
people" in the company of "wig people" and, to deal with the situation, he
learned to "turn myself off": "I snapped myself into invisibility" and "felt the

strangulation of all my feelings" (294). "I could bear no references to the wig," he wrote, and he treated it as if "It just wasn't there. Nothing was there. It was just something that didn't exist, like a third arm, so how could you talk about it? But it hurt, it hurt" (295).

Ironically, while Chester was openly queer fifteen years before Stonewall and seems to have escaped most of the trauma of living in a sexual closet, he was terrorized by another kind of closet—by a perceived need to disguise his baldness and by leading parallel "secret" lives beneath his hat and his wig.[12] Early in life, Chester learned to create his own definition of reality: to deny the existence of his wig, to make himself invisible, to turn off his feelings. This early intimacy with denial and masquerade would have a decisive effect on his adult life, when he came to suspect that nothing around him was "real." In Morocco, Chester reached a point at which he began to suspect that he was really dead, that he was "the only creature in existence," and that his purgatory was to live with the knowledge that "my friends, family, are scenery, depthless, selfless props, populating the illusion" (269). He relates this particular paranoid fantasy in *The Foot*, Chester explains, because it was necessary to describe his fear of utter isolation and entrapment in order to explain why he left Morocco: "I thought New York must be real. My old vampire mother must be real. Edward my friend must be real. And then I won't be dead" (269). Edward Field explains that, in fact, Chester was thrown out of Morocco because of his increasingly erratic behavior, but it was important for Chester to establish this other explanation, to name the search for reality as the reason for his rather sudden departure from the place he had earlier described as paradise ("A Biographical Sketch," 307). If Chester is dead, then Morocco is his hell, for it is only an illusion of paradise. "Larbi too is an illusion," Chester adds, "the worst of all illusions. Because if he were here now with his lips softly against mine, I wouldn't care if he were an illusion. I remember those last days in Morocco saying to myself: this cock is real. (Both of them.) This orgasm is real. So I am alive" (*Head of a Sad Angel,* 269).

While all the rest of experience may be fraudulent in Chester's eyes, in *The Foot* he establishes the grounds of reality through sexual experience and through desire. There is a certain confusion between the subject of desire and the object of desire ("this cock," which is also "Both of them"), but this confusion itself fashions Chester's reality and consequently his existence ("I am alive" because my/his/our "orgasm is real"). The cock of this moment is real in and through its materiality, just like the foot that appears elsewhere in the text; in fact, cock and foot are real in relation to each other, the one standing in for the other. Moreover, it is cock and foot that ground the "reality" of Chester's psychological and social relations in a string of linkages: Dris—Arab—Morocco—Africa. If Chester insists rather too much on the reality of these body parts, it is because they are in fact not real—or, rather, the real objects have been left behind along with Dris—and, without a cock and a foot to buttress the edifice his desire has constructed, Chester's psyche crumbles.

In Praise of Alfred Chester

Chester did not invent the logic expressed in the series Dris—Arab—Morocco—Africa. Rather, his desire was shaped by common discourses about race, colonialism, and the Orient. Nor did these linkages occur only after Chester arrived in Morocco. As we have already seen in regard to Bowles and Burroughs, sexual tourists and expatriates in Tangier brought their conceptions about the East with them from home—whether the contents of that luggage were declared or not. The writing Chester produced before arriving in Morocco provides some important clues that help to explain how and why racial difference shaped sexual desire in his later writing. For example, his short story "In Praise of Vespasian" (1961) explores the love of one man for racially othered men by describing the life and death of a friend named Joaquin. While this story was written in New York, it is set in Paris; it opens with Joaquin already dead, having succumbed to a mysterious intestinal illness he seems to have contracted during his first sexual experience and that seems to bring him closer to death with each subsequent sex act. Joaquin, a Catalan, becomes aware of his sexual attraction to men at the age of eighteen. He falls in love with a gypsy laborer who passes by the seminary in Spain where Joaquin is a student. After watching his beloved disappear into the forest with another student, Joaquin is confused—until he accompanies another man into the same forest. This event sends Joaquin to the infirmary and eventually leads to his death, but it leads him first to give up his studies and flee to Paris. There he devotes his life to a new altar of worship in the city's public toilets, seeking men who resemble the gypsy he had loved only from afar: he pursues some working-class French men, but primarily he seeks dark Algerians with small "Kikuyu" ears and "curly black oil-soaked hair" (*Head of a Sad Angel*, 178). The gypsy man whom Joaquin loved and lost (or, rather, whom he lost before love could unfold) was from the working class and had dark features and small ears, so this is the type of man Joaquin seeks. But the repeated emphasis given to specifically small "Kikuyu" ears, to a "Mohammedan head," to powerful shoulders, strong hands, and large cocks, underscores the way that Joaquin's desire, first activated by the sight of a specific gypsy man, comes to be excited by a range of body parts that signal for him generic racial and class difference.

Joaquin finds men easily enough, and with each encounter he tells himself that "*This*, this surely is love" (179), but after sex the love evaporates as easily as it arrived, and he sets off on yet another quest for his gypsy. No amount of *having* sex can satisfy Joaquin, for, as he describes his need for the gypsy man, "I envied him his freedom, his dark skin, his beauty, his ears, that enormous basket. I wanted to *be* him" (174). Joaquin envies, rather than admires; he wants to be, rather than to possess. As the narrator puts it, "From men he sought love—not theirs but his own" (173). And, while Joaquin can have any number of beautiful Algerian men, he can never become other than what he is: a "good-looking, nearly beautiful" young bourgeois Catalan. He cannot cross the lines of race and class that separate him from his objects of desire, and yet desire will not stop. As he discovers in the stall of a public toilet, "the walls of the Unconscious begin about twenty inches above the ground," and sex can take place in that space, but "there exists the problem of how two Unconsciousnesses are going to become one when a partition separates them, has in fact created them" (182). His answer to this problem is to accept the partition for what it is, to accept desire for what it is, and to pursue it relentlessly, even though it leads to unhappiness and, eventually, to his death.

The narrator of the story refuses what would appear to be an unhappy ending. He begins the story with "a fixed image of Joaquin," a still photo of him "caught, somewhat blurred, in the midst of walking rapidly past a plane tree on the Boulevard St. Germain." Joaquin is merely looking for love but the narrator declares: "I refuse to free him . . . because if the still turns to motion, death will wall Joaquin's young life into its myriad urinals" (172). In this story, Chester demonstrates how memory may be manipulated in an attempt to create a new reality. Like that kiss memorialized in *The Foot*, Joaquin's search for love can be frozen in time—life and love can be preserved through memory and through fiction. The still photo of Joaquin is reminiscent of those "perfect moments" captured by Robert Mapplethorpe on film: images of flowers, celebrities, nude black men, and S/M practitioners immobilized by a refined aesthetic, frozen by studio lights, hardened in black and white. Chester does unfreeze the frame long enough to let the story of Joaquin unroll but then preserves his memory in another "perfect moment" at the story's end. "Once more, and finally, Joaquin will move," the narrator tells us, and this final cruise takes him to a Parisian toilet where he encounters an "extraordinary figure," a "monument of a man," with a "powerful" neck, "dark" eyes, and ears that are "round and small like the Kikuyu." His race is obscure but all the more exciting in its obscurity: "Asia or Africa must at one time have raped his ancestry and his complexion, since . . . the color of his skin is not altogether European" (191–92). There are twenty men in the room, all of whom worship this stranger, but he chooses Joaquin, who, in the image with which the story ends, "closes his eyes, drops to his knees violently as if suffering a conversion or a revelation and, throwing wide his arms to grasp him who comes to them, opens his lips upon Life Everlasting" (193). To pursue relentlessly and perpetually a desire that is forged by the very walls of race and class that frustrate its fulfillment is an act of faith. Joaquin, the former seminarian, is nothing if not faithful, and this perfect moment of religious ecstasy rewards him not with death but with eternal life.

The problem of insatiable, frustrated desire forged in the face of racial and class difference also appears in a more personal story from this same period of Chester's career—more personal in the sense that characters and events are clearly based on Chester's own experience. "Ismael" relates the events of a long weekend in New York City. It opens on a Friday night with the conversion ceremony of John Anthony (né Morris), a Jewish friend and former lover who becomes Catholic because of his "buried ravenous dream of living the good life as advertised by Pepsi Cola or General Motors" (*Head of a Sad Angel,* 203). John Anthony also attempts to convert from homosexuality to heterosexuality. The narrator, whom we can infer is Chester himself, is made nauseous by the hypocrisy of both conversions, and for the remainder of the weekend he seeks solace in love. Saturday at dawn he meets Ismael, a dark but "fairer than mulatto" Puerto Rican boy, with whom he has sex, and with whom he falls in love. "Ah, the taste of a stranger's mouth!" he later tells a friend, "Love is the only ecstasy, the only religion on this island," and, for him, sudden devotion to a total stranger is the highest form of worship (207). This is a complex love, however, and more than casually related to the disgust the narrator feels for the wholesome America John Anthony seeks in Catholicism and heterosexuality. Ismael, wrote Chester, "loves himself with a joy that is foreign" and adds that, after having sex, "My hands now smell of him, washed clean by his sweat and his come of grimy America" (206). In Ismael, the narrator seeks an antidote to middle-class America. On Saturday, he attends a party overflowing with "Smart young moderns" and says, "Ugh to it all": "Publishing people. Advertising people. Oh, I am dying, Egypt, dying!" (207). In a striking anticipation of the same cry made to Dris in *The Foot,* the narrator calls upon Ismael/Egypt to save him through love. Disgusted by the party, he leaves for the gay bars but finds "Madison Avenue represented in force . . . an army of Tom Sawyers. God preserve us from the invasion of good fairies. Where are the screaming queens, the gigolos, the outrageous Harlem faggots—where is Ismael?" (207–8).

On Sunday, the narrator finds the physical if not the fantasmatic Ismael and declares his love, only to be rebuffed. Ismael warns him that "Frankie is the only person in this world I love" (209). Frankie, it turns out, is a Tom Sawyer, one of the "All-American boys who at thirty or forty or fifty are still All-American boys," wearing "dacron suits crowned by vacant, stupid, unlived faces" (208, 207). Ismael, on the other hand, is a "Nigger Jim" according to the narrator, who implicitly casts himself in the role of Huck. The narrator presses Ismael with a question: does Frankie love him?

"Frankie says: Ismael, I love you But."
"But what?"
He hesitates, then shrugs, smiles sourly. "I am a Puerto Rican. I don blame him. I don like my people either." (209)

The narrator hates middle-class professional America, Ismael hates Puerto Ricans, John Anthony hates his Jewishness and his sexuality—we do not learn enough about Frankie to know what love or hate mean to him, but all the other characters turn in disgust from those central categories that structure their identities and they attempt through desire to make contact with someone unlike themselves. Like Joaquin, the narrator of "Ismael" wants to be rather than to have, and he encounters the object of his desire only to discover that such desire can be sustained but not fulfilled. He and Ismael have sex again, "But it isn't like the first time. We have lost our innocence, our anonymities" (210). Ismael is now a person to the narrator, rather than an idea, a subject with his own desires: "Not only does my body want his, but my heart wants his, and his wants Frankie's, and Frankie's wants—whose? How many men are here with us in bed, flailing and laboring with us, locked with us not only in the body's terrific heat but in the heart's terrible romance?" (210). No one is able to get what he wants—not even John Anthony, who is too cowardly to go "the whole hog, so to speak, and become a Methodist or a Presbyterian" (203).

The affair, which begins early Saturday morning, lasts only until the narrator and Ismael meet again on Sunday. Paradoxically, it could have lasted much longer—but only if they had never seen each other again. The narrator's love for Ismael is as sweet as the "taste of a stranger's mouth" but becomes bitter once that mouth is no longer strange and no longer foreign. On Sunday, they meet and have sex, but after the sex the narrator provokes an argument with Ismael: he creates a scene in public by camping about, mocking Ismael's masculinity and exposing the sexual interest of their interaction. This provocation has the intended effect of angering Ismael, who ends the conversation and severs their young relationship. In this way the narrator arrives at "The moment of truth and love—the instant of separation" (212). Like Joaquin's desire, desire in "Ismael" is forged in the face of the wall that separates self and other—a wall constructed variously by race, class, nationality, and religion. But, whereas the narrator of "Vespasian" can memorialize and freeze Joaquin in the pursuit of his desire, the narrator of "Ismael" cannot memorialize or freeze himself. Instead, he provokes a separation from the object of his desires in order to seek in that separation "the moment of truth and love," the reconstruction of a barrier that will sustain desire. Separation also leads to loss, however, and loss to grief. The narrator does in fact wake up Monday morning "in a nameless, faceless misery like mud" (212). Ordinarily, we would expect the narrator to mourn the loss of his beloved, Ismael. Chester, however, suggests a different possibility: he mourns neither the object of desire nor desire itself (which never goes away) but rather the loss of love. Love is lost outside the moment of separation, and, except for this moment, the narrator is cut off from other people, terribly alone as he writes the script of his own life. Facing "another day without love and without God, with nothing but a few more sheets of scrawled paper," the narrator insists that "the name and face of my grief [is] not Ismael, but another day. One more morning to pass through and invent" (213).

When Chester escaped New York for Morocco, he hardly left behind this grief or the need to invent himself through writing every day. In fact, his writing in Morocco became more "inventive" insofar as he left realism behind and devised a new, surreal fictional world in *The Exquisite Corpse*. While this novel marks a new phase of Chester's career, it is rooted in the experience that also created his Parisian and New York short stories. Connections with "Ismael" are especially explicit, since several of the realistic characters from that story appear in surreal form in *The Exquisite Corpse*. Ismael himself is there, although, when writing to an advice columnist, he invents a new name for himself, Isobel, and soon Isobel has her own life and story. Ismael's lover Frankie is in *The Exquisite Corpse,* as well, although he is renamed Tommy (after Tommy's bar in the story, where Ismael and the narrator drink). This Tommy is, of course, a Tom Sawyer, but there is another Tom Sawyer in *The Exquisite Corpse,* named Ferguson (also known as John Doe), and a new "Nigger Jim," named Tomtom Jim. John Anthony shows up as well, although he quickly splits into Baby Poorpoor and James Madison, as well as maintaining the identity of John Anthony (drag name: Veronica).

Other references in *The Exquisite Corpse*—to the ambivalence felt toward a dying father, to a mother who refuses financial or emotional support, to former lovers like Extro (after whom Xavier is named, even though if Xavier resembles any living person it is Chester himself), to Susan Sontag (Mary Poorpoor, although this association becomes more clear in *The Foot*)—mark biographical connections between Chester's life and his novel. Although *The Exquisite Corpse* was written in Morocco, it works through material that had been troubling Chester in Europe and in the United States. As I have mentioned, his troubles centered around his experience of self as a situational phenomenon, which was both a widespread postwar cultural problem and an intensely personal problem for Chester regarding identity and desire. Like Joaquin and the narrator of "Ismael," Chester seems to have acted upon his sexual desires with success but not without question. He placed his identity under scrutiny, as well, especially regarding the categorization of identity by sexuality, race, religion, class, and nation.

"In Praise of Vespasian" and "Ismael" express many of the thoughts Chester had about identity and desire before he embarked for Morocco. Both stories focus on a kind of desire that is made both possible and impossible by the walls that exist between men. Anonymous sex is celebrated, and the separation that ensures anonymity is figured as racial difference. What is especially interesting about the way Chester represented desire for a racial other is the way that the categorization of otherness was so mobile. In France, racial otherness floated between "gypsy" and "Arab" or "Algerian" but was also associated with working-class appearance. In the United States, this same mobility associated a Puerto Rican boy who was "lighter than mulatto" with Mark Twain's character Jim. (In *The Exquisite Corpse*, the ability to reinvent racial otherness to suit one's needs is demonstrated by the English man who cruises Ismael because he wants to have sex with an Arab.) Racial difference shades into class difference, most notably in Joaquin's story, but class is an issue in "Ismael," as well. The narrator repudiates his own class affiliations ("Ugh!" to use his word), and seeks his "Ismael" in the economic and social underclass: "the screaming queens, the gigolos, the outrageous Harlem faggots" are equivalent to each other and to Ismael by virtue of being abstractly, fantasmatically different from the narrator.

Both Joaquin and the narrator of "Ismael" accept their desires, and neither seems interested in or troubled by the way that those desires mobilize a variety of race and class markers in a singular logic of difference. But both stories and especially "Ismael" are troubled by the impact desire has on identity. Both Joaquin and the narrator of "Ismael" are confused by (dis)identification with the objects of their desire and by the contradictory needs to have and to be those objects. Desire is celebrated in the stories, but especially in "Ismael"; identity is in crisis, for a mobility of desire leads to a mobility in identity. The wall of strangeness that shapes the perfect moment of love is perpetually falling down and being reconstructed; the narrator grieves the ensuing loss of permanence and stability in himself, in his relation to that wall, and in his relation to shifting objects of desire. He grieves as well the new day—the passage of time—for each movement forward is a loss of perfection and of love; each new day requires him to seek new objects and to reinvent himself in relation to them.[13]

When Chester left for Morocco, he did not travel lightly: he carried with him a complex set of relations to race and class difference that weighed heavily on his identity, his desires, and his search for love, sex, and joy in Morocco. One indication that his relation to racial difference in the United States was carried over into his encounter with Morocco is provided by the offhand remark that "sometimes I call Dris 'You big nigger' even though he's more or less white."[14] Chester used this appellation as a term of endearment, much the same way that Bellew called Clare "Nig" in Nella Larsen's *Passing*. Both Dris and Clare are fondly eroticized by being named "black" in spite of their fair complexions. To call Dris "you big nigger" marks racial difference upon his body in order to make that body mysterious and unknowable, so that, while the sex Chester and Dris have could hardly be called anonymous, they could be said to have anonymous love: a deep mutual affection combined with a superficial mutual understanding. One clue that part of Chester's fascination for Dris was precisely this lack of understanding is found in the dedication to *The Exquisite Corpse*:

For Driss Ben Hussein El Kasri
For Dris Kasri
For Dris
For You—whatever your name is and whoever you are
—with love and admiration

This dedication, presumably written in New York after Chester was expelled from Morocco, suggests that not only was Dris unavailable after the breakup but that in a substantial way he was "unavailable" or unknowable even during the course of the relationship.

In this regard, Chester's relationship with Dris resembles Bowles's relationship with Yacoubi more than Burroughs's relationship with Kiki. Burroughs was interested not so much in dispelling as ignoring Orientalist notions of mystery, the inscrutability of exotic sex partners, and so forth. Chester, on the other hand, entered Morocco with a relatively common and unquestioned relationship to Orientalism, so that his understanding of racial difference in the United States was inserted into a discourse of exoticism, mystery, and sexual stereotypes. In short, at the beginning of his stay in Morocco, Chester's encounter with the Orient as such, and with Moroccan men, resembled the sort of encounter Bowles had already made famous in his fiction. In fact, it is important to bear in mind that Chester came to Morocco through Bowles, in a concrete as well as a metaphorical way. While Bowles claimed never to have invited anyone to come to Tangier, Chester's letters show that he not only invited but actively urged Chester to come and take up residence there.[15] The letters he wrote to Bowles before setting out for Morocco indicate that Chester accepted rather than critiqued common attitudes and stereotypes about North African sexual culture and the interaction of Western expatriates with Moroccan boyfriends. "Maybe I can have myself a little Arab wife in Morocco?" Chester wrote on one occasion, and, on another, "I want someone nice who doesn't need pampering; and can look after my apartment and me and the dogs. Like a servant one screws."[16] Bowles responded by locating not only an apartment for Chester but "a little Arab wife" as well: he set Chester up with Dris.[17]

During the first weeks of his stay in Morocco, Chester was captivated by Bowles's fame and personality, but that fascination turned to an intense love and hate relationship as Chester was drawn to Bowles's intellect but repelled by the colonial relations in which his life and work were steeped. In September 1963, Chester provoked a dramatic fight with Bowles because he suspected that Bowles had cheated Larbi Layachi out of a fair share of royalties from *A Life Full of Holes*. During this fight, he called Bowles a "big queen" and threatened to "expose him to the world for the monster he is."[18] Couched in terms of "exposure," this threat demonstrates Chester's continuing obsession with reality versus fakery; for him, the "real" Bowles was queer and colonial—

specifically, an exploitative colonial—and the mask of heterosexuality and gentility behind which Bowles hid, in Chester's view, wreaked violence upon the world—or at least upon Chester's world. Bowles had "done everything to mess my life up," Chester wrote; "He has been a monster in my life here."[19] Chester referred specifically to his fear that Bowles was maneuvering to break up his relationship with Dris, but also more generally to his fear that Bowles mysteriously controlled his life.

The transformation of Bowles from friend to monster happened suddenly and figured prominently in Chester's experience of Morocco. While early in Chester's Moroccan stay Bowles had been a formative influence on him and had shaped his ideas about sexual relations between Moroccan and Western men, Chester later repudiated his own writing on this subject in the story "Glory Hole" as "superficial, untrue and a vision imposed on me by Paul Bowles."[20] It is not especially surprising that Chester would criticize Bowles for remaining in the closet—as I noted, Chester was quite open about his own sexuality, and he had a special fear of masquerade and illusion. Moreover, he thought Bowles's reticence needlessly old-fashioned. After a second incident involving the potential "outing" of Paul Bowles, Chester wrote, "It is a drama between generations and Paul is asking to have his generation destroyed."[21] What is perhaps more surprising is the related criticism Chester leveled against Bowles for being "an old fashioned colonial type."[22] In this case, the charge of fakery would seem not to apply, because there is no substantive distance between the sort of life Bowles lived and the sort of life he wrote about. Yet, in a fictionalized account of a day spent with Bowles, Chester described being terrified by his colonial life, and particularly by the belief that Bowles produced and controlled a false, illusory reality. In "Safari," Bowles is called Gerald, and Chester wrote that "Gerald has lived here so long that magic and sorcery are more part of his nature than science or the ten commandments. . . . He is a witch doctor using the body of a mild English missionary. I believe his mind can create things, can make them up as he goes along, *real* things (so to speak), like this road we were on" (*Head of a Sad Angel,* 238). This passage is just one of many in Chester's fiction and letters from 1964 and later that indicates the central role his relationship with Bowles played in Chester's psychological decline. As Chester began to doubt the solidity of any sort of reality, including his own existence, Bowles came to represent for him a demonic father figure capable of creating and destroying "reality." The ascription of such powers to Bowles arose from the initial invitation to come to Morocco, as well as from the introduction to Dris. In New York and quite mad, in 1966, Chester wrote to Bowles, "I love you as I loved my father whom I hated," because "you gave me the greatest gift I've ever had, by which I mean, in short, of course, what else, Morocco."[23]

It is precisely because Bowles gave Chester this gift that he became, in Chester's paranoid view, an omnipotent figure: God the father, the lawgiver. Moreover, the law that this God handed down was the law of colonial desire. When Bowles "gave" Chester Dris and Morocco, he also "bestowed" upon him the legacy of centuries of sexual exchange between East and West in Tangier. As I have shown, Chester in fact brought with him to Morocco a well-developed set of expectations concerning race and desire, and those expectations were inserted into a preexisting regime of exoticization that construes Moroccan men to be unfathomably, mysteriously different. When he began to develop a critique of colonial relations, however, Chester did not turn inward; he did not examine the ways in which his own identity and his sexual desires were produced by the social dynamics of American culture or of Orientalism. Moreover, he did not have a specific political criticism to make of colonialism; his discomfort with colonial relations was registered rather through references to "artificiality" and incongruity with modern life. Ultimately, Chester's critique was grounded in what seemed most real to him: his desire and love for Dris. In *The Foot*, as his own identity came to seem increasingly unreal, this desire for Dris provided Chester with his most secure anchor. Meanwhile, Bowles came to represent that force that would separate him from his beloved. Chester's suspicion that Bowles wanted to come between the two lovers was not simply paranoia but rather reflected a growing hostility to the structures of colonial desire, which Bowles represented (in his writing) and embodied (in Chester's mind). In "Vespasian" and "Ismael," Chester indicated a willingness to accept separation as the price of love—in fact, he indicated that love is possible only at the moment of separation. In his letters from Morocco, however, and later in *The Foot*, Chester demonstrated that he was no longer willing to accept this logic. In spite of his frequent fights with Dris, he dreaded the ensuing separations and wanted to put an end to them while preserving love.

Chester sought to overturn the law of colonial desire—the law of Bowles the father—and he undertook this effort through writing *The Exquisite Corpse* and *The Foot*. In its subject matter, *The Exquisite Corpse* does not concern itself with colonial relations as such; rather, it processes and represents the problems of desire and identity Chester brought with him to Tangier from Europe and the United States. But *The Exquisite Corpse* could not have been written without Morocco, for it arose out of Chester's attempt to resist the logic of colonial desire as it enforces a separation between himself and Dris. To an extent that is difficult to trace, the novel also arose out of Chester's experience with kif and out of his growing insanity. Kif highs encouraged Chester to see associations among his characters that link them, dream-like, through proximity, metonymy, splitting, and merging. The question of where Chester's insanity left off and where his creative writing began is more difficult; however, it is safe to say that *The Exquisite Corpse* was written between

two periods of severe psychotic breakdown, and, while the events of the
novel ultimately seem under the control of an authorial consciousness, in
Diana Athill's words, "one inch madder, and it would have been too mad"
(*Stet*, 195).

Chester named the novel after the game the French surrealists had played
in the 1930s, in which a folded piece of paper was passed around a circle, and
each participant would draw a body part on a square. Only after the squares
had been filled would the paper be unfolded and the entire corpse revealed.
The title makes his tribute to surrealism obvious, but Chester chose it because
he liked the sound of the phrase, not because of any direct descent from the
collaborative production of sketched corpses to his own imaginative project.
The surrealists embarked through art on a political mission with revolutionary
ambitions, and the movement fragmented in part over political strategies and
the failure to realize those ambitions. One of those strategies, as Maurice
Nadeau points out, was to conceive of desire as capable of overturning the
established order. "Was it [desire] not in essence protean, revolutionary, and
capable of disguising itself in order to conquer?" Nadeau asks, and hence particularly well suited for use by people who seek freedom, who seek "'to transform the world', 'to change life' by an objectification of desire, the omnipotent
force capable of producing every miracle" (*The History of Surrealism*, 245).
Chester did not share the political ambitions of the surrealists, but, after coming to Morocco, he did share this notion of desire and the hope that desire could
change the world. His realistic short stories "Vespasian" and "Ismael" explore
the pleasure and pain of desire but view it as an inevitable product of an alienated and hierarchical relation between subject and object. But his surrealistic
novel *The Exquisite Corpse* conceives of desire as a protean force capable of
rupturing hierarchy and difference—a force that could make the distance
between subject and object irrelevant.

The novel represents the force of such desire through a series of interlock-
ing stories that fade in and out of each other, each one going everywhere and
nowhere. For example, there is the story of Ismael, which reworks the characters and dynamics of the short story by that name. In the novel, the "Tom
Sawyer" lover is named Tommy, and he carries on a passionate romance with
Ismael until, as a side effect of cancer surgery, his face becomes horribly dis-
figured. We learn about the surgery and its aftermath through a letter Ismael
writes to the advice columnist Dr. Franzblau. Ismael loves Tommy in spite of
his new face, but Tommy can no longer love himself and goes out of his way
to highlight the disfigurement, daring Ismael and the world to hate him. As
Ismael describes it, the face "was sort of pulled around to one side, but it didn't
always stay there. It dropped sometimes. It slid around here and there like it
was alive or something" (*Exquisite Corpse*, 59). Not only does the face move
around this way but so also do the characters in the novel. When Ismael writes

his letter to Dr. Franzblau, he signs it "Isobel" in order to disguise his gender and the fact that the love affair is between two men. Stepping in the closet is a realistic choice for Ismael, but then, surrealistically, Isobel becomes a separate character in the novel with her own story. We learn through a second letter to Dr. Franzblau that she has become a prostitute in Amsterdam and is engaged to a sailor named Dickie. Dickie is also the name, the "real" name or birth name, of a character who prefers to be called Xavier. This Xavier is a young Jewish man from New York with a complicated relationship with his father—he is much like Alfred Chester—but at the same time, the "X" of Xavier also makes him Extro, the Canadian hippie boyfriend with whom Chester broke up before sailing for Morocco. Xavier/Dickie is a confusion and a refusal of the difference between Chester and his ex-lover; but Dickie does not stop here. Dickie is also Dickie Gold (who is black as well as gold), a gigolo with whom John Anthony had been infatuated in Paris. Finally, Dickie is also Christ crucified, for John Anthony calls the Christ hanging on his bedroom wall "Dickie." (He is a "rugged boyish Jesus," "clean shaven" with a "crew cut" and a "white terry-cloth towel around his muscular waist" [93].) All these Dickies are different characters, and yet simultaneously they are all the same: they are all Dickie, and, by association, they are all "dick." Like a dream, they fade in and out of focus and slide in and out of one another, not in order to build up any sort of heavy-handed symbolism but rather to link various parts of the novel together as if by chance, as if any mutation is possible and all mutations are senseless, absurd, and anarchic.

Meanwhile, as the story of Isobel unravels, Tommy sells all his possessions, leaves the money to his beloved Ismael, and becomes homeless, turning up after several adventures at the Catholic charity managed by John Anthony. John Anthony is a drag queen with special talent not only for costume but also for making masks, and he devises a mask of Tommy's old face that he can wear as he goes in search of Ismael. The mask works brilliantly, except that Ismael refuses to believe this handsome man is his lover: "Listen, mister . . . you're not my Tommy . . . my Tommy has a sweet crippled face now and a heart of gold. And I love him" (190–91). Enraged at this rejection, Tommy screams, "Stop calling me mister, you black slut" (191), and he rips the mask off his face. Ismael recognizes his true love, but, still enraged, Tommy thrusts the mask on Ismael's own face. With red and yellow fire, the mask burns Ismael's face away, leaving him "even uglier" than his beloved (238). At the close of the novel, the lovers are happily united by this ugliness. John Anthony makes another mask for them, this time modeled after Ismael's former face, but it is Tommy who puts it on, telling Ismael, "Look into the mirror, darling. Look at your own loveliness" (239), as he looks at his own ugliness in Ismael's deformed face. Tommy also wears Ismael's mask when they have sex so that Ismael can see "himself" and vice versa. The erotics of racial difference are not abandoned by this exchange of masks, but they are transformed: the "white" face has been obliterated, and the "black" face can be worn or not at will. Subject and object are reduced to a game of masks, beauty and deformity are equalized, and desire and identity become fluid and interchangeable. Through its strategic surrealism, this episode and the novel as a whole work to demystify human relations and to reconceptualize complex interactions as a simple game of assuming and discarding masks. In the world of *The Exquisite Corpse,* identity is superficial, rather than essential, and subjectivity is susceptible to sudden shifts and splits. Moreover, the entire novel is written with a hilarious camp sensibility that stands in sharp contrast to the agonized tone of *The Foot.* In that sense, *The Exquisite Corpse* is Chester's "gayest" piece of fiction: not only in the sense of manipulating the idioms of camp but also insofar as it is more lighthearted than his stories or his final novel fragment. *The Exquisite Corpse* adopts in literature the strategies of an openly queer and defiant queen, assuming and discarding personas with humor, parody, and biting satire. It is in this sense that writing and sexuality came together in Chester's writing in a strikingly different way from that in Bowles's and Burroughs's writing. While sexuality is "closeted," displaced, and sublimated in Bowles, and while it is obscene and outside the bounds of the law in Burroughs, in Chester it is out and about, cruising and joyful.

It is in this sense that Chester claimed the future for his own writing. Just as he found a third way to be queer, he found a third way to write about sexuality. Similarly, he found a third way to be an expatriate in Tangier and imagined that alternative course in *The Foot.* Bowles lived in perfect form the role of the studious colonial or expatriate who, while keeping his own lifestyle separate from "native" life, knew the local language, befriended local people, and lived as an alien and alienated "insider." This is the model of expatriation he wrote about so incisively in "The Time of Friendship" and in *The Spider's House.* Burroughs, on the other hand, lived in Tangier as an "outsider" who refused to learn Arabic and had no interest in North African culture. This position "outside" led him to write a very political novel, *Naked Lunch,* in which he refused to recognize, much less critique, the politics of colonialism that helped structure his experience and his novel. Alfred Chester refused the dichotomy of "inside" versus "outside." In Morocco, he made a confused and abortive attempt to "go native": to immerse himself in Moroccan culture, to cut ties with his own culture and cultural identity, and to deny the difference he nonetheless strongly felt between himself and the object of his desire, Dris. He refused the alienation that Bowles accepted and Burroughs avoided and refused the loss that alienation enforced as he was separated from his beloved. In Morocco, writing *The Exquisite Corpse,* Chester began to imagine a surreal world in which difference did not matter, or at least where it mattered differently because difference—and reality itself—could be bent to one's will.

He was successful in writing the novel but not in replicating this vision as a sustainable mode of expatriate life, and so he left Morocco, exchanging expatriation for exile. Finally, in *The Foot* Chester attempted through an imaginative reworking of the conventions of fetishism to reject change, loss and grief, to memorialize Dris rather than mourn him, and to freeze love into permanence. This attempt also produced fascinating literature but provided an extremely unstable and "unrealistic" solution to Chester's psychological decline.

The epigraph that heads this chapter celebrates queer life in Morocco, proclaiming that it is better to be an old queen there than a king in America. But Chester attached one stipulation to this claim: "provided, of course, that you're free." In *The Foot,* Chester suggested what such freedom meant to him:

I want freedom. Even more than Morocco I want to sniff every green and barren corner of this earth. I want to make love in seven hundred languages to seven million Africans—South Americans and Asians too, perhaps, though they do seem a bit overrefined, already too much like fine porcelain and martini glasses. I want to make love with those of the hot regions where water is drunk out of the palm of the hand. And where drums beat. I want a magic carpet to visit the unfactoried corners of the world, the places that are not New York. If there are any left. (*Head of a Sad Angel,* 275)

Chester sought the freedom to love not only Dris but all of the nonindustrialized world! And while the scarcity of industry increased the appeal to him of "unfactoried" Africa, South America, and Asia, it was the primitive drum beats and magic of the tropics that he especially yearned for but knew he could not have. He was restrained from them not because he lived in exile in New York but because these "seven million Africans" were exotic fantasies and as such were unrealizable to a man for whom "reality" had dropped away. As much as *The Foot* elegizes Dris and this magic, primitive world, and as much as Chester attempted through writing to resurrect his life in Morocco, *The Foot* also concedes that the freedom to do so is not forthcoming—is in fact nonexistent. The life of an old queen in Morocco is not so ideal after all. Bowles and Burroughs were no less constrained by this lack of freedom, but they found ways to write and live around it. Chester imagined a new, third path, but it did not lead to an exit.

5

Translating Homosexuality
Paul Bowles's Collaborations with Larbi Layachi,
Mohammed Mrabet, and Mohamed Choukri

Chapter 1 introduced the notion of interzone literature, and subsequent chapters have focused on the interzone literature Paul Bowles, William Burroughs, and Alfred Chester wrote in response to the very different personal experiences each author had in Tangier. Just as the International Zone of Tangier was created by foreign powers, so one might think of interzone literature strictly as the creation of expatriate imagination and expression. But I argue in this chapter that Moroccans were also active in Tangier's unique "writers colony" and that Larbi Layachi, Mohammed Mrabet, and Mohamed Choukri in particular offer important and compelling representations of identity, desire, and male subjectivity in Tangier.

Like the American expatriate authors, Layachi, Mrabet, and Choukri created literary interzones that responded to colonial relations—including colonial sexual relations—they witnessed in Tangier. But the Moroccan authors offer very distinct perspectives on colonial sexuality. The melancholia and nostalgia so pervasive in Paul Bowles's representations of colonial desire are wholly absent in the work of Layachi, Mrabet, and Choukri. Neither do they, in the mode of Burroughs or Chester, turn to fantasy or surrealism to explore identity and desire. Rather, in the texts I analyze here, Layachi, Mrabet, and Choukri narrate realistic stories that emphasize the economic dimensions of sexuality in Tangier. Specifically, their texts represent sexual relations with foreign men in the context

111

of poverty, prostitution, homosocial bonds among Moroccan men, male adolescence, and marriage as a rite of passage into adulthood.

We might be tempted to understand the sexual relations between foreign and
Moroccan men in Tangier as transparently exploitative. Indeed, texts by Layachi, Mrabet, and Choukri do at times invite us to consider how power relations in the international political economy are mapped directly onto
interpersonal experience. The exploitation of one nation or one race by another
can be a useful metaphor for understanding the power dynamics of sex acts
and sexual culture; such a metaphor can even be constitutive of one's identity
and desire. But Layachi, Mrabet, and Choukri also invite us to approach these
matters carefully, for the exercise of power in the interzone is not as transparent or simplistic as it might seem.

As I have argued in previous chapters, colonial discourse perpetuates binary
modes of relation and enforces rigidity in the roles assigned "colonizer" and
"colonized." These roles are often cast in racial terms (for example, white versus black) and in gender terms (masculine versus feminine). In this chapter,
I explore how male homosexual relations can be assimilated to such a binary
structure by gendering sexual roles (masculine domination, effeminate submission) or by specifying other kinds of difference (the older, wealthier gay
man who purchases sex from the younger, straight hustler). Nationalist discourse can be equally rigid, especially when it regards normative masculinity and heterosexuality as loyal and effeminacy or homosexuality as
treacherous. A simplistic analysis of Tangier's sexual economy could construe
all sexual relations between Moroccan and foreign men as acts either of
betrayal on the part of Moroccans or exploitation on the part of foreigners.
But literary representations of male homosexuality in Tangier challenge such
binary, rigid modes of interpretation. My aim in this chapter is to offer a more
nuanced analysis of interzone sexuality by examining works of literature that
unsettle—even as they are unsettled by—stereotypes and facile binarisms.

Paul Bowles's renderings of stories told to him by Moroccan collaborators
are curiously situated outside the boundaries of any national literature. As interzone literature, the texts speak to matters of race and sexuality, of identity and
desire, and of nation and culture through a complex interplay of textual and
extratextual signification. The translations recirculate many of the stereotypes
that work to shore up the boundaries of binary difference between racially and
nationally coded subjects and objects of desire, but in this recirculation the texts
also work to undermine binary structures by calling into question the capacity of stereotypes to represent experience. Moreover, the translations of texts
spoken to Bowles in Maghrebi Arabic are shaped by a set of erotic demands
and contradictions that exceed the limits that are normally thought to define
national, racial, and sexual identities. Excesses of desire are associated with
the excess of translation itself, and this combined flood of signification produces a highly unstable politics of representation.

Transacting Translations

The translations Paul Bowles rendered of fiction and autobiographies authored by Larbi Layachi, Mohammed Mrabet, and Mohamed Choukri provide an intriguing place to interrogate narratives of identity, especially because the way these texts are produced calls into question the distinction between "author" and "translator." These texts exhibit a marked fascination with male-male sexual activities and desires; their representations of sex and sexuality include both encounters between Moroccan men and encounters between Moroccans and foreigners. Moreover, the texts themselves were generated through literary encounters between Moroccans and a foreigner that in some ways mimic the dynamics of an erotic encounter. Layachi, Mrabet, and Choukri wrote about the economic demands that structure male-male sexual activity in Tangier, and their writings were themselves produced within an economy of erotic exchange. I turn to a close examination of these economic relations later in this chapter and also look closely at the work performed by the recirculation of certain stereotypes. But in order to understand representations of sex and sexuality in these texts, I first examine the extratextual pressures of collaboration and translation that shaped their production and reception.

Bowles's collaborative translations were produced for the most part in the twenty-five years following Moroccan independence in 1956, but many of them—especially the more autobiographical works—refer to life in colonial times. Larbi Layachi's autobiography, *A Life Full of Holes,* was first published in 1964, but it relates events from Layachi's life that date from the 1940s. Mrabet began collaborating with Paul Bowles in the mid-1960s and published most of his work in the 1960s and 1970s. Choukri first worked with Bowles on his autobiography, *For Bread Alone* (1973). In the twenty-five years from 1956 to 1981, the euphoric expectation that independence would bring prosperity to all sectors of Moroccan society had diminished, and the writings of Layachi, Mrabet, and Choukri all respond in their own ways to the poverty and inequalities perpetuated under a neocolonial economic system. The vision of male-male sex presented in these writings was profoundly shaped by the economic situation in which the authors found themselves: Layachi, Mrabet, and Choukri survived through occasional manual labor and petty crime before they began to earn money as writers. The perspective these writers brought to their portrayal of Moroccan society is different from that of such internationally recognized Moroccan writers as Tahar Ben Jelloun and Abdelkebir Khatibi, who have formulated critiques of contemporary Morocco based on quite different personal experiences. Ben Jelloun and Khatibi write in French from the perspective of the highly educated elite. As we will see, Layachi and Mrabet did not "write" in the traditional sense but rather spoke into a tape recorder. Moreover, Layachi and Choukri were born into such severe poverty that they were lucky to have survived at all, let alone to have found ways to publish their literature. Lay-achi, Mrabet, and Choukri became authors while living on the periphery of Tangier's economic and intellectual life, and the system of representation that these three men developed in their texts marks out the ground upon which their voices spoke from the margins of Moroccan society.

Mohamed Choukri's career and his literary vision differ significantly from those of Layachi and Mrabet. Choukri had written two novels in Arabic before he met Paul Bowles. His autobiography, *For Bread Alone,* first appeared in English, and he published two additional books with Bowles.[1] These collabora-tions helped establish Choukri's international reputation, but it was his Arabic-language writing that moved him from the margins toward the center of Moroccan intellectual life. Layachi and Mrabet, on the other hand, remained on the margins. Layachi left Morocco entirely, emigrating to the United States, where he learned to write in English and where he published *Yesterday and Today* (1985) and *The Jealous Lover* (1986). Mrabet remained in Morocco, but he "wrote" only through Bowles's translations. Moreover, the primary audi-ence for their books lived not in Morocco but in the United States and in Europe. While Laychi and Mrabet did manage to find novel ways to set their thoughts on paper and publish them, the process of translation and overseas publication placed their texts between nations and between languages. From this rather unusual position, Layachi and Mrabet formulated a critique of the role of the nation and nationalism in relation to culture, language, and litera-ture. This critique emerged in response to the pressures experienced by the authors in the colonial and postcolonial eras and was complicated by the ways their texts were collaboratively produced.

The first complication is that of writing itself: who writes these books? Lay-achi was illiterate when he collaborated with Bowles on *A Life Full of Holes*; while Mrabet could read, he did not "write" any of his books. Both men com-posed in their heads and told their stories in the unwritten colloquial Arabic of Morocco. They recorded their narratives on a tape recorder so that Paul Bowles could later simultaneously transcribe and translate them into English. Choukri, on the other hand, wrote *For Bread Alone* in standard Arabic, but, since Bowles did not know this language, Choukri translated his own writing into spoken Spanish so that Bowles could translate the spoken word back into writing, this time in English.[2] A second complication, which follows from the first, is that of language: while Layachi and Mrabet told their stories in Maghrebi Arabic, the stories were published and read in English or other European languages (French, Spanish, Portuguese, Italian, and German edi-tions have been issued over the years). Did Layachi and Mrabet "write for" an American or European reader? Are their books to be considered Moroccan literature, since they were first published in English and entered Morocco only in French translation? Are they to be considered American literature, since they

From left to right: Mohamed Choukri, Jean Genet, Hassan Oukrim, and Mohamed Zerrad at Café de France, Tangier, 1969 (Provided by the Swiss Foundation for Photography, Paul Bowles Photographic Archive © 2001 Artists Rights Society (ARS), New York/Pro Litteris, Zurich.)

were produced in collaboration with an American writer and translator? Choukri achieved fame by telling his autobiography to Bowles in Spanish, but now he publishes in Arabic—does this make him a more authentic Moroccan author than Layachi or Mrabet?

Choukri would probably answer the latter question affirmatively; certainly he has criticized Mrabet for writing for a Western audience. Choukri raises the question of readership in order to distinguish his own writing from that of the Mrabet/Bowles and Layachi/Bowles collaborations: Choukri's claim that Mrabet and Layachi write for a Western reader is also a claim that his own writing is destined for a Moroccan reader and that therefore he is a legitimate cultural producer.[3] This claim is formed within the terms of a literary criticism that seeks to define national literature not only in terms of language and audience, but also in terms of a proper national consciousness. Layachi's and Mrabet's books do not exhibit a nationalist consciousness per se. Both authors relate their experience of surviving on the margins of Moroccan society, and when their texts criticize authority they do not draw a distinction between national and (neo)colonial oppression. For example, in *A Life Full of Holes* Layachi describes a period in his life when he cannot find employment and when his hunger drives him to steal copper wire from a French company's warehouse in order to survive. He is arrested, and at his trial he does not in his defense denounce a colonial system that encourages unemployment to keep labor costs down but instead blames the prejudice of his compatriots, who will not hire him because he comes from a different region. While serving time in prison, he supports the rights of two fellow prisoners to equal and fair treatment, for which he is unjustly punished by a corrupt French guard—but, while Layachi disapproves of the guard's corruption, he reserves the highest blame for the Moroccan prison director, who allows such corruption to take place. It could be said that Layachi has not achieved a proper consciousness of the international dimensions of injustice or of the divide-and-rule tactics of the French, but the propriety of Layachi's consciousness is beside the point: in spinning a narrative of his own experience, Layachi's text offers a coherent and moving critique of a corrupt and inhumane system of injustice that remains in place under a national state. Taken as a whole, *A Life Full of Holes* relates a life story that spans the end of formal colonialism and the coming of independence and suggests that life for common people does not change after 1956.

Ironically, it is in part Layachi's position as a common Moroccan who dictates his story in a common, unwritten Maghrebi variant of Arabic that makes his text so difficult to classify as Moroccan literature. The ongoing debate among writers and critics in Morocco concerning the proper language for literary production is for the most part limited to a choice between French and standard written Arabic. There are a number of reasons for ignoring the potential to create literature in colloquial speech: the sacred character of Arabic, the prestige of Arabic's long literary tradition, an aspiration to unify the nation around a national language, and a readiness to ignore the voices of those who can speak only in colloquial languages. The texts of people like Layachi and Mrabet, who write neither French nor Arabic—who do not write at all—cannot easily be absorbed into the dichotomous terms of the attempt to define Moroccan national literature. Since Moroccan culture is rooted in the Arab-Muslim world, some literary critics argue that Arabic-language literature is more authentic than French-language literature.[4] The fragility of this argument lies in the fact that, while it is relatively easy to move from one language to another, it is much more difficult to isolate the political meaning of that move. Colonial power may be projected or consolidated through indigenous languages (missionary publications in indigenous languages are the best example), or anticolonial struggles may be waged through colonial languages. The politics of using any given language are in no way pure. Moreover, the necessity of translation puts the notion of authenticity in question. In Morocco, translation is a way of life and a way of survival. In spite of the fact that Arabic is the national language, the cultural and economic life of the nation is conducted in several languages at once. Educated people speak and write standard Arabic and French, but the majority of Moroccans speak regional varieties of colloquial Arabic or variants of Berber. In addition, Spanish is widely spoken in the north, and other foreign languages, particularly English, are used in the commercial and tourist sectors of the economy. In this polyglot, postcolonial society, it is impossible to locate one language in which the experience and imagination of all Moroccans resides. While the importance of written Arabic continues to grow in Morocco and while it is one component of anticolonial struggles, written Arabic can also be used to delegitimate and disempower colloquial spoken Arabic. No single Moroccan language can speak universally to and for all Moroccans; rather, Moroccans must daily translate among themselves, whether in the quotidian scene of a marketplace transaction or in the formation of literary narratives, both written and oral.

Like the Moroccan nationalist critics who object to his translations for political reasons, Paul Bowles was also interested in authenticity—but for different reasons. Bowles thought of himself as both an anthropologist who worked to preserve a record of a disappearing culture and as a translator who made foreign texts available to Westerners. It is necessary that the tales of Layachi and Mrabet be considered "really" Moroccan for Bowles's translations to carry out the function assigned them: to secure the borders of the West by producing knowledge about the West's Others. Bowles dismissed the significance of his participation in the production of these texts in order to establish the authenticity of the Moroccan authors and of their narratives—but this authenticity proved difficult to maintain. Bowles insisted that he did not change the narratives when he transcribed and translated them. He objected to the word "collaboration" to describe his interaction with Lay-achi and Mrabet; in the introduction to *A Life Full of Holes,* he states, "At the outset I had seen that the translation should be a literal one, in order to preserve as much as possible of the style. Nothing needed to be added, deleted, or altered" (8).[5] He then proceeds to describe the one principal exception to his self-imposed rule, an occasion when Layachi wished to delete a section of one chapter and Bowles disagreed. The episode in ques-tion describes a local belief in a spiritual figure who is thought to appear at night near the tomb of a local saint. Layachi and Bowles both found the episode incidental to the rest of the chapter, but Bowles insisted that it should be included in Layachi's autobiography because it illustrated the persistence of a pre-Islamic belief that has been grafted onto Islam. Bowles found this phenomenon interesting and wanted to relate it to the reader. The disagree-ment between Layachi and Bowles points to the different desires each of them brought to their collaboration: Layachi wanted to tell his life story, but Bowles wanted to have something told about Morocco and Moroccan lives in general. Moreover, Layachi objected to "any suggestion to the effect that his ancestors had been something else before embracing Islam" (9), whereas Bowles insisted that it was precisely this fact that makes Islam in Morocco especially interesting. In overruling Layachi and including the tomb episode in the published autobiography, Bowles acted the part of the anthropolo-gist/translator who places his own fascinations with and interpretations of Moroccan culture above those of his "informant." In effect, he claimed a posi-tion of objective authority from which he arbitrated what is and is not "authentic" about Moroccan religious practice.

Bowles took the categorical position that a "literal" translation is one in which no change occurs; this position reveals a certain nervousness about the question of who "wrote" the books of Layachi and Mrabet. Bowles revealed his anxieties about seeming too much "like" Mrabet when he told an interviewer: "Usually I don't use Moroccan source material [in my own writing] purposefully, because the pieces would be too similar to the translations I do of Mohammed Mrabet's stories."[6] Taking this precaution, however, did not suffice to protect Bowles from the suspicion that he was at the very least an active participant in the creation of Mrabet's work. In a 1968 review of *Love with a Few Hairs,* Jerome Stern points to the similarity in style between this text and Bowles's own writing and raises the question of whether Bowles and Mrabet just happened to think in sim-ilar ways or whether Bowles's "'inimitable prose' . . . transmutes a story in a particular way" ("Moroccan Viewpoint," 30). Suspicions were raised again when the matter of authorship and authenticity became a legal and financial question. In *Yesterday and Today,* Larbi Layachi relates the story of how, when Paul Bowles was overseeing the publication of *A Life Full of Holes*, he approached Layachi with a letter from the Library of Congress requesting the author's real

Larbi Layachi, Tangier, 1963 (Provided by the Swiss Foundation for Photography, Paul Bowles Photographic Archive © 2001 Artists Rights Society [ARS], New York/Pro Litteris, Zurich. Photograph by Paul Bowles.)

name and the tapes on which his story was recorded.[7] It seems that the Library of Congress wished either to determine that Paul Bowles had written the book under a Moroccan pseudonym or to possess the proof or signature of a spoken text—in this case, the original tapes.

Skeptics from both sides of the Atlantic questioned the authorship of texts published under the names of Layachi and Mrabet. The Library of Congress suspected that Bowles was the "real" author behind these names; even when the existence of Layachi and Mrabet was proven, doubt lingered in the minds of readers who noticed that Bowles's sparse style resonated in his translations from Maghrebi Arabic. Moroccan nationalist critics suggested that Bowles authored the texts signed by Layachi and Mrabet—or else, like Choukri, they claimed that Bowles's collaboration made these texts irrelevant to Morocco.[8] Since a Western language and consciousness had intervened in the production of, for example, *A Life Full of Holes* and *Love with a Few Hairs*, these books were considered impure and foreign. Some Moroccan readers and some Western readers were troubled by the "inauthenticity" of Mrabet's and Layachi's work—not for identical reasons, although in a way their arguments began to resemble one another. Nationalist critics who dismissed as impure literature that lacked a proper language or consciousness and "colonial" critics who nervously decried the lack of borders that are supposed to divide West from East both fastened their arguments upon the unstable ground of authenticity. The texts produced by Larbi Layachi and Mohammed Mrabet in collaboration with Paul Bowles demonstrate why this ground is shaky and why it is not the best foundation for anticolonial cultural production.

In *Paul Bowles: Le Reclus de Tanger,* Mohamed Choukri argues that, when Bowles translated Layachi and Mrabet, he adapted and recast the raw material provided in taped narratives (51). A comparison of Bowles's original English transcriptions with the published English texts supports Choukri's view. When translating Layachi and Mrabet, Bowles would listen to a segment of taped narrative (or, in some cases, listen to a live recitation) and then transcribe the narrative in English in a notebook. The original transcription of, for example, Mrabet's *Look and Move On* differs substantially from the published version.[9] The transcription bears marks of oral story telling, such as repetition and circularity, that do not appear in the published book. Passages extending more than thirty pages in length have been entirely cut. The result is a much more streamlined and precise narrative that builds dramatic tension using the conventions of written, rather than spoken, story telling. These stylistic changes also alter the content. For example, the original transcript of *Look and Move On* includes a great deal of boasting about Mrabet's skills as a boxer and places even more emphasis on violence in his life than does the book. But it is also important to note that many sentences and even entire scenes in the transcription appear word for word in the published version. Mrabet's words did carry

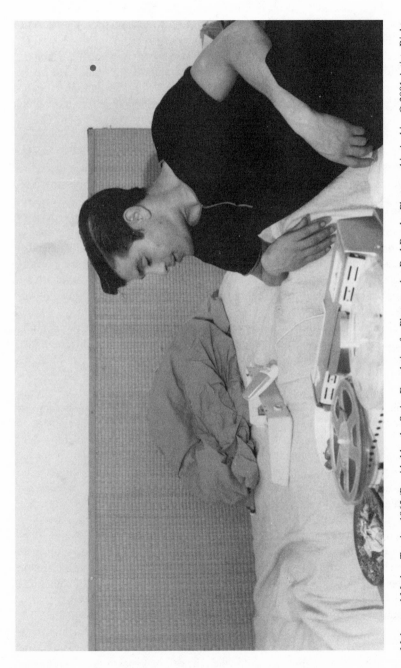

Mohammed Mrabet, Tangier, 1965 (Provided by the Swiss Foundation for Photography, Paul Bowles Photographic Archive © 2001 Artists Rights Society (ARS), New York/Pro Litteris, Zurich. Photograph by Paul Bowles.)

through the process of recording, translating, transcribing, and editing them, but Bowles was an active editor in this process, which can hardly be considered the act of producing a "literal" translation.[10]

Mrabet responded in an oblique way to those people who, like Choukri, questioned the legitimacy of his speaking voice and the relevance to Morocco of his narratives. In the autobiographical *Marriage with Papers* (1986), the following incident occurs: while in the hospital, Mrabet encounters an intern who writes poetry and who is curious to read the books by Mrabet that are available in French. Mrabet lends him a copy of *L'amour pour quelques cheveux*, which the intern praises, declaring that it is "really Moroccan" (48). Mrabet lays his own claim to legitimacy not through a critical or theoretical discourse but through this testimony, which occurs, not accidentally, in a passing conversation—which is to say, in an informal and unofficial discourse. It is precisely informal and unofficial discourse that, Mrabet implies, can lead to cultural criticism and political change. Later, the intern gives Mrabet one of his poems, written in Spanish. The entire episode in the hospital, Mrabet implies, is "really Moroccan"—the exchange of languages, the sharing of narratives in a variety of forms, both in speech and in writing, and, above all, the ability and necessity to represent the experience of living in Morocco in different languages at different times.

Unlike those cultural producers who secure their position in the national culture by writing in standard Arabic, Mrabet expressed a different idea about what constitutes national culture and the national "reality." In Mrabet's writing, Moroccan "reality" is a multilingual fluidity in which life unfolds within the stream of a constant translation, a constant negotiation between languages. This quotidian commerce of expressions and knowledges suggests that translation is a matter of bartering and exchange. To say that translation is a matter of exchange is to emphasize that it is not a matter of reproduction, of faithfully mirroring the thought of one language in another. In the linguistic marketplace of daily life in Morocco, there is always the risk and the hope that something will be lost and something else gained in the process of translation. Translation also exhibits this capacity for loss and growth when literature is passed from one language to another. In the founding essay of contemporary translation theory, "The Task of the Translator," Walter Benjamin demonstrates "that no translation would be possible if in its ultimate essence it strove for likeness to the original. For in its afterlife—which could not be called that if it were not a transformation and a renewal of something living—the original undergoes a change" ("The Task of the Translator," 73). As Paul de Man points out in his reading of Benjamin, the original text is dead until it is reborn in translation, which is, of course, also an interpretation. Certainly, in the case of Bowles's collaborations with Layachi and Mrabet, a great deal of change occurred when the original spoken word, entombed on magnetic tapes, was resurrected in English. In translation another voice enters—another consciousness, another grammar, another culture—and, in marketing those translations, the original narratives are uprooted from the scene of their narration: they appear in a variety of languages, in a number of unpredictable places, both foreign and domestic, subject to unanticipated interpretations. All these changes keep the texts alive.

Benjamin argues that the notion of faithful devotion to an original or "authentic" text does not help us understand the process and promise of translation. A work of literature undergoes multiple translations over time because no single version—not even the original—can speak in a language "pure" enough to express its ideas adequately. In a metaphor widely cited in translation theory, he compares translations to the fragments of a broken vessel that fit together to form a "greater language." The examples Benjamin draws upon in order to develop his theory of translation are taken from classical and contemporary European languages and literatures, and his argument does not take into consideration the ways languages relate to each other within complex fields of social relations. Paul Bowles's translations from Maghrebi Arabic raise a set of questions that Benjamin ignores when discussing German translations of Sophocles or Baudelaire. Mohammed Mrabet's work points to the economic aspect of the exchange between languages in Morocco, and this economy is formed within certain relations of power between languages: standard Arabic maintains its dominance as a written language over colloquial vernacular languages, for example, and French maintains prestige as a language through which one can gain access to education, certain technical fields of knowledge, and higher income. English translations allowed Mrabet and Layachi to earn money from "private" and unofficial speech; ironically, English translations also launched Choukri's international reputation as an Arabic-language writer.

The power differentials that structure encounters between languages in Tangier grew out of the history of colonialism in Morocco—and not only recent colonialism: the tension between Arabic and Berber dates to the invasion of Arab armies in the seventh century. Benjamin does not postulate the existence of a force that has broken his "vessel" of pure language—the cause of the rupture that translation seeks to repair—because there never has been a universal language. But the metaphor of the vessel suggests a desire, perhaps wistful, for wholeness and completion. This is the desire, Jacques Derrida points out, behind the urge to construct the Tower of Babel. It is an imperial desire that the world be brought to peace and reason through monolingualism. The destruction of the tower brings an end to peace, says Derrida, but also creates a need for translation, and it is precisely this necessity that contests linguistic imperialism ("Des Tours de Babel," 174). In their own fashion, the translations of Larbi Layachi, Mohammed Mrabet, and even

Mohamed Choukri engage in anti-imperial struggle by virtue of their status as translations. These texts suggest that Moroccan experience cannot be confined to any one language and that Moroccan lives can indeed be represented in translation. In fact, translation is a matter of survival, not only of the *survie,* or "afterlife," of a work that is reborn in translation but the literal survival of authors who live on the streets and whose only hope of earning money by writing is to have it sold in English abroad.

Even for writers who do not live and write on the economic margins of a postcolonial nation, translation theory suggests ways in which translation is a necessary and integral part of anticolonial cultural production. Homi Bhabha has refashioned Benjamin's metaphor of the vessel of language as a way of thinking about his own position as an intellectual who resides in a colonial metropole and who writes in English. The comparison of language to a fragmented vessel and translation to the renewal of that vessel suggests to Bhabha that translation provides the possibility of forging alliances across national and linguistic barriers and that the cultural splits that divide immigrant and diasporic peoples can be overcome. He argues that transformations take place in translation and that "Culture as a strategy of survival is both transnational and translational" (*The Location of Culture,* 172). His writings consistently look to an "in-between space"—that of hybridity and of cultural translation—in order to conceive of a way out of the hegemonies of colonial discourse.

Larbi Layachi and Mohammed Mrabet are not the sort of metropolitan hybrid writers that Bhabha celebrates: they neither bridge poststructuralist theory with postcolonial experience, as does Abdelkebir Khatibi, nor join disparate literary and cultural traditions, as does Salman Rushdie. But the writings of Layachi and Mrabet certainly fall "in between" languages, and they do engage in strategies of cultural survival. Published in translation under a double signature, this group of texts confounds notions both of authorial and of national authenticity. In the Moroccan oral tradition, narratives are repeated and adapted by storytellers in cafés and marketplaces; stories live as long as they continue to circulate, and the meaning of the story resides in its reception, not in the name of the speaker. While the writings of Layachi and Mrabet bear traces of the oral tradition, they are not traditional oral stories. Layachi wrote a book-length autobiography, while Mrabet's work includes fictionalized autobiography, novels, and short stories that mix traditional tales, dreams, and myths. Both writers combine conventions of the oral tradition with conventions of literary authorship: they foreground an organizing consciousness that filters experience and puts that experience in writing. But the collaborative production of the translations calls the conventions of authorship into question: a second consciousness, and language, is also present in these texts. The "in-betweenness" of the writings of Layachi and Mrabet as translated by Bowles suits them neither to a celebration of "Moroccanness" nor to nostalgia about traditions or oral narrative expression. On the contrary, it is the very "impurity" of these texts that calls for celebration, because it is in the mixing of authorship, languages, and literary traditions that these texts call attention to and critique the oppressive restrictions of calls for "authenticity" within both colonial and postcolonial discourses. Just as Layachi and Mrabet ensured their personal survival in a difficult economic situation by having their words translated and published abroad, so is translation itself a strategy of intellectual survival and ideological critique.

Who, in the final analysis, did "write" the books published under the names of Mohammed Mrabet and Larbi Layachi? This question provoked anxiety from almost all corners: from Bowles, from nationalist critics, and from readers on both sides of the Atlantic. Paul Bowles found it expedient to appeal to the authenticity of Mrabet's and Layachi's experiences and voices in order to claim that authorship was theirs alone and that his own distinct function was that of translator. Nationalist critics appealed to authenticity in a different way, in order to claim that translation made the texts impure. Neither Mrabet nor Layachi, on the other hand, exhibited any anxiety about whether they "owned" their authorship. When their narratives comment on the process of speaking-translating-transcribing, they relate the straightforward facts of economic activity: the stories were told to Paul Bowles so that they could be sold abroad.[11] Layachi and Mrabet were not interested in questions of authenticity; on the contrary, the "in-betweenness" of the texts they produced together with Bowles suggests that their thoughts were expressed, as their lives were lived, in translation. "Writing" these texts was an innovative strategy of survival, both in the economic sense of earning money and in the cultural sense of undermining oppressive ideological structures. The enterprise of transcription and translation made possible rather than impossible the articulation of lived experience, so that people without access to writing and publishing were able to find a way to make their voices heard—and to benefit materially from that speech. The texts of Layachi and Mrabet suggest that recourse to a notion of authenticity is not necessary in order to form a practice of reading or writing. Translation opened some doors to them, while it closed others; the circulation of their texts in translation opened up the works to new interpretations and allowed them to perform innovative cultural work. In the next section, I examine one particular type of cultural work performed by the writings of Layachi and Mrabet: the circulation and rearticulation of racial and sexual stereotypes.

Oral Fixations: Telling Stories about Sex

Encounters between Western and Moroccan men in Tangier are governed by the set of stereotypes each group has of the other. These stereotypes include the notions that all North African boys are available for sex and that all North African men are extremely virile, aggressive, and willing to have sex with other men—at least in exchange for money. Taken together, these ideas are condensed into a myth, frequently articulated in the United States and Europe, that all "Arab" men are "really bisexual." For example, the British travel writer and amateur historian Rom Landau wrote, in 1952, that Moroccan men are governed in their sexual behavior by "great virility combined with inability to refuse its dictates" and that, since that virility is "exceptionally unbridled, the average Moor may not be overparticular in the choice of an object for gratifying his urge. . . . Without necessarily being homosexual, he will often indulge in homo-erotic practices" (*Moroccan Journal,* 180). More recently, in a journalistic piece titled "An Italian in Morocco," Gianni De Martino expressed a similar idea but couched it more obviously within the language of his own fantasies about and desires for Moroccan men: "Since the Moroccan has a hard-on all the time, the tourist gets what he wants" (29).[12]

De Martino's interest in overly virile men is one expression of a familiar narrative of gay male sexual tourism that anticipates the availability of wild, exotic, limitless sex in Morocco. The exoticism of such sex, which some sexual tourists seek and find, resides not only in the crossing of an imprecise racial/cultural divide but also in the crossing of another boundary: that of sexual identity. According to Landau and De Martino, sexual identity is something that Western tourists in Morocco "have," while Moroccans do not, and it is this difference, De Martino explains, that makes the sexual exchange between Westerners and Moroccans particularly complicated and exciting. De Martino describes Moroccan men, in contrast to Americans and Europeans, as practicing a sexuality based on "undifferentiated desire" (31); Paul Bowles also describes Moroccan men as sexually "undifferentiated."[13] Gay travel guides to North Africa invariably comment on the "bisexual nature" of North African men. The special erotic appeal of difference conceived in this way is that it becomes possible for a Western gay man to have sex not with another *gay* man but with a *man* whose masculinity is uncompromised.

Western visitors are also stereotyped in the discourse that surrounds Tangier's sexual tourism: all male travelers are assumed to be gay men, usually effeminate gay men, looking for sex and willing to pay for it. In contemporary gay argot, these stereotypes are succinctly expressed in terms of chicken hawks looking for boys and queens looking for rough trade. But in Tangier, the concept of "boys," "rough trade," and "queens" has a racial twist: it is not all boys who are available but all "Arab" boys, not all men who are extraordinarily virile but all "Arab" men. Queens, on the other hand, come from the West. The construction of racial and sexual difference along these dichotomous lines has two effects. In the first place, such a stark delimitation of the boundaries of sexual desire and activity obscures the broad range of male-male sexual experience and fantasy. For example, if one takes the stereotypes seriously, one might forget that a variety of roles and positions are available to Moroccan men for male-male sexual activity depending on age, social and economic position, urban or rural residence, and inclination. The experiences and fantasies of Western tourists are equally polymorphous and diverse. In the second place, the discourse of which these stereotypes are a condensed expression works to establish an essential, "racial" difference between Western and Moroccan men and an essential, "racial" difference between Western and Moroccan sexuality. The ideas of boy and chicken hawk, of rough trade and queen are refracted through the lens of race, through the opposition of "Arab" to "Nazarene," with the result that not only desire but also identity is constructed and perpetuated through these racial and sexual stereotypes.[14]

Is it possible to break out of the framework constructed by such racially based sexual stereotypes? It is clear that such stereotypes are deployed to produce and regulate subjectivities, but is such regulation unassailable? Stereotypes emerge from a complexly articulated discourse; they endure with such force because they perpetually rearticulate the discourse that creates them. Such discourse does not exist in an historical or social void but is part and parcel of the human experiences it helps shape. Stereotypical discourse is not separable from "reality": it helps to produce the very "reality" upon which it is grounded. For this reason, it is possible to say that "undifferentiated" North African sexuality is both a stereotype and a "fact." The most recent sociological research into North African sexuality serves to confirm the stereotypes that De Martino reiterates in his own sensational and journalistic way. According to this research, male sexuality in Morocco is constructed along the lines of a "Hellenistic" model the salient feature of which is an active/passive dichotomy. The man is the penetrator, and neither his masculinity nor his identity are differentiated according to whether the passive position is occupied by a woman, a boy, or a tourist.[15] Malek Chebel's *L'Esprit de sérail*, the most thorough recent analysis of sexual relations and activities in North Africa, is a scholarly book that has little in common with the travelogues of Landau and De Martino, yet all three works do share similar representations of male-male sex and masculinity in Morocco.[16] Western tourists, Western sociologists, and Moroccan scholars all share the idea that male sexuality in Morocco is traditionally structured by a dichotomy between masculine "activity" and feminine "passivity."

Since it is impossible to dislodge stereotypes from the "reality" they help to create, a useful way to interrogate the meaning stereotypes have for culture is to ask to what uses stereotypes are put. How are subjectivities forged not in spite of them but precisely through them? These are the questions I address through the works of Mohammed Mrabet, Larbi Layachi, and Mohamed Choukri. I am primarily interested in the representational work performed by the staging of the erotic encounters between Moroccan boys and Western men in their autobiographies. These representations accrue meaning both from the context of colonial Tangier out of which they are written and from the context of Orientalisms within which they are read, for these contexts produce the racial and sexual stereotypes that the autobiographies of Mrabet, Layachi, and Choukri circulate and rearticulate.

The autobiographies of Larbi Layachi, Mohammed Mrabet, and Mohamed Choukri share a great many characteristics and concerns. In addition to the generic autobiographical work of explaining how one arrives at adult male subjectivity through the processes of childhood and adolescence, these texts are concerned with the specific constellation of social pressures exerted upon boys and young men in colonial Tangier. Mrabet, Layachi, and Choukri all grew up on the streets of Tangier and survived extraordinary hardships of hunger, poverty, and violence. From an early age, Layachi worked in cafés and fishing boats and as a house boy for Western expatriates; Mrabet came from a middle-class family but left school for an adventurous life on the street hustling tourists. Choukri's family moved to Tangier when he was a small child in order to escape famine in the Rif Mountains. The poverty in which he grew up was extreme, and his survival was made even more precarious by his own father, who murdered Choukri's infant brother to silence the starving boy's cries.[17]

In the autobiographies of Layachi, Mrabet, and Choukri, one common central theme stands out: a boy who would become a man in colonial Tangier must struggle against and negotiate with the structures of male authority that govern him. Of special interest to these texts are paternal and state structures of authority; the latter are coded not only as male but also as colonial—as saturated with the power relations that result from foreign occupation and economic domination of Tangier. Layachi and Mrabet in particular make it clear that to cross the frontier from boyhood to manhood—a crossing the success of which is marked by the sexual and economic transaction of marriage—one must secure some kind of sexual and economic advantage in a fiercely competitive and hierarchical male world. The boys of these autobiographies confront male colonial power in the figure of the Western tourist or expatriate, and it is in this meeting that the young Mrabet and the young Layachi literally work their way into adult subjectivity.

Mrabet and Layachi represent Westerners in Tangier by making use of common stereotypes about them: they are wealthy and they are effeminate—and they are easily taken advantage of because they are wealthy and effeminate. It is presumed that Western male tourists come to Tangier looking for sex with boys or men, a stereotype that is based in and helps to produce the "reality" of encounters between Moroccans and Westerners without ever being exactly accurate or fully descriptive of that experience. There is a cultural difference in the sexual encounter between West and East that is also construed to be a racial difference. In the broadest of terms, the dramas that Mrabet and Layachi stage are read against this backdrop of representative sexual difference: homosexual men—conceived of as a species—travel from the West to Tangier in order to have sex with Moroccan men and boys who do not possess a sexuality in the Western sense. The autobiographies of Mrabet and Layachi are told from the point of view of the street boys of Tangier. In these autobiographies, boys struggle against the poverty and the multiple disentitlements that constrain them, and, through their economic and erotic exchange with foreigners, they strive to attain adult male subjectivity. The attainment of this goal is marked by marriage, which in turn marks sexual and economic prowess—the man is expected to provide both a home and a sizable bride price.

Mrabet's life story, as related in *Look and Move On,* provides one example of how Western men participate in this romance/financial transaction. When Mrabet is sixteen and working as a golf caddie, he meets two Americans traveling together, Maria and Reeves. Mrabet begins sexual relationships with both of them; while the autobiography speaks more explicitly about the sex with Maria, it is through the relationship with Reeves that Mrabet earns five hundred thousand francs, with which he buys a house. After Mrabet has spent several months with Maria and Reeves, his life takes a perhaps less than exemplary turn: he travels to America, to live first with Maria in New York, then with Reeves in Iowa. For Mrabet, this is clearly a business trip. He has no great love for travel but uses his position to get as much money as possible from his two lovers. After a hilarious encounter with Midwestern propriety, Mrabet returns to Tangier a wealthy man—or, more exactly, a wealthy boy. For he is not yet married, and, once home, he turns his attention toward that end.[18]

Mrabet's personal experience is echoed in the fictional life of the boy Mohammed in his first novel, *Love with a Few Hairs.* This Mohammed is seventeen years old when the novel opens and has been living and sleeping with a British man named Mr. David for four years, but the "love" of the novel's title refers to Mohammed's stormy marriage with a girl named Mina. Mohammed and Mr. David have a classic patron/client relationship in which the man provides the boy with the money he needs to marry. In comparison to the marriage, which is quickly ruined by jealousy and greed, the love between patron and client is portrayed as almost idyllic. By the end of the novel, Mohammed has divorced Mina and she has poisoned him, but he continues to live happily with Mr. David—having sex with women on the side, but never making the mistake of falling in love with them.[19]

The autobiography of Larbi Layachi develops a similar narrative of heterosexual marriage transacted through the financial advantage of a sexual relationship with a Western man. Layachi comes from an extremely impoverished background, and, after a short career as a petty thief, he secures a job as a watchman at a café. Twice Layachi meets women he would like to marry, and twice he is rebuffed by their families because of his poverty: the women are married off to wealthier men. Eventually, he secures a better job as a house boy and carpenter for François and Marcel, a gay couple from France. Marcel leaves when François's Moroccan lover, Omar, moves in; Omar is extraordinarily successful at separating François from his money and property, with which Omar sets up his own house and marries a woman. Layachi watches Omar's fortunes rise as his own decline—having declined to enter a sexual relationship with a wealthy foreigner, Layachi earns only a modest salary, and, by the end of the book, when François has given away all his money, Layachi is once again unemployed and on the streets.

The autobiographies of Mrabet and Layachi are centrally concerned with the role played by wealthy gay foreign men in the struggle of a certain group of impoverished Moroccan boys to attain a position of adult authority and prestige. Manhood may be defined or marked by heterosexual conquest and marriage, but that goal is attained through male prostitution. The way that sex between Western men and Moroccan boys is represented in these texts resonates with stereotypes found in the writings of Americans like Paul Bowles and William Burroughs but betrays a certain dissonance, too. Tangier's status as a Mecca for sexual tourism is based on the popular understanding that, in Morocco, any man—or, more often, any boy—is available for sex. Because casual prostitution has a long history in Tangier, and because poverty is widespread, sexual tourists—like De Martino—can pretty much find what they want. The types of desires and fantasies that motivate the sexual tourist are innumerable, but his insertion into the sexual economy of Tangier is governed by Orientalist discourse and by the power relations that obtain under colonialism— that is to say, by the respective positions occupied by man and boy, foreigner and Moroccan, "homosexual" and "merely sexual." As I have already noted, these structures enforce a dominant fantasy of a gay man sleeping with a straight man, but a straight man with a "racial" difference. All this can be seen in the autobiographies and in Mrabet's *Love with a Few Hairs*: the Western men have a clearly defined interest in sex exclusively with other men and view the fact that their Moroccan sex partners also sleep with women to be at worst a nuisance and at best the source of a special erotic appeal.

The vision of the relationship between the "homosexual" and the "merely sexual" in works by contemporary Western writers differs in an important respect from the vision presented by Layachi, Mrabet, and Choukri. In contemporary European and American representations, an axis of difference separates those who have a sexual identity from those who do not. In sharp contrast, texts by Layachi, Mrabet, and Choukri represent difference through axes such as dominance versus submission, activity versus passivity, and masculinity versus femininity. In *A Life Full of Holes* and *Look and Move On*, nearly every European or American man who appears wants to have sex with boys, but the texts do not necessarily understand these men as "homosexual" in the Western sense. For example, in Mrabet's autobiography, the American man Reeves travels to Morocco with his friend Maria, and, while a sexual relationship between Reeves and Maria is never mentioned, within the terms of *Look and Move On* their relationship is understood as heterosexual. The expectations of patriarchal culture in Tangier provide Maria and Reeves with a cover for their sexual acts in the same way that marriage provided a cover for Jane and Paul Bowles. But even two gay men who live together are not necessarily seen as "gay" in the Western sense. In *A Life Full of Holes*, Larbi Layachi, writing under his pseudonym Ahmed, has a revealing conversation with Marcel in which Marcel states that he likes boys and Ahmed states that he likes girls (177). Later, François also declares, "I like dark boys" (122). These are declarations of preference, not of orientation or identity, and as such they do not differentiate Western gay men from "merely sexual" Moroccan men.

Texts written by Layachi, Mrabet, and Choukri do, however, differentiate between "masculine" men—those who penetrate—and "*maricones*"—those who are penetrated. The idea of the *maricón* or faggot functions as a category of difference against which masculinity is defined. Significantly, in his translations, Bowles retains the use of the Spanish word maricón, as if to emphasize the locality and untranslatability of this concept, just as he retains words like *sebsi* (kif pipe) or *jefatura* (police station). The retention of Spanish, French, and Maghrebi words in the English translation also conveys a sense of the linguistic complexity of colonial Tangier. The concept "faggot" is expressed not with the Maghrebi word *zamel* but with the Spanish word maricón in order to enact a double othering—to assert that effeminacy and penetration are as foreign to masculinity as Spaniards are to Morocco and to suggest that only Moroccan men are truly or sufficiently masculine. For example, in *For Bread Alone*, Choukri does not specify the nationality of the maricón who pays fifty pesetas to fellate him, but the conversation is conducted in Spanish, implying that the man is a Spaniard or at least from the West. Spain stands in here for the West in general, but the linguistic linkage of "West" and "effeminacy" is not a simple or general accusation of homosexuality. As noted, the texts do not necessarily label Western gay men "maricones." Rather, the concept of the maricón is used to regulate the behavior of all men—Moroccans as well as foreigners.

One of the most important representational tasks performed in the autobiographies of Mrabet, Choukri, and Layachi is the consolidation of masculinity. As mentioned earlier, in these texts young men struggle against various structures of male authority and attempt to secure adult male subjectivity by attaining a position of economic and sexual advantage. One facet of this struggle is the competition between Moroccan men for sexual dominance over each other. Both Choukri's *For Bread Alone* and Mrabet's novel *The Lemon* (1969) portray this competition as an effort by older men to seduce or rape younger

men, while boys and young men try in all ways possible to protect their
asses—and their masculinity—from violation.[20] The young Choukri of *For
Bread Alone* and Abdelslam of *The Lemon* are threatened not only by rape but
also by the possibility that they could be seduced and, most important, by the
possibility that that seduction could become public knowledge. In "Chico," a
short story Mrabet appended to *Marriage with Papers*, the regulatory power
of public discourse about one's sexual behavior is vividly dramatized. When
the narrator of the story fights with his friend Chico, he speaks the greatest
insult possible: in front of women, the narrator says that Chico is a *zamel*, that
they have slept together, and that Chico willingly plays the passive role. The
story does not represent male-male sex outside this insult, and the accusation
remains as ambiguous for the reader as it is for the female friends of Chico
who hear it. It is precisely this ambiguity that regulates masculinity, for the
potential for all men to be penetrated and to enjoy being penetrated leads those
who wish to conform to dominant notions of masculinity to actively, even violently, disavow deviant desire.

If these representations of male-male sex in Tangier sound familiar, if you
already feel acquainted with the machos and maricones of *For Bread Alone* or
Look and Move On, the reason is that these narratives repeat information that
has long been available through Orientalist discourse. Mrabet, Layachi, and
Choukri confirm something that anthropological literature has already told us:
that honor and shame regulate Mediterranean social behavior, that it is shameful for men to have sex, especially shameful to be the receptive partner, and
terribly shameful to ask for it. Moreover, these autobiographies and novels confirm that the circulation of knowledge—who knows what, what is said, what
is left unsaid—is a large part of gender, sex, and sexuality. Not only is the circulation of knowledge about sex internally important to the texts discussed in
this chapter, but it is also important to the way these texts function in the West.
The question of who speaks, what is said, and what is left unsaid returns us
to the issues discussed in the previous section, for Mrabet, Layachi, and
Choukri produced their texts in collaboration with Paul Bowles, and it was
through him, through his translations and his reputation, that their writings
came to the West.

One of the functions of these texts is to recirculate for Western readers the
familiar notion of "Oriental bisexuality" and to "fix" representative sexual difference. These texts also work to consolidate masculinity and adult male subjectivity for their narrators. These functions came into operation through an
unusual collaborative process in which Paul Bowles acted as editor, agent, tran-
scriber, and translator. As translations, the autobiographies of Layachi, Mrabet, and Choukri are supposed to represent "authentic" and "original"
Moroccan experience—but the way the texts were produced calls authenticity
and originality into question. Authenticity is vital if sexual difference between

West and East is to be effectively delimited and maintained; originality is key because the authors stake their subjectivity on it. But contrary to the humanistic underpinnings of the translation project, the translator is strikingly present in these texts—a presence that undermines their status as "auto" biographies as well as their claims to authenticity and originality. Ironically, while Bowles's translation project pretended to enable self-representation and to fix sexual difference, the collaborative writing of that project destabilized its politics of representation.

How, then, are we to understand male erotic exchange in these extraordinarily compelling narratives? As a model, let's return to the ending of Larbi Layachi's autobiography, *A Life Full of Holes*. I noted earlier that, since Layachi chooses not to seek out sexual relationships with wealthy foreigners as does Omar, he is left homeless, unemployed, and unmarried. There is, however, an extratextual continuation to this story, for Layachi produced an autobiography, from which he earned enough money to marry.[21] For Layachi, the narrative in which one attains adult subjectivity through boyhood prostitution was displaced into the process of literary production. Mrabet provides a fictional representation of this displacement in his novel *Chocolate Creams and Dollars* (1992), in which the protagonist, Driss, records stories on tape, as did Mrabet and Laychi, with the intention of selling them and securing adult subjectivity. Bowles acted as Layachi's patron, but the exchange that took place was one of money for words: words allowed Western access to an "authentic" Moroccan life story, and money allowed Layachi to marry. The Bowles translations can best be understood as an erotic exercise in their own right, an exercise that reflects the patron/client model of sexual commerce between West and East in Tangier.

In fact, it is possible to trace Bowles's personal investment in translating oral stories to his experience as the patron of Ahmed Yacoubi, the person who first taught Bowles to speak colloquial Arabic.[22] During the early years of their relationship—before Yacoubi had established his own career as a successful painter—Yacoubi entertained his patron with stories that, in Bowles's words, "issued from the repertory of Moroccan folk humor, which took on new meaning as it was propelled by his untrammeled imagination."[23] Bowles was drawn to the young man because, again in his own words, "Yacoubi was 'primitive,'" a designation that for Bowles suggested the immediacy of Yacoubi's worldly experience and expressions and the authenticity of his Moroccanness ("How Could I Send a Picture into the Desert?" 224). Bowles's relationship with Yacoubi, in both its sexual and literary dimensions, was motivated at least in part by a desire to secure access to Moroccan thought and culture. Among the uncounted stories Yacoubi told him, Bowles translated only three from the "private" realm of conversation into the "public" realm of transcription, and these three stories do not concern themselves directly or narratively with matters of male-male desire.

Bowles and Yacoubi pursued their relationship with discretion, and the stories they published collaboratively assist, at least passively, in maintaining that silence. But it is possible to locate the original impetus for Bowles's interest in translating narratives from Maghrebi Arabic in the nexus of desires that sustained his interest in the young Yacoubi: this included a desire to achieve access to an "authentic" Morocco and to represent that Morocco in English by letting a Moroccan voice speak "through" him, "unmediated," in translation.

By tapping into the "primitive" narratives of Yacoubi, and, more famously, into the tales and autobiographies of Layachi, Mrabet, and Choukri, Bowles attempted to erase his own interests and position as an American writing about an "Oriental" culture. But the texts he produced through collaboration frustrate this attempt. The autobiographies of Layachi, Mrabet, and Choukri in particular call attention to themselves as "colonial" texts and foreground the economic and sexual dimensions of their production. By doing so, they repeat the pattern we have seen emerge in the writing of Paul Bowles, William Burroughs, and Alfred Chester. These authors also wrote interzone literature that explores colonialism and sexuality in Tangier and that celebrates Tangier as a place suspended between languages and cultures and nations. Ultimately, however, the literature of all six authors remains framed by the structures and stereotypes of colonial discourse. Interzone literature imaginatively engages colonial discourse with diverse representations of sex, sexuality, identity, and desire in Tangier. It deploys a fascinating array of traditional and experimental literary techniques to creatively redefine boundaries of male subjectivity. But these freshly articulated visions of male subjectivity and desire remain shadowed by the historical, material, and psychological legacy of colonialism.

Notes
Bibliography
Index

Notes

Chapter 1. Colonial Desire in the "Interzone" of Tangier

1. Burroughs to Allen Ginsberg, Tangier, 29 October 1956, *The Letters of William S. Burroughs*, 339.

2. Neither the word "queer" nor "gay" nor "bisexual" comprehensively describes the sexual orientation of men who sought sex with men in Tangier. Some male expatriates had a gay or bisexual identity and some female expatriates had a lesbian or bisexual identity, but many did not experience sexuality within the frame of identity. I lack the space to detail biographical facts here, but the following list of artists and writers is evocative and includes people of all sexual orientations. In addition to Paul and Jane Bowles, William Burroughs, and Alfred Chester, several less well-known people were associated with Tangier's expatriate community: the artist and writer Brion Gysin, the poets Ira Cohen, John Giorno, and Ted Joans, the journalists Christopher Wanklyn and David Woolman, the novelists John Hopkins and Charles Wright, the editors Irving Rosenthal and Mark Schleifer, and the translator Norman Glass. In addition, many prominent cultural producers vacationed in Tangier, most of them drawn there to some extent by the Bowleses, Burroughs, or Chester: Charles Henri Ford, Djuna Barnes, Aaron Copland, Robert Rauschenberg, Tennessee Williams, Truman Capote, Gore Vidal, Allen Ginsberg, Peter Orlovsky, Alan Ansen, Gregory Corso, Harold Norse, Susan Sontag, Edward Field, and Neil Derrick. Several European artists and writers also lived or vacationed in Tangier during these years, including Francis Bacon, Joe Orton, Roland Barthes, Jean Genet, Robin Maugham, Angus Stewart, and Rupert Croft-Cooke. More recently, Rupert Everett, Aldo Busi, and Juan Goytisolo have written about Tangier and

Morocco. Samuel Clemens, Gertrude Stein, Oscar Wilde, André Gide, Edith Wharton, and Claude McKay passed through Tangier in the late nineteenth and early twentieth centuries.

3. For a discussion of this treaty, see Jerome B. Bookin-Weiner and Mohamed El Mansour, *The Atlantic Connection,* 19–29 and especially 26.

4. The United States joined the Sanitary Council in 1797; see Stuart, *The International City of Tangier,* 31–39. Stuart calls the Hygiene Commission, which replaced the Sanitary Council in 1893, "to all extents and purposes a city council for Tangier" (36). See also Luella J. Hall, *The United States and Morocco,* 741. For a discussion of the Cape Spartel lighthouse and of the various foreign postal services in Tangier, see Stuart, *The International City of Tangier,* 39–53.

5. Great Britain acknowledged French dominance of Morocco in exchange for a free hand in Egypt; France and Spain divided Morocco between themselves, with the Spanish zone centered in Tetuan in the north, across the straits from Spain. See Stuart, *The International City of Tangier,* 62–64, and Hall, *The United States and Morocco,* 343.

6. The signatories to the convention were Germany, Austria-Hungary, Belgium, Denmark, Spain, the United States, France, Great Britain, Italy, Morocco, the Netherlands, Portugal, Russia, and Sweden (Stuart, *The International City of Tangier,* 26, 70–71). Hall points out that the Algeciras conference marks a historic intrusion by the United States into "European" affairs, a striking departure from the Monroe Doctrine (*The United States and Morocco,* 570).

7. France maintained indirect control of the sultan's appointed representatives and so was able to dominate the assembly. The statute provided for a number of administrative bodies, including separate judicial systems for Moroccans and foreigners. A court of French, Spanish, and British magistrates held authority over foreign residents. See Stuart, *The International City of Tangier,* 126–28, and the text of the statute, 239–316.

8. Ibid., 117–18, 123–26, 153–54, 221–24.

9. For an excellent analysis of American involvement in international trade through the lens of world-system theory, see Thomas J. McCormick, *America's Half Century.*

10. For example, in *Imperial Leather,* a groundbreaking study of colonialism and heterosexual perversion, Anne McClintock demonstrates that regimes of domination and subordination extend from the domestic space of the Victorian bourgeois home to the overseas domains of the British empire. Robert Young explores the cultural consequences of interracial reproductive sex in *Colonial Desire.* Other studies approach the question of colonial sexuality from a different bent and concern themselves specifically with homosexuality. In *Empire Boys* Joseph Bristow argues that homosexual practices in British boarding schools developed through formations of masculinity and athleticism that were themselves produced by the needs of imperial expansion. In *Britain's Imperial Century* and *Empire and Sexuality,* Ronald Hyam explores the ways that construction of the British Empire was enabled by the sublimation of homosexual desire. Making use of a much more nuanced approach to psychoanalysis, Christopher Lane argues that the confluence of homosexuality and colonialism is best studied in terms of paradox and ambivalence. In *The Ruling Passion,* a study that ranges across some of the most significant literary products of British imperialism, Lane explores the ways that homosexual desire disrupted Great Britain's dominant narratives of nationhood and empire.

11. Joseph Boone, "Framing the Phallus in the *Arabian Nights*"; "Mappings of Male Desire in Durrell's *Alexandria Quartet*"; "Rubbing Aladdin's Lamp"; "Vacation Cruises; or, The Homoerotics of Orientalism."

12. In the years immediately after independence, police harassment did increase, a question I take up in chapter 3.

Chapter 2. Paul Bowles

1. What brings an American writer to Tangier in the 1930s and keeps him there most of his life? This question has fascinated critics, reviewers, and interviewers for fifty years and was asked of Bowles repeatedly. Not surprisingly, he repeated his answer: In 1931, Gertrude Stein and Alice B. Toklas suggested that he travel to Tangier, and so he went. See interview by Ira Cohen, 1965, in Bowles, *Conversations with Paul Bowles*, 10. See also Bowles, *Without Stopping*, 123, and Lawrence D. Stewart, *Paul Bowles*, 11–12. He liked Morocco and returned to North Africa in each of the following three years, traveling also in the Algerian Sahara. During World War II, Bowles lived in New York and Mexico, but in 1947 he returned to Tangier and aside from various travels lived there until his death in 1999. Staying in Tangier was never a conscious decision, he insisted; he simply found himself there at a time in his life when he did not want to move anymore and found Tangier a less objectionable place to live than any other. See Bowles, *Without Stopping*, 366, and his interview with Daniel Halpern, 1975, *Conversations with Paul Bowles*, 86.

2. Bowles to Ruth Fainlight, Tangier, 10 April 1986, in Bowles, *In Touch*, 528.

3. I doubt that this nostalgia is limited to the 1980s and 1990s, but it certainly became especially visible during those years. During the late 1980s, I was living in Kenya, and it was at that time that I first noticed the phenomenon of colonial nostalgia, especially among tourists who came to Kenya in search of a khaki-clad colonial-style adventure. Significantly, most of these tourists (at least those who dressed for the role) were Americans. Besides *Out of Africa*, a number of other books and films centered on colonial Kenya were produced or reissued in the 1980s: the book and film *White Mischief*, the film version of *The Flame Trees of Thika*, and the reissue of Beryl Markham's *West with the Night*. Other examples of major motion picture fantasies about colonial nostalgia are *Raiders of the Lost Ark*, *King Solomon's Mines*, *A Passage to India*, and *The Gods Must Be Crazy*, but these Anglo-American examples are only a small sampling of texts that cross high and popular culture throughout the West.

4. Christopher Sawyer-Lauçanno called his biography of Bowles *An Invisible Spectator* on the basis of a comment Bowles once made to him that he would like to be "an invisible spectator" at the reunion of the Bowles fan club in Japan. Sawyer-Lauçanno makes this remark into a metaphor for Bowles's life. Bertolucci plays upon this idea in his film by placing Bowles before the camera and making him visible as he silently watches the characters Port, Kit, and Tunner. See Bowles to Allen Hibbard, Tangier, 10 May 1990, *In Touch*, 543.

5. Interview by Soledad Alameda, 1990, *Conversations with Paul Bowles*, 222.

6. Bowles describes the nostalgia for Tangier that swept over him, and how he sketched out the entire novel in his mind on the Fifth Avenue bus in the spring of 1947. See Bowles, *Without Stopping*, 274–75.

7. Rosaldo, "Imperialist Nostalgia," in *Culture and Truth,* 68–87.

8. Rosaldo points to transportation as an example of how his research benefits from the social forces that are helping to transform the culture he studies: he rides in a missionary airplane when conducting his research.

9. See Mary Louise Pratt's *Imperial Eyes* for a discussion of the trope of "virgin" land and the possession of that land through seeing.

10. Mungo Park, *Travels into the Interior of Africa.* Pratt points out that Park's book is emblematic of the genre of sentimental travel writing, and as such Park is looking for reciprocity in his relations with Africans. This idea of reciprocity is also evident in Bowles—see the discussion of "The Time of Friendship" later in this chapter.

11. See Pratt for a discussion of eighteenth-century sentimental travel writing (*Imperial Eyes,* 69–107).

12. Interview by Catherine Warnow and Regina Weinreich, 1988, *Conversations with Paul Bowles,* 216.

13. The connection to surrealism begins with his youthful surreal poetry and is sustained throughout his work through the notion of unconscious writing and the linkage made between the unconscious mind and primitive life. Bowles—the first American translator of *No Exit*—has also been associated with existentialism ever since the publication of *The Sheltering Sky.*

14. See Sigmund Freud, "Mourning and Melancholia" and *The Ego and the Id.*

15. This last point is my reading of Butler, rather than Butler's reading of Larsen. See Judith Butler, "Passing, Queering" in *Bodies That Matter,* 167–85.

16. Bowles names this story his favorite in an interview by Catherine Warnow and Regina Weinreich, 1988, *Conversations with Paul Bowles,* 213. He based the character Fräulein Windling on a Swiss woman he met in Algeria in 1948 and the character Slimane on her young friend Suliman.

17. See Allen Hibbard, *Paul Bowles,* 56. Hibbard also connects this story to Gide's *L'Immoraliste,* suggesting that it is a rewriting of that novel, with heterosexual desire substituted for homosexual.

18. This marriage dismayed nearly everyone on both sides of the Mediterranean. For an excellent discussion of Eberhardt's attempt to assimilate, and of her intervention against the binaries colonizer/colonized, Christian/Muslim, see Laura Rice, "Nomad Thought'."

19. See Pratt, *Imperial Eyes,* 69–85, on Mungo Park and sentimentality.

20. John Maier argues that, over the course of his career, Bowles stretched his ability to bridge the cultural gap between his experience and the lives of the Moroccans among whom he lived. See "Penetrating the Ramparts: Morocco in the Fiction of Paul Bowles" and "Two Moroccan Storytellers in Paul Bowles's *Five Eyes*: Larbi Layachi and Ahmed Yacoubi" in *Desert Songs.*

21. The Istiqlal Party encourages these demonstrations and riots; though their movement is secular and they would prefer to wrest independence from both the French and the sultan, they fan the flames of mass anger to reach their ends.

22. I define the word "fetish" in greater detail in chapter 4, but both here and in that chapter I use it to describe an erotic relation in which a person projects a complex set of desires on an object and does so at least in part in order to ward off the fear of loss.

23. After Stenham and Lee reverse their views about humanity, Amar leaves the scene and the Americans have sex. This "resolution" to triangulated love is palpably unsatisfying, and Paul Bowles later agreed, remarking that he added the sex scene only upon the insistence of his editors at Random House. Apparently the editors felt that some form of heterosexual closure was necessary at this point, perhaps in order to break the circuit of fetishized desire that implicates both colonial and neocolonial positions. See Bowles to Wendy Lesser, Tangier, 15 May 1983, *In Touch*, 518.

24. Bowles to James Leo Herlihy, Tangier, 30 April 1966, *In Touch*, 381. These deceptions began in childhood, as strategies to avoid the censorship and displeasure of his father. See Marilyn Moss, "The Child in the Text."

25. Bowles interview conducted in the documentary *Let It Come Down*.

26. Yacoubi's stories first inspired Bowles to attempt to translate and publish the work of Moroccan collaborators. Yacoubi built his career not as a writer, however, but as a painter. Yacoubi eventually settled in the United States. Jeffrey Miller indicates that Yacoubi was born in 1931 (*In Touch*, 571). Michelle Green states that Yacoubi died of cancer in 1986 (*The Dream at the End of the World*, 340–41).

27. In addition to the Bowles/Yacoubi segment, the other seven "movements" included as performers Man Ray, Marchel Duchamp, Jean Arp, Jacqueline Matisse, Yves Tanguy, Julien Levy, Richard Huelsenbeck, Alexander Calder, Jean Cocteau, Dorothea Ernst, Max Ernst, Frederick Kiesler, Ceal Bryson, and Eugene Pellegrini.

28. Bowles to Regina Weinreich, Tangier, 8 November 1983, *In Touch*, 521.

29. Bowles to Aaron Copland, Westhampton, Mass., summer 1933, *In Touch*, 116–17.

Chapter 3. The Sexual Re-Orientations of William S. Burroughs

1. Jamie Russell offers an extensive analysis of "effeminophobia" in Burroughs's life and texts. Russell's *Queer Burroughs* is the first book to thoroughly analyze Burroughs as a queer writer in relation to queer theory.

2. Ted Morgan's 1988 biography is longer and more detailed, but Barry Miles's 1993 biography and Graham Caveney's 1998 illustrated biography are more current.

3. Jennie Skerl's *William S. Burroughs* is an exception to this practice, which is most forcefully exemplified by David Lodge in "Objections to William Burroughs." For another virulent denunciation of Burroughs see John Willett, "UGH . . ."

4. Ihab Hassan is one well-known critic who appreciated Burroughs early and has analyzed his work in several essays; see especially "The Subtracting Machine." See also the following: Timothy S. Murphy, *Wising up the Marks;* Robin Lydenberg, *Word Cultures;* Alvin J. Seltzer, *Chaos in the Novel, The Novel in Chaos,* especially 330–74; Cary Nelson, "The End of the Body"; Michael Bliss, "The Orchestration of Chaos"; Michael Leddy, "'Departed Have Left No Address'"; Charles Russell, "Individual Voice in the Collective Discourse"; and Frederick M. Dolan, "The Poetics of Postmodern Subversion."

5. The first edition of *Junky*, published by Ace, was spelled *Junkie*. Burroughs referred to the opiates he used by the generic term "junk"; more specifically, he used at various times opium, heroin, morphine, dilaudid, pantapon, eukodol, paracodeine, dionine, codeine, demerol, and methodone. See his "Letter from a master addict to dangerous drugs," appended to *Naked Lunch*, 240.

6. The disguise was a thin one: Lee is the maiden name of Burroughs's mother.

7. Burroughs wrote to Jack Kerouac that Mexico "is an Oriental country that reflects 2000 years of disease and poverty and degradation and stupidity and slavery and brutality and psychic and physical terrorism." Burroughs to Kerouac, Mexico City, May 1951, in Burroughs, *The Letters of William S. Burroughs,* 91.

8. Burroughs to Ginsberg, Pharr, Texas, 1 May 1950, *Letters of William S. Burroughs,* 69.

9. Burroughs to Kerouac, Mexico City, 18 September 1950, *Letters of William S. Burroughs,* 71.

10. As Burroughs discovered on his 1953 excursion to Colombia and Peru, yage is used throughout the region of the Amazon shared by those two countries together with Ecuador—he was, however, especially unlucky and inept on his first try.

11. The writing of *Junky* bled into the writing of *Queer,* and Burroughs tried to negotiate with Ace Books to publish both volumes, either as one text or separately. Ace declined to publish *Queer.* See Burroughs to Lucien Carr, Mexico City, 5 March 1951, *Letters of William S. Burroughs,* 81, and Burroughs to Ginsberg, Mexico City, 22 April 1952, *Letters of William S. Burroughs,* 119.

12. Burroughs discusses possession by the Ugly Spirit in the context of what caused him to act out the William Tell routine in which he killed his wife, Joan Vollmer. Her death occurred soon after he returned from Ecuador with Marker, but *Queer* was written after her death. "[T]he book is motivated and formed by . . . the accidental shooting death of my wife, Joan, in September 1951" (*Queer,* xvii–xviii).

13. Burroughs to Ginsberg, Mexico City, 5 May 1951, *Letters of William S. Burroughs,* 85–86.

14. Angelo is one of the few names not disguised as Burroughs renders his life in *Junky*—he had a happy casual relationship with Angelo for two years in Mexico City.

15. So that, for example, his shooting of his wife was caused not by misogyny and an unconscious wish to eliminate her but rather by the Ugly Spirit that invaded his body and directed his actions.

16. Burroughs to Ginsberg, Mexico City, 20 December 1951, *Letters of William S. Burroughs,* 97.

17. Burroughs to Ginsberg, Mexico City, 22 April 1952, *Letters of William S. Burroughs,* 119–20, emphasis in original.

18. Burroughs specified the age group 18–25 when asked what exactly he meant when referring to sex with "boys." See his interview by Laurence Collinson and Roger Baker, in *Gay Sunshine Interviews,* 11.

19. Burroughs to Ginsberg, Tangier, 26 April 1954, *Letters of William S. Burroughs,* 230.

20. Burroughs to Ginsberg, Quito, 22 April 1953, *Letters of William S. Burroughs,* 160.

21. Burroughs to Ginsberg, Lima, 8 July 1953, *Letters of William S. Burroughs,* 179–80.

22. Ibid., 180.

23. Burroughs to Ginsberg, Lima, 12 May 1953, *Letters of William S. Burroughs,* 162.

24. Burroughs to Ginsberg, Lima, early July 1953, *Letters of William S. Burroughs,* 176.

25. Burroughs to Ginsberg, Tangier, 13 December 1954, *Letters of William S. Burroughs*, 243, and Burroughs to Ginsberg, Tangier, 6 January 1955, *Letters of William S. Burroughs*, 251. The title *Naked Lunch* was suggested to Burroughs by Jack Kerouac several years before he started writing the book that would eventually be published under that name. The title "Interzone" was eventually used for a collection of Burroughs's early short pieces edited by James Grauerholz in 1989, including some material excised from the published version of *Naked Lunch*.

26. Burroughs to Kerouac and Ginsberg, Tangier, 2 November 1955, *Letters of William S. Burroughs*, 302.

27. Burroughs to Ginsberg, Tangier, 9 January 1955, *Letters of William S. Burroughs*, 254.

28. Burroughs to Ginsberg, Tangier, 9 February 1954, *Letters of William S. Burroughs*, 196–97.

29. Burroughs to Ginsberg, Tangier, 29 October 1956, *Letters of William S. Burroughs*, 337.

30. In 1957, Ahmed Yacoubi was arrested and imprisoned, falsely accused of seducing a fourteen-year-old German boy. Early in 1958, Paul and Jane Bowles flew to Portugal rather than be called as witnesses in his trial or be expelled. Yacoubi was acquitted, and they returned later that year. In August 1958, Burroughs wrote to Ginsberg, "Tanger [*sic*] is finished. . . . Many a queen has been dragged shrieking from the Parade, the Socco Chico, and lodged in the local box where sixty Sons of Sodom now languish" Burroughs to Ginsberg, Tangier, 25 August, 1958, *Letters of S. William Burroughs*, 395.

31. The dedication of *Junky* is to "A. L. M." (Adelbert Lewis Marker); Burroughs noted in a letter that "I wrote *Queer* for Marker." Burroughs to Ginsberg, Mexico City, 6 October 1952, *Letters of William S. Burroughs*, 138.

32. Burroughs to Ginsberg, Tangier, 12 January 1955, *Letters of William S. Burroughs*, 255. Similarly, ten months later, "Writing now causes me an almost unbearable pain. This is connected with my need for you, which is probably not a sexual need at all, but something even more basic. I wonder if we could collaborate?" Burroughs to Ginsberg, Tangier, 10 October 1955, *Letters of William S. Burroughs*, 286.

33. Burroughs to Ginsberg, New York, early October 1954, *Letters of William S. Burroughs*, 235.

34. Ibid., 236.

35. See Eric Mottram, *William Burroughs,* for a discussion of Burroughs's treatment of addiction. "Image addiction" and "morality addiction" are Lydenberg's terms; see *Word Cultures*, 3–18.

36. Burroughs to Ginsberg, Paris, 11 September 1959, *Letters of William S. Burroughs*, 424.

37. The process was not totally random; the more interesting cut-ups are those Burroughs selected for their fruitful juxtapositions. For a detailed explanation of the cut-up method see Lydenberg, *Word Cultures*; Burroughs, Brion Gysin, Gregory Corso, and Sinclair Beiles, *Minutes to Go*; and Brion Gysin, *Brion Gysin Let the Mice In*. Burroughs's cut-up period produced not only the three novels but also numerous short pieces that he published in small literary magazines. Many of these pieces are collected in William Burroughs, *The Burroughs File* and in *Exterminator!*

38. Writing about *Queer,* Burroughs said, "The Oil-Man and Slave Trader routines are not intended as inverted parody sketches à la Perelman, but as a *means* to make contact with Allerton and to interest him." Burroughs to Ginsberg, Mexico City, 23 May 1952, *Letters of William S. Burroughs,* 126.

39. Burroughs to Kerouac, Tangier, 7 December 1954, *Letters of William S. Burroughs,* 241; Burroughs to Ginsberg, Tangier, 13 December 1954, *Letters of William S. Burroughs,* 243; Burroughs to Ginsberg, Tangier, 7 February 1955, *Letters of William S. Burroughs,* 259–62; Burroughs to Ginsberg, Tangier, 20 April 1955, *Letters of William S. Burroughs,* 273; Burroughs to Ginsberg, Tangier, 21 October 1955, *Letters of William S. Burroughs,* 288; Burroughs to Ginsberg, Tangier, 26 February 1956, *Letters of William S. Burroughs,* 309; Burroughs to Ginsberg, Tangier, 13 October 1956, *Letters of William S. Burroughs,* 330 and 332.

40. Burroughs to Kerouac, Tangier, 22 April 1954, *Letters of William S. Burroughs,* 205.

41. Burroughs to Ginsberg, Tangier, 7 April 1954, *Letters of William S. Burroughs,* 201.

42. Burroughs to Ginsberg, Tangier, 24 June 1954, *Letters of William S. Burroughs,* 216.

43. Burroughs to Ginsberg, Tangier, 19 October 1957, *Letters of William S. Burroughs,* 372.

44. This literature is exemplified by many of the essays collected in Skerl and Lydenberg, *William S. Burroughs at the Front.*

45. Burroughs to Ginsberg, Tangier, 29 October 1956, *Letters of William S. Burroughs,* 339.

46. Burroughs to Ginsberg, Tangier, 26 January 1954, *Letters of William S. Burroughs,* 195.

47. Burroughs to Ginsberg, New York, early October 1954, *Letters of William S. Burroughs,* 236.

Chapter 4. Alfred Chester's Multiple Exiles

1. Alfred Chester to Norman Glass, Tangier, 20 February 1964, "Voyage to Destruction." I am grateful to Edward Field for sharing with me the manuscript of Chester's letters, which he has edited for future publication under the title "Voyage to Destruction: Letters from Morocco." Used by permission of the Alfred Chester Estate. Edward Field has deposited this manuscript in the Edward Field Alfred Chester Archives at the University of Delaware Library, Special Collections Department.

2. Chester's book review of *City of Night* and his essay "Mailer in Search of His Hero" are reprinted in *Looking for Genet.*

3. Chester to Edward Field, Arcila, Morocco, 2 October 1963, "Letters from Morocco," 310.

4. Chester to Dennis Selby, Tangier, 1 December 1963, "Voyage to Destruction."

5. Chester to Dennis Selby, Arcila, Morocco, 22 July 1963, "Voyage to Destruction."

6. This one friend was Robert Friend; see his short piece "The Last Days of Alfred Chester." Dennis Selby describes Chester's paranoia in New York in the late 1960s in "The Sodden, Stoned, Cold-Water, Fantasticks Blues."

7. References to *The Foot* refer to *Head of a Sad Angel,* an edition of collected stories and other pieces.

8. Chester's objection to colonialism was not articulated as a political or ideological critique but rather was communicated through his letters as a pervasive discomfort with the relations he witnessed and experienced in Morocco. Part of Chester's unease was related to the way that race and racism structured identities and desires in his Moroccan encounters; at times, his letters brought this discomfort to consciousness. While Chester did not systematically confront or challenge racism as a key organizer of his experience, his discomfort with it did differentiate him from Bowles and Burroughs, who never adequately questioned the racism that informed and shaped their relationships with Morocco.

9. Edward Field notes that, during Susan Sontag's visit to Tangier late in the summer of 1965, Chester suffered a serious psychotic breakdown, part of which involved the fear that Sontag had come to steal Dris from him. Chester wrote about this fear in *The Foot*, suggesting also a confusion between himself and Sontag, and Dris. See Edward Field, "Tea at Paul Bowles's." The final breakup with Dris seems to have occurred during this period. In *The Foot* Chester mentions receiving a letter from Dris, who migrated to Europe to work, but the two men apparently never met again after 1965.

10. Chester to Edward Field, Tangier, 9 January 1964, "The Nazarene and the Native," 27.

11. A certain mystery surrounds this disease, since Chester was reluctant to discuss it or his baldness even with close friends. Edward Field wrote in his "Biographical Sketch," included in *Head of a Sad Angel,* that the disease was scarlet fever and that Chester contracted it at the age of seven. In *The Foot*, Chester suggested that the baldness was caused not by a disease but rather by x-rays, but this explanation seems to be part of a larger paranoid fantasy—or metaphor—that he was an alien creature transplanted into a human body. See *Head of a Sad Angel,* 279–80 and 303.

12. Unlike so many gay or queer writers, Chester did not write about his early sexual experiences or about coming out of the closet. His letters do suggest a certain amount of what today we call internalized homophobia. But even his first novel and early short stories deal frankly with homosexuality, and biographical accounts suggest that he was open about and comfortable with his sexuality beginning at least in his twenties, when he lived in Paris. Cynthia Ozick knew Chester before he moved to Paris and discusses their friendship in "Alfred Chester's Wig."

13. "Ismael" and "In Praise of Vespasian" are perfectly sane stories that represent these problems of identity and desire in conventional, realistic fiction. Nonetheless, both stories also begin to experiment with the sorts of writing practices Chester would employ in Morocco as he found less sane and more surreal ways of "inventing" self, other, and future: "Vespasian" freezes a perfect moment, "Ismael" practices camp. The former strategy is developed more fully in relation to the fetish in *The Foot*; the latter is brilliantly executed in *The Exquisite Corpse.* Already in "Ismael," however, camp as a writing strategy is associated with those drag queens and Harlem faggots, and in *The Exquisite Corpse* it is developed as a way of perverting and subverting conventional reality.

14. Chester to Harriet Zwerling, 23 November 1964, "Voyage to Destruction."

15. Edward Field discusses this invitation and provides a detailed analysis of the complex relationship between Chester and Bowles in "Tea at Paul Bowles's."

16. Chester to Bowles, New York, 19 March 1963, and Chester to Bowles, New York, 25 May 1963, both in "Voyage to Destruction."

17. Edward Field specifies that Bowles found Dris to be rather dangerous and introduced him to Chester in order to see what might result when these two strong personalities encountered each other; see "Tea at Paul Bowles's," 106.

18. Chester to Harriet Sohmers (Zwerling), Tangier, 10 October 1963, "Voyage to Destruction." Edward Field discusses this incident in "Tea at Paul Bowles's," 104 and 108, and Norman Glass discusses it in "The Decline and Fall of Alfred Chester," 338–40.

19. Chester to Harriet Sohmers (Zwerling), 23 September 1963, "Voyage to Destruction." Chester to Edward Field, Arcila, Morocco, 2 October 1963, "Letters from Morocco," 310.

20. Chester to Edward Field, 15 July 1964, "Voyage to Destruction." "Glory Hole" was first published in *Evergreen Review* in March 1964 and is reprinted in *Head of a Sad Angel.*

21. Chester to Norman Glass, Tangier, 28 February 1964, "Voyage to Destruction." This second incident involved Irving Rosenthal, who wrote a passage in a novel that maligned Bowles's abilities as a fellator, and Ira Cohen, who had to decide whether to publish the lines in his magazine *Gnaoua*. Chester encouraged Cohen to publish, but Burroughs, Jane Bowles, and Paul himself strongly objected, and Cohen eventually decided against publication.

22. Chester to Dennis Selby, Arcila, Moroco, 22 July 1963, "Voyage to Destruction."

23. Chester to Paul Bowles, New York, 5 March 1966, "Voyage to Destruction."

Chapter 5. Translating Homosexuality

1. Mohamed Choukri befriended Jean Genet and Tennessee Williams when they visited Tangier, and he wrote two books based on his experiences with them, *Jean Genet in Tangier* and *Tennessee Williams in Tangier.*

2. Choukri indicated that Spanish was the language most centrally used in his translation work with Bowles. See Mohamed Choukri, *Paul Bowles: Le Reclus de Tanger,* 50. Bowles indicated as much in the introduction to *Five Eyes,* by Abdelslam Boulaich et al. (8), but, curiously, in his introduction to *For Bread Alone,* by Mohamed Choukri (5), he claims to have worked with Choukri primarily through dialectical Maghrebi Arabic. The misrepresentation in the latter case is telling, for it suggests a wish on Bowles's part to highlight his facility with a Moroccan language and to present the translation project as a Moroccan enterprise.

3. For Choukri's criticism of Mrabet see Iain Finlayson, *Tangier: City of the Dream,* 346.

4. For articles in English on this subject see Marc Gontard, "Francophone North African Literature and Critical Theory"; Jean Déjeux, "Francophone Literature in the Maghreb: The Problem and the Possibility"; and M'hamed Alaoui Abdalaoui, "The Moroccan Novel in French."

5. In an interview in 1971, Bowles insisted that his translations were "not exactly collaborations. I only get the authors to talk, you see. The stories are their own. My function is only to translate, edit, and to cut; now and then I have to ask a question to clarify a point." Interview by Oliver Evans, 1971, in Bowles, *Conversations with Paul Bowles,* 53.

6. Interview by Stephen Davis, 1979, in *Conversations with Paul Bowles*, 107.

7. Layachi had used the name "Driss" as a pseudonym as he told his life story. He relates the incident involving the Library of Congress in *Yesterday and Today,* 129–30.

8. Paul Bowles in a 1981 interview: "What little notice [Mrabet has] received here has been adverse. . . . They feel that a foreigner can present a Moroccan only as a performing seal. They scent neocolonialism in a book translated directly from *darija* [colloquial Moroccan Arabic]. At first they wrote that he didn't exist, that I'd invented him. Then they accused me of literary ventriloquy. I'd found some fisherman and photographed him so I could present my own ideas under the cover of his name, thinking that would give them authenticity. What they seem to resent most of all is not that the texts were taped, but that they were taped in the language of the country which, by common consent, no one ever uses for literary purposes" (Interview by Jeffrey Bailey, 1981, in *Conversations with Paul Bowles*, 133).

9. Bowles's notebook transcriptions of *Look and Move On, For Bread Alone,* and several other published and unpublished translations are held by the University of Delaware Library, Special Collections Department, in the Paul Bowles Papers and Paul Bowles Collection.

10. Unlike the Mrabet/Bowles text, the transcription of Choukri's *For Bread Alone* is very similar to its published version. Since Choukri wrote pages of his autobiography by day in Arabic, then read them aloud to Bowles in the evening in Spanish, the written style of the text was established from the beginning. Alterations from the transcribed to the published version are minor: for example, editing for consistency in verb tense or for a more precise choice of adjective or syntax.

11. Layachi repeatedly comments on the importance of making money through writing in *Yesterday and Today*; this is also a major theme in Mrabet's *Marriage with Papers* and *Chocolate Creams and Dollars.*

12. For an extended account of an Italian vacation in Morocco that shares many of the concerns of De Martino's article, see Aldo Busi, *Sodomies in Elevenpoint.*

13. Interview by Jeffrey Bailey, 1981, in *Conversations with Paul Bowles*, 130.

14. The word "Arab" is frequently used by Americans and Europeans to refer to North Africans whether they are Arab or Berber in origin; the word "Nazarene" (meaning Christian) is used by Layachi and Mrabet to refer to all Westerners, no matter their religious affiliation. Both words assume racial connotations, and both collapse a wide array of stereotypes into a compact sign.

15. For a good account in English of this social analysis of sexuality see Arno Schmitt's introductory essay in *Sexuality and Eroticism among Males in Moslem Societies,* 1–24. It is the more careful and academic version of De Martino's article in the same volume, 25–32. In that collection see also Andreas Eppink, "Moroccan Boys and Sex." For other Western accounts of Arab sexuality, see Stephen O. Murray and Will Roscoe, *Islamic Homosexualities,* and David F. Greenberg, "The House of Islam" in *The Construction of Homosexuality,* 172–82.

16. Chebel makes use of psychoanalytic theory to understand a wide range of sexual practices as they function within North African society. More than merely describing sexual practices, the book argues that "perverse and marginal sexualities" cast light upon "normality" and structure a wide range of social relations. The book does not directly address cross-cultural sexual relations. For a critical account in English that is sensitive to Maghrebian definitions of sexuality see Jarrod Hayes, *Queer Nations*.

17. Layachi was born in 1937 in Menarbiyaa and moved to Tangier in 1940. Mrabet was born around 1940 in Tangier. Choukri was born in 1935 at Beni Chiker in the Rif Mountains and moved to Tangier as a small boy.

18. Mohammed Mrabet does not "purchase" his wife, Zohra, through a bride price; since the woman he loves is betrothed to a more wealthy man, Mrabet "steals" her by "taking" her virginity away from her before her wedding. The illicit sex is discovered, and Zohra and Mohammed have to marry.

19. Mrabet's autobiographical *Marriage with Papers* makes a critique of married life similar to that expressed in Mohammed Mrabet, *Love with a Few Hairs*. The same elements are there: jealousy, a struggle for money and power, the use of magic and poison in the battle of spouses, a fight over the children, the involvement of extended families, the juridical power of patriarchy, and, above all, violence.

20. *For Bread Alone* provides a good example of what it means for one boy to rape another (Mohamed rapes a neighbor, 46) and what it means to fear being raped in turn: Mohamed witnesses a "fake" rape (22), a boy tries to seduce him (69), men at the Fondaq rape boys (72), a drunkard follows him (74), and he savagely beats a man who propositions him (116). *A Life Full of Holes* represents the fear of rape in a similar way: a policeman tries to rape the eight-year-old Ahmed (11), and a French prison guard rapes boys (119). *The Lemon* begins when Abdelslam refuses to be disciplined by his effeminate French school teacher. He moves in with an older friend, Bachir, who threatens to rape him. Abdelslam fends off the rapist with cunning and violence.

21. Paul Bowles explains in his autobiography that Layachi's own autobiography was marketed as a novel in order to compete for a literary award. "[I]t sold well in several languages and went quickly into paperback editions in both America and the United Kingdom, with the result that Larbi made enough money from it to look for a bride" (*Without Stopping*, 350).

22. Bowles related how Yacoubi taught him to speak Maghrebi Arabic during the initial months of their sexual relationship. See Bischoff's interview with Bowles in *Paul Bowles Photographs*, "How Could I Send a Picture into the Desert?" especially pages 224, 227, and 231.

23. Bowles makes these comments in his preface to *Five Eyes*, a collection of short pieces by Boulaich et al. (7). This collection includes three tales told to Bowles by Ahmed Yacoubi: "The Man Who Dreamed of Fish Eating Fish," "The Game," and "The Night before Thinking."

Bibliography

Abdalaoui, M'hamed Alaoui. "The Moroccan Novel in French." *Research in African Literatures* 23.4 (winter 1992): 9–33.

Athill, Diana. *Stet: A Memoir*. New York: Grove Press, 2000.

Benjamin, Walter. "The Task of the Translator." In *Illuminations,* translated by Harry Zohn, 69–82. New York: Schocken Books, 1969.

Bersani, Leo. "Is the Rectum a Grave?" In *AIDS: Cultural Analysis, Cultural Activism,* edited by Douglas Crimp, 197–222. Cambridge, Mass.: MIT Press, 1988.

Bhabha, Homi. *The Location of Culture*. London: Routledge, 1994.

Bliss, Michael. "The Orchestration of Chaos: Verbal Technique in William Burroughs' *Naked Lunch*." *Enclitic* 1 (spring 1977): 59–70.

Bookin-Weiner, Jerome B., and Mohamed El Mansour, eds. *The Atlantic Connection: Two Hundred Years of Moroccan-American Relations*. [Rabat?]: Edino Press, 1990.

Boone, Joseph. "Framing the Phallus in the *Arabian Nights:* Pansexuality, Pederasty, Pasolini." In *Translations/Transformations: Gender and Culture in Film and Literature*, edited by Cornelia Moore and Valerie Wayne, 22–33. Honolulu: University of Hawaii Press, 1993.

Boone, Joseph. "Mappings of Male Desire in Durrell's *Alexandria Quartet*." In *Displacing Homophobia*. Special issue of *South Atlantic Quarterly* 88 (1989): 73–106.

Boone, Joseph. "Rubbing Aladdin's Lamp." In *Negotiating Lesbian and Gay Subjects,* edited by Monica Dorenkamp and Richard Henke, 148–77. New York: Routledge, 1995.

Boone, Joseph. "Vacation Cruises; or, The Homoerotics of Orientalism." *PMLA* 110 (January 1995): 89–107.

Boulaich, Abdelslam, Mohamed Choukri, Larbi Layachi, Mohammed Mrabet, and Ahmed Yacoubi. *Five Eyes*. Edited and translated by Paul Bowles. Santa Barbara, Calif.: Black Sparrow Press, 1979.

Bowles, Paul. *Collected Stories 1939–1976*. Santa Barbara, Calif.: Black Sparrow Press, 1979.

Bowles, Paul. *Conversations with Paul Bowles*. Edited by Gena Dagel Caponi. Jackson: University Press of Mississippi, 1993.

Bowles, Paul. "How Could I Send a Picture into the Desert?" Interview with Simon Bischoff. In *Paul Bowles Photographs*, edited by Simon Bischoff, 205–55. Zurich: Scalo, 1994.

Bowles, Paul. *In Touch: The Letters of Paul Bowles*. Edited by Jeffrey Miller. New York: Farrar, Straus and Giroux, 1994.

Bowles, Paul. *Let It Come Down*. 1952. Reprint, Santa Barbara, Calif.: Black Sparrow Press, 1980.

Bowles, Paul. *The Sheltering Sky*. 1949. Reprint, New York: Vintage-Random House, 1990.

Bowles, Paul. *The Spider's House*. New York: Random House, 1955.

Bowles, Paul. *Too Far from Home: The Selected Writings of Paul Bowles*. Edited by Daniel Halpern. New York: Ecco Press, 1993.

Bowles, Paul. *Up above the World*. 1966. Reprint, New York: Ecco Press, 1982.

Bowles, Paul. *Without Stopping*. 1972. Reprint, New York: Ecco Press, 1985.

Bristow, Joseph. *Empire Boys: Adventures in a Man's World*. London: HarperCollinsAcademic, 1991.

Burroughs, William. *The Adding Machine: Selected Essays*. 1986. Reprint, New York: Arcade, 1993.

Burroughs, William. *The Burroughs File*. San Francisco: City Lights Books, 1984.

Burroughs, William. *Conversations with William S. Burroughs*. Edited by Allen Hibbard. Jackson: University Press of Mississippi, 1999.

Burroughs, William. *Exterminator!* New York: Viking, 1974.

Burroughs, William. Interview by Laurence Collinson and Roger Baker. In *Gay Sunshine Interviews*, edited by Winston Leyland, vol. 1, 11–21. San Francisco: Gay Sunshine Press, 1978.

Burroughs, William. *Interzone*. Edited by James Grauerholz. New York: Viking, 1989.

Burroughs, William. *The Job: Interviews with William S. Burroughs*. Edited by Daniel Odier. New York: Penguin, 1989.

Burroughs, William. *Junky*. 1953. Reprint, New York: Penguin Books, 1977.

Burroughs, William. *The Letters of William S. Burroughs: 1945–1959*. Edited by Oliver Harris. New York: Viking, 1993.

Burroughs, William. *Naked Lunch*. 1959. Reprint, New York: Grove Weidenfeld, 1992.

Burroughs, William. *Nova Express*. 1964. Reprinted in *Three Novels*. New York: Grove Press, 1988.

Burroughs, William. *Port of Saints*. 1973. Reprint, Berkeley, Calif.: Blue Wind Press, 1980.

Burroughs, William. *Queer*. 1985. Reprint, New York: Penguin Books, 1987.

Burroughs, William. *The Soft Machine*. 1961. Reprinted in *Three Novels*. New York: Grove Press, 1988.

Burroughs, William. *The Ticket That Exploded*. 1962. Reprint, New York: Grove Press, 1968.

Burroughs, William. *The Wild Boys*. 1969. Reprinted in *Three Novels*. New York: Grove Press, 1988.

Burroughs, William, and Allen Ginsberg. *The Yage Letters*. San Francisco: City Lights Books, 1963.

Burroughs, William, Brion Gysin, Gregory Corso, and Sinclair Beiles. *Minutes to Go*. Paris: Two Cities Editions, 1960.

Busi, Aldo. *Sodomies in Elevenpoint*. Translated by Stuart Hood. London: Faber and Faber, 1993.

Butler, Judith. *Bodies That Matter: On the Discursive Limits of "Sex."* London: Routledge, 1993.

Butler, Judith. *Gender Trouble: Feminism and the Subversion of Identity*. London: Routledge, 1990.

Caponi, Gena Dagal. *Paul Bowles*. New York: Twayne, 1998.

Caponi, Gena Dagal. *Paul Bowles: Romantic Savage*. Carbondale: Southern Illinois University Press, 1994.

Caveney, Graham. *Gentleman Junkie: The Life and Legacy of William S. Burroughs*. Boston: Little, Brown, 1998.

Chauncey, George. *Gay New York: Gender, Urban Culture, and the Making of the Gay Male World, 1890–1940*. New York: Basic Books, 1994.

Chebel, Malek. *L'Esprit de sérail: Perversions et marginalités sexuelle au Maghreb*. Paris: Lieu Commun: 1988.

Chester, Afred. *The Exquisite Corpse*. 1967. Reprint, New York: Carroll & Graf, 1986.

Chester, Alfred. "Flung Out." *Christopher Street* 145 (1990): 28–29, 31–33, 35, 37, 39–40.

Chester, Alfred. *Head of a Sad Angel: Stories 1953–1966*. Edited by Edward Field. Santa Rosa, Calif.: Black Sparrow Press, 1990.

Chester, Alfred. *Jamie Is My Heart's Desire*. 1956. Reprint, New York: Vanguard Press, 1957.

Chester, Alfred. "Letters from Morocco." *Confrontation* 37–38 (spring-summer 1988): 305–17.

Chester, Alfred. *Looking for Genet: Literary Essays & Reviews*. Edited by Edward Field. Santa Rosa, Calif.: Black Sparrow Press, 1992.

Chester, Alfred. "The Nazarene and the Native." *New York Native* 48 (10 November 1986): 26–31.

Chester, Alfred. "Voyage to Destruction: Letters from Morocco." Edited by Edward Field. Unpublished manuscript.

Choukri, Mohamed. *For Bread Alone*. Translated by Paul Bowles. 1973. Reprint, San Francisco: City Lights Books, 1987.

Choukri, Mohamed. *Jean Genet in Tangier*. Translated by Paul Bowles. New York: Ecco Press, 1974.

Choukri, Mohamed. *Paul Bowles: Le Reclus de Tanger*. Translated by Mohamed El Ghoulabzouri. Paris: Quai Voltaire, 1997.

Choukri, Mohamed. *Tennessee Williams in Tangier*. Translated by Paul Bowles. Santa Barbara, Calif.: Cadmus Editions, 1979.

Déjeux, Jean. "Francophone Literature in the Maghreb: The Problem and the Possibility." *Research in African Literatures* 23.2 (summer 1992): 5–19.

de Man, Paul. "'Conclusions': Walter Benjamin's 'The Task of the Translator.'" *Yale French Studies* 69 (1985): 25–46.

De Martino, Gianni. "An Italian in Morocco." In *Sexuality and Eroticism among Males in Muslim Societies,* edited by Arno Schmitt and Jehoeda Sofer, 25–32. New York: Haworth Press, 1992.

Derrida, Jacques. "Des Tours de Babel." Translated by Joseph F Graham. In *Difference in Translation,* edited by Joseph F. Graham, 165–207. Ithaca: Cornell University Press, 1985.

Dillon, Millicent. *A Little Original Sin: The Life and Work of Jane Bowles*. New York: Holt, Rinehart, and Winston, 1981.

Dillon, Millicent. *Out in the World: Selected Letters of Jane Bowles, 1935–1970*. Santa Barbara, Calif.: Black Sparrow Press, 1985.

Dillon, Millicent. *You Are Not I: A Portrait of Paul Bowles*. Berkeley: University of California Press, 1998.

Dolan, Frederick M. "The Poetics of Postmodern Subversion: The Politics of Writing in William S. Burroughs's *The Western Lands.*" *Contemporary Literature* 32.4 (winter 1991): 534–51.

Drugstore Cowboy. Directed by Gus Van Sant. Avenue Entertainment. 1989. 101 minutes.

8 X 8: A Chess Sonata in Eight Movements. Directed by Hans Richter. Self-produced by Hans Richter. 1957. 81 minutes.

Eppink, Andreas. "Moroccan Boys and Sex." In *Sexuality and Eroticism among Males in Muslim Societies,* edited by Arno Schmitt and Jehoeda Sofer, 33–41. New York: Haworth Press, 1992.

Fanon, Frantz. *Black Skin, White Masks*. Translated by Charles Lam Markmann. 1952. Reprint, New York: Grove Weidenfeld, 1967.

Fiedler, Leslie. "The New Mutants." *Partisan Review* 32.4 (fall 1965): 505–25.

Field, Edward. "A Biographical Sketch." In *Head of a Sad Angel: Stories 1953–1966,* edited by Edward Field, 303–9. Santa Rosa, Calif.: Black Sparrow Press, 1990.

Field, Edward. "Tea at Paul Bowles's." *Raritan* 7 (winter 1993): 92–111.

Finlayson, Iain. *Tangier: City of the Dream*. London: HarperCollins, 1992.

Freud, Sigmund. "Fetishism." In *The Standard Edition of the Complete Psychological Works*, edited by James Strachey, vol. 21, 152–57. London: Hogarth Press, 1961.

Freud, Sigmund. *The Ego and the Id*. In *The Standard Edition of the Complete Psychological Works of Sigmund Freud,* edited by James Strachey, vol. 19, 1–59. London: Hogarth Press, 1961.

Freud, Sigmund. "Mourning and Melancholia." In *The Standard Edition of the Complete Psychological Works of Sigmund Freud,* edited by James Strachey, vol. 14, 237–58. London: Hogarth Press, 1961.

Friend, Robert. "The Last Days of Alfred Chester." In *Head of a Sad Angel: Stories 1953–1966*, edited by Edward Field, 366–77. Santa Rosa, Calif.: Black Sparrow Press, 1990.

Glass, Norman. "The Decline and Fall of Alfred Chester." In *Head of a Sad Angel: Stories 1953–1966*, edited by Edward Field, 338–40. Santa Rosa, Calif.: Black Sparrow Press, 1990.

Gontard, Marc. "Francophone North African Literature and Critical Theory." *Research in African Literatures* 23.2 (summer 1992): 33–38.

Green, Michelle. *The Dream at the End of the World: Paul Bowles and the Literary Renegades in Tangier*. New York: HarperCollins, 1991.

Greenberg, David F. *The Construction of Homosexuality*. Chicago: University of Chicago Press, 1988.

Gysin, Brion. *Brion Gysin Let the Mice In*. Edited by Jan Herman. West Glover, Vt.: Something Else Press, 1973.

Hall, Luella J. *The United States and Morocco, 1776–1956*. Metuchen, N.J.: Scarecrow Press, 1971.

Hassan, Ihab. "The Subtracting Machine: The Work of William Burroughs." In *William S. Burroughs at the Front: Critical Reception, 1959–1989,* edited by Jennie Skerl and Robin Lydenberg, 53–67. Carbondale: Southern Illinois University Press, 1991.

Hayes, Jarrod. *Queer Nations: Marginal Sexualities in the Maghreb*. Chicago: University of Chicago Press, 2000.

Hibbard, Allen. *Paul Bowles: A Study of the Short Fiction*. New York: Twayne, 1993.

Hyam, Ronald. *Britain's Imperial Century 1815–1914: A Study of Empire and Expansion*. London: Batsford, 1976.

Hyam, Ronald. *Empire and Sexuality: The British Experience*. Manchester: Manchester University Press, 1990.

JanMohammed, Abdul. "Sexuality on/of the Racial Border: Foucault, Wright, and the Articulation of 'Racialized Sexuality.'" In *Discourses of Sexuality: From Aristotle to Aids,* edited by Donna C. Stanton, 94–116. Ann Arbor: University of Michigan Press, 1992.

Landau, Rom. *Moroccan Journal*. London: Robert Hale, 1952.

Lane, Christopher. *The Ruling Passion: British Colonial Allegory and the Paradox of Homosexual Desire*. Durham, N.C.: Duke University Press, 1995.

Larsen, Nella. *Passing*. New York: Knopf, 1929.

Layachi, Larbi. *The Jealous Lover*. Bolinas, Calif.: Tombouctou Books, 1986.

Layachi, Larbi. *A Life Full of Holes*. Translated by Paul Bowles. 1964. Reprint, New York: Grove Press, 1982.

Layachi, Larbi. *Yesterday and Today*. Santa Barbara, Calif.: Black Sparrow Press, 1985.

Leddy, Michael. "'Departed Have Left No Address': Revelation/Concealment Presence/Absence in *Naked Lunch*." *Review of Contemporary Fiction* 4.1 (1984): 33–40.

Let It Come Down: The Life of Paul Bowles. Directed by Jennifer Baichwal. Requisite Productions. 1998. 72 minutes.

Lodge, David. "Objections to William Burroughs." In *William S. Burroughs at the Front: Critical Reception, 1959–1989,* edited by Jennie Skerl and Robin Lydenberg, 75–84. Carbondale: Southern Illinois University Press, 1991.

Lydenberg, Robin. *Word Cultures: Radical Theory and Practice in William S. Burroughs's Fiction*. Urbana: University of Illinois Press, 1987.

Maier, John. *Desert Songs: Western Images of Morocco and Moroccan Images of the West*. Albany: State University of New York Press, 1996.

McClintock, Anne. *Imperial Leather: Race, Gender and Sexuality in the Colonial Contest*. New York: Routledge, 1995.

McCormick, Thomas J. *America's Half Century: United States Foreign Policy in the Cold War*. Baltimore: Johns Hopkins University Press, 1989.

McHale, Brian. *Constructing Postmodernism*. New York: Routledge, 1992.

Miles, Barry. *William Burroughs: El Hombre Invisible*. New York: Hyperion, 1993.

Morgan, Ted. *Literary Outlaw: The Life and Times of William S. Burroughs*. New York: Henry Holt, 1988.

Moss, Marilyn. "The Child in the Text: Autobiography, Fiction, and the Aesthetics of Deception in *Without Stopping*." *Twentieth Century Literature* 32.3/4 (1986): 314–33.

Mottram, Eric. *William Burroughs: The Algebra of Need*. Buffalo, N.Y.: Intrepid Press, 1971.

Mrabet, Mohammed. *Chocolate Creams and Dollars*. Translated by Paul Bowles. New York: Inanout Press, 1992.

Mrabet, Mohammed. *The Lemon*. Translated by Paul Bowles. 1969. Reprint, San Francisco: City Lights Books, 1986.

Mrabet, Mohammed. *Look and Move On*. Translated by Paul Bowles. Santa Barbara, Calif.: Black Sparrow Press, 1976.

Mrabet, Mohammed. *Love with a Few Hairs*. Translated by Paul Bowles. 1967. Reprint, San Francisco: City Lights Books, 1986.

Mrabet, Mohammed. *Marriage with Papers*. Translated by Paul Bowles. Bolinas, Calif.: Tombouctou Books, 1986.

Murphy, Timothy S. *Wising up the Marks: The Amodern William Burroughs*. Berkeley: University of California Press, 1997.

Murray, Stephen O., and Will Roscoe. *Islamic Homosexualities: Culture, History, and Literature*. New York: New York University Press, 1997.

Nadeau, Maurice. *The History of Surrealism*. 1964. Reprint, Harmondsworth, U.K.: Penguin Books, 1973.

Naked Lunch. Directed by David Cronenberg. Recorded Picture Company. 1991. 115 minutes.

Nelson, Cary. "The End of the Body: Radical Space in Burroughs." In *William S. Burroughs at the Front: Critical Reception, 1959–1989*, edited by Jennie Skerl and Robin Lydenberg, 119–32. Carbondale: Southern Illinois University Press, 1991.

Ozick, Cynthia. "Alfred Chester's Wig." *New Yorker* 68 (30 March 1992): 79–84, 86–98.

Park, Mungo. *Travels into the Interior of Africa*. 1799. Reprint, London: Eland, 1983.

Pietz, William. "The Problem of the Fetish, I." *Res* 9 (spring 1985): 5–17.

Pratt, Mary Louise. *Imperial Eyes: Travel Writing and Transculturation*. London: Routledge, 1992.

Rice, Laura. "'Nomad Thought': Isabelle Eberhardt and the Colonial Project." *Cultural Critique* (winter 1990–91): 151–76.

Rogin, Michael. "'Make My Day!' Spectacle as Amnesia in Imperial Politics." In *Cultures of United States Imperialism*, edited by Amy Kaplan and Donald Pease, 499–534. Durham, N.C.: Duke University Press, 1993.

Rosaldo, Renato. *Culture and Truth: The Remaking of Social Analysis*. Boston: Beacon Press, 1989.

Russell, Charles. "Individual Voice in the Collective Discourse: Literary Innovation in Postmodern American Fiction." *SubStance* 27 (1980): 29–39.

Russell, Jamie. *Queer Burroughs*. New York: Palgrave, 2001.

Said, Edward W. *Culture and Imperialism*. New York: Knopf, 1993.

Said, Edward W. *Orientalism*. New York: Pantheon Books, 1978.

Sawyer-Lauçanno, Christopher. *An Invisible Spectator: A Biography of Paul Bowles*. New York: Weidenfeld & Nicolson, 1989.

Schmitt, Arno, and Jehoeda Sofer, eds. *Sexuality and Eroticism among Males in Muslim Societies*. New York: Haworth Press, 1992.

Sedgwick, Eve Kosofsky. *Between Men: English Literature and Male Homosocial Desire*. New York: Columbia University Press, 1985.

Selby, Dennis. "The Sodden, Stoned, Cold-Water, Fantasticks Blues." In *Head of a Sad Angel: Stories 1953–1966,* edited by Edward Field, 314–20. Santa Rosa, Calif.: Black Sparrow Press, 1990.

Seltzer, Alvin J. *Chaos in the Novel, the Novel in Chaos*. New York: Schocken Books, 1974.

Sheltering Sky, The. Directed by Bernardo Bertolucci. Sahara Company. 1990. 138 minutes.

Skerl, Jennie. *William S. Burroughs*. Boston: Twayne, 1985.

Skerl, Jennie, and Robin Lydenberg. *William S. Burroughs at the Front: Critical Reception, 1959–1989*. Carbondale: Southern Illinois University Press, 1991.

Stern, Jerome H. "Moroccan Viewpoint." *Saturday Review* 51 (6 April 1968): 30–31, 40.

Stewart, Lawrence D. *Paul Bowles: The Illumination of North Africa*. Carbondale: Southern Illinois University Press, 1974.

Stuart, Graham H. *The International City of Tangier*. Stanford: Stanford University Press, 1931.

Suleri, Sara. *The Rhetoric of English India*. Chicago: University of Chicago Press, 1992.

Twain, Mark. *Traveling with the Innocents Abroad*. Norman: University of Oklahoma Press, 1958.

Willett, John. "UGH . . ." In *William S. Burroughs at the Front: Critical Reception, 1959–1989*, edited by Jennie Skerl and Robin Lydenberg, 41–44. Carbondale: Southern Illinois University Press, 1991.

Young, Robert J. C. *Colonial Desire*. New York: Routledge, 1995.

Index

157